The Fundamentals and Practice of Marketing

The Institute of Marketing

Marketing means Business

The Institute of Marketing was founded in 1911. It is now the largest and most successful marketing management organisation in Europe with over 20,000 members and 16,000 students throughout the world. The Institute is a democratic organisation and is run for the members by the members with the assistance of a permanent staff headed by the Director General. The Headquarters of the Institute are at Moor Hall, Cookham, near Maidenhead, in Berkshire.

Objectives: The objectives of the Institute are to develop knowledge about marketing, to provide services for members and registered students and to make the principles and practices of marketing more widely known and used throughout industry and commerce.

Range of activities: The Institute's activities are divided into four main areas:
    Membership and membership activities
    Corporate activities
    Marketing education
    Marketing training

OTHER TITLES IN THE SERIES

Marketing Communications
Colin J. Coulson-Thomas

Marketing Research for Managers
S. Crouch

Case Studies in International Marketing
Peter Doyle and Norman Hart

The Principles and Practice of Selling
Alan Gillam

Essentials of Statistics in Marketing
C. S. Greensted, A. K. S. Jardine and J. D. Macfarlane

A Career in Marketing, Advertising and Public Relations
N. A. Hart and G. W. Lamb

The Practice of Advertising
N. A. Hart and J. O'Connor

Glossary of Marketing Terms
N. A. Hart and J. Stapleton

The Practice of Public Relations
Wilfred Howard

Legal Aspects of Marketing
J. L. Livermore

A Modern Approach to Economics
F. Livesey

Marketing Plans
M. H. B. McDonald

Case Studies in Marketing, Advertising and Public Relations
Colin McIver

Business Analysis for Marketing Managers
L. A. Rogers

Profitable Product Management
John Ward

Behavioural Aspects of Marketing
K. Williams

Business Organization
R. J. Williamson

Management Controls and Marketing Planning
R. M. S. Wilson

Bargaining for Results
John Winkler

Pricing for Results
John Winkler

The Fundamentals and Practice of Marketing

JOHN WILMSHURST

M.A., F.C.A.M., M.Inst.M., A.M.B.I.M.

Second Edition

Published on behalf of the Institute of Marketing
and the CAM Foundation

HEINEMANN PROFESSIONAL PUBLISHING

Heinemann Professional Publishing Ltd
Halley Court, Jordan Hill, Oxford OX2 8EJ

OXFORD   LONDON   MELBOURNE   AUCKLAND   SINGAPORE
IBADAN   NAIROBI   GABORONE   KINGSTON

First published 1978
Reprinted 1979, 1980, 1981, 1983 (twice)
Second edition 1984
Reprinted 1985, 1986, 1987, 1988, 1989

ISBN 0 434 92331 1

Photoset by Deltatype, Ellesmere Port
Printed at The Bath Press, Avon

Preface to First Edition

This book sets out to present as clearly, comprehensively and simply as possible what is generally recognized as being the best of current thinking in the marketing field.

It was written solely with the teaching/learning situation in mind. Whilst it is especially geared to the Institute of Marketing and CAM Certificate Syllabuses in Marketing students and teachers of marketing for other professional courses embodying marketing (DMS for example) will also find it valuable.

Thus, whilst I have used many examples, most of them from direct practical experience, I hope I have avoided making it a largely anecdotal book and kept a clear statement of important principles as the main objective throughout.

The questions at the end of each chapter, some of them from past papers of the Institute of Marketing examinations, have all been thoroughly tested in the lecture room as 'discussion starters' and as essay subjects.

The sources on which I drew are first my own practical experience of working full-time in the marketing field for nearly twenty years, including consultancy work for a wide range of British and overseas companies in many different industries during the past few years.

Secondly, my six years of lecturing to mature students for the Institute of Marketing Diploma and the Diploma in Management Studies together with running and taking part in post-experience marketing seminars at an advanced level in the U.K., other parts of Europe, Africa and South America.

Thirdly, my reading of large numbers of books and articles on marketing topics, many of which are referred to here.

Finally, and most important of all, I am indebted to the many clients, colleagues and friends with whom I have worked over the years. Those particularly deserving mention in this respect are Pete Parker and Harold Parkin of Roles and Parker Limited; Norman Hart, Director of the CAM Foundation; Edgar Hibbert, Ted Jenner, and Jacqueline Marrian of the Institute of Marketing; Peter Doyle, Professor of Marketing at Bradford University; Marcos Porto, Chairman of Marpro Marketing Projects Ltda of Sao Paulo in Brazil.

The whole manuscript was thoroughly read on behalf of the Institute of Marketing by two highly experienced marketing people. It now embodies their valuable comments but is still my personal responsibility.

My thanks are due and freely given to my wife and business partner Patricia to whom this book is dedicated. Without her vision, support and patience, it would never have been started, let alone completed. Sonia Chambers coped with most of the massive amount of typing involved and – incredibly – never complained of the complexity, volume or illegibility of the handwritten material I dumped on her. Gladys Field dealt – most efficiently – with amendments, getting approvals for quotes and generally tidying up the manuscript. Malcolm Stern and Robert Lomax at Heinemann provided very necessary encouragement and guidance at crucial stages. Margaret Calvey deserves special thanks for loaning (and later selling to us) the sea-side cottage where most of the book was written.

John Wilmshurst

Preface to Second Edition

Reactions to the First Edition have been so strongly and universally favourable that no change has been made to the basic treatment and layout. The revisions that have been made fall into the following categories:

1 Figures, e.g. of advertising expenditures, have been updated wherever possible and obvious changes like the replacement of the old JICTARS television audience research with the current BARB system.
2 More subtle but more far-reaching changes in the economic situation, industrial structure, etc. have been reflected in an even greater emphasis than before on the dynamic nature of effective marketing management.
3 Some key areas of subject matter, notably sales promotion, pricing and marketing planning, have been strengthened by the addition of extra material.
4 More recent examination questions have been included in the 'Questions for Discussion' at the end of each Chapter and the CAM Certificate papers as well as the IM Certificate papers have been drawn on for this.
   In addition some short case histories have been added for the benefit of students and lecturers or trainees wanting to use case histories as a basis of discussion without having to 'scratch around' for suitable material.
5 Various comments from lecturers, examiners and others have also been incorporated and my thanks go to them for their interest and support.

John Wilmshurst

Contents

Preface to First Edition   v
Preface to Second Edition   vii

THE FUNDAMENTALS OF MARKETING

 1 What Marketing is All About   1
 2 Gathering Facts for Marketing   16
 3 The Right Mixture and the Vital Spark   26
 4 The Ever-changing Product   35
 5 The Search for New Products   49
 6 Where Price Comes In   62
 7 Getting the Goods to the Customers   78
 8 The Message and the Medium   90
 9 Where the Marketing Department Comes In   101
10 The Changing Climate of Marketing   112

THE PRACTICE OF MARKETING

11 What Marketing Research Can Do   124
12 How Marketing Research Works   139
13 How Personal Selling Works   150
14 How Selling is Managed   164
15 What Advertising and Sales Promotion Can Do   173
16 How the Advertising Business Works   185
17 How Sales Promotion Works   197
18 How International Marketing Works   210
19 How Marketing Planning Works   211

Index   237

1. *What Marketing is All About*

'Marketing is the management process responsible for identifying, anticipating and satisfying customer requirements profitably.'

Institute of Marketing Definition

1.1 What Marketing Means

The term 'marketing' is used in different ways by different people; so, to avoid talking at cross purposes, it is necessary to disentangle these differences at the out-set. Commonly, there are three ways in which people use the term:

1 As a description for some part of the company's organization or in a person's function or job title, such as the 'marketing department' or the 'marketing director'.
2 To describe certain techniques within a company. Such activities as advertising, market research, and sometimes sales or product development, can be conveniently described by the collective term 'marketing' to distinguish them from other activities coming under the heading of 'production', 'finance' and similar main sub-divisions of a company.
3 To indicate a particular approach to business, or a management attitude, in relation to customers and their needs. This 'business philosophy' has become known as the 'marketing concept'.

It is in this third way that the term is mainly used in this book, and the meaning and implication of the marketing concept are discussed fully later in this chapter. However, we must look briefly at the other two uses of the term in order to get them in perspective.

1.11 *Marketing as an Organizational or Functional Term*

There are fashions in management jargon as in everything else. In recent years 'marketing' has become one of the more fashionable management words. This means it is often used widely without too much attention to its true meaning. For example, many a sales department has been renamed 'marketing department' over-night with no change in its function or attitudes. The term is used to describe advertising and public relations activities, market research or merchandising. All this simply means is that it is sometimes wise to ask 'What do *you* understand by "marketing"?'

1.12 *Marketing to Describe Certain Techniques*

Many activities are particularly concerned with a company's relations with its customers – for example, market research, public relations, customer enquiries,

1

and advertising. Often these activities are grouped together under the collective term 'marketing'.

While there is some virtue in this, there is danger, too. As we shall see in the next section, marketing in its fullest sense must motivate the whole company. The managing director, production men, accountants, typists, all must be concerned with marketing. To put the marketing label on some parts of the business can be read as indicating that they and only they are concerned with marketing. This in turn would mean that only they are concerned about the customers on which the business depends. The saying 'Marketing is too important an activity to be trusted to the marketing department' contains a great deal of truth. A fairly common solution to the problem is to label these specialist departments 'Marketing Services' (see Section 9.2).

Be that as it may, we do commonly find within a company structure a marketing department set up something along the following lines:

> Marketing is one of the three basic divisions of effort in the typical industrial enterprise. It begins by influencing the form the product should take to secure maximum acceptance in the market, as well as the prices at which and the quantities in which it should be offered in any given period to secure the maximum return to the enterprise in the long term.
>
> It normally includes:
> 1 Market assessment and sales forecasting
> 2 Formulation of marketing policy
> 3 The planning and operation of the marketing organization – internal and external – for achieving the desired level of sales and for dealing with customers
> 4 Sales promotion in all its forms
> 5 The costing and budgeting of marketing effort
> 6 The measurement of results by reference to internal data and the results of market research.[1]

This is a perfectly valid and worthwhile approach, provided it does not obscure the need for the whole company to be committed to the process that 'identifies, anticipates and satisfies customer requirements efficiently and profitably'.

1.2 The Marketing Concept

During the 1960s there emerged what is known as the 'marketing concept'. This is how we refer to the way in which many modern businesses have come to look at the total activity of their company in a different light. William J. Stanton, Professor of Marketing at the University of Colorado, says:

> The marketing concept is based on two fundamental beliefs. First, all company planning, policies, and operations should be oriented toward the customer; second, *profitable* sales volume should be the goal of a firm. In its fullest sense, the marketing concept is a philosophy of business which states that the customer's want satisfaction is the economic and social justification of a company's existence. Consequently, all company activities in production, engineering, and finance, as well as in marketing, must be devoted first to determining what the customer's wants are and then to satisfying those wants while still making a reasonable profit.[2]

A marketing executive at the General Electric Company, one of the first companies formally to recognize and implement the marketing concept, expressed the philosophy nicely when he said: 'We feel that marketing is a fundamental business philosophy. This definition recognizes marketing's functions and methods of organizational structuring as *only the implementation* of the philosophy. These things are not, in themselves, the philosophy.'

But the best-known writer on the subject is Professor Theodore Levitt of Harvard. He had this to say:

> Every major industry was once a growth industry. But some that are not riding a wave of growth enthusiasm are very much in the shadow of decline. Others which are thought of as seasoned growth industries have actually stopped growing. In every case the reason growth is threatened, slowed, or stopped is not because the market is saturated. It is because there has been a failure of management.
>
> The failure is at the top. The executives responsible for it in the last analysis are those who deal with broad aims and policies.
>
> Thus, the railroads did not stop growing because the need for passenger and freight transportation declined. That grew. The railroads are in trouble today not because the need was filled by others (cars, trucks, airplanes, even telephones), but because it was not filled by the railroads themselves. They let others take customers away from them because they assumed themselves to be in the railroad business rather than in the transportation business. The reason they defined their industry wrong was because they were product-oriented instead of customer-oriented.[3]

The terms 'product-oriented' and 'customer-oriented' have become important in marketing and in business management generally.

Peter Drucker, the world's leading writer on the whole field of management, says:

> It is the customer who determines what a business is. It is the customer alone whose willingness to pay for a good or service converts economic resources into wealth, things into goods. What the business thinks it produces is not of first importance – especially not to the future of the business and to its success . . . What the customer thinks he is buying, what he considers value, is decisive – it determines what a business is, what it produces and whether it will prosper. And what the customer buys and considers value is never a product. It is always utility, that is, what a product or service does for him . . . *Because its purpose is to create a customer, the business enterprise has two – and only these two – basic functions: marketing and innovation. Marketing and innovation produce results; all the rest are 'costs'* (Drucker's italics).[4]

It is vital for every company regularly to ask this question 'what business are we in?' and to answer it in terms of what its customers buy not in terms of what it produces.

1.3 The Need for the Marketing Concept

Even in the 1960s there was nothing new in the idea that the entire activity of a business should be devoted to serving its customers' interests. One of the first writers on economics, and still the most famous, was the Scotsman Adam Smith. He says:

> Consumption is the sole end and purpose of all production; and the interest of the producer ought to be attended to, only so far as it may be necessary for promoting that of the consumer. The maxim is so perfectly self-evident that it would be absurd to attempt to prove it. But in the mercantile system, the interest of the consumer is almost

constantly sacrificed to that of the producer; and it seems to consider production, and not consumption, as the ultimate end and object of all industry and commerce.[5]

So why has 'marketing' and the 'marketing concept' come into prominence only fairly recently as an important aspect of management? Largely because the growing complexity of modern industrial nations has tended to obscure the relationship between supplier and user. Some important aspects of this relation are the following:

1 The chain of communication between basic producer and ultimate consumer can be very long. The manufacturer supplies wholesalers or overseas agents who, in turn, supply retailers from whom the consumer buys. Manufacturer may never meet consumer. The relation between Allied Bakeries or Rank Hovis McDougall's and their customers is quite different from that between the village baker of 100 years ago and his customers.
2 The big development of the Industrial Revolution was mass production. Many goods became available for consumption or use by ordinary people for the first time, because they could be produced in vast quantity and therefore cheaply. Production on an ever-bigger scale was often the major factor in supplying customers' needs.
3 As basic needs become satisfied, people turn to more and more complex goods and services. It is likely that this will require a more sophisticated approach from suppliers, more investigation of customers' needs, greater communication with customers. When a car was a new wonder suddenly made available cheaply by Henry Ford's production line, turning out more cars was top priority. As more and more choice becomes available, as the steep increase in demand tails off or perhaps turns into a decline (as it did in 1977), then manufacturers need to consider more and more what kind of transportation their customers truly need. For example, there is continuing research for a cheap electric car which would be quiet, non-polluting and convenient for shopping etc.
4 As companies themselves become bigger and more complex, there is a greater tendency for objectives to become confused. The entrepreneur running a small localized business, dealing with sales, production and finance himself, stands a much better chance of correctly divining how to turn customers' needs into profitable business. (This is not to say that the marketing concept is not applicable to small businesses, merely that it is perhaps easier for them to stay constantly aware of their customers' needs.)
5 With ever-increasing social economic and technological changes, the need to monitor and respond to changing customer requirements on a planned basis.

Professor Kotler (see p. 33 for reference) sees a changing emphasis in management through the decades, as follows:

1910 Emphasis on engineering
1920 Financial restructuring, mergers, etc.
1930 Accounting, 'making the books look better' throughout the depression
1940 Production – getting more goods out faster
1950 Sales – as production overtook demand
1960 Marketing – to develop new products and markets

1970 Greater emphasis on strategic planning

1980 To ensure optimum use of resources.

To summarize, the marketing concept had become necessary to correct the following:

1 The preoccupation with production as the overriding business activity.
2 The communication gap that had developed between customers and their suppliers.

1.4 Present Status of the Marketing Concept

To many people, at least until recently, marketing had an important part to play in the state of the economy. A modern 'market economy' (i.e. one operated by individuals' decisions as to how they will deploy their personal spending power) depends on a high level of commercial activity to generate a high level of employment and prosperity. To quote Stanton again: 'American marketing activity has the task of encouraging the consumption of the vast output of goods and services of American business and industry.'[6]

However, as the idea that our planet's resources are finite grows, and as careful husbandry rather than ever-increasing consumption becomes for many the desirable aim, this approach comes under fire from some quarters: Stanton continues:

> Mass-production industries are impelled by a great drive to produce all they can. The prospect of steeply declining unit costs as output rises is more than most companies can usually resist. The profit possibilities look spectacular. All effort focuses on production. The result is that marketing gets neglected.
>
> John Kenneth Galbraith contends that just the opposite occurs. Output is so prodigious that all effort concentrates on trying to get rid of it. He says this accounts for singing commercials, desecration of the countryside with advertising signs, and other wasteful and vulgar practices. Galbraith has a finger on something real, but he misses the strategic point. Mass production does indeed generate great pressure to 'move' the product. But what usually gets emphasized is selling, not marketing. Marketing, being a more sophisticated and complex process, is ignored. The difference between marketing and selling is more than semantic. Selling focuses on the needs of the seller, marketing on the needs of the buyer. Selling is preoccupied with the seller's need to convert his product into cash; marketing with the idea of satisfying the needs of the customer by means of the product and the whole cluster of things associated with creating, delivering, and finally consuming it.
>
> In some industries the enticements of full mass production have been so powerful that for many years top management in effect has told the sales departments: 'You get rid of it; we'll worry about profits.' By contrast, a truly marketing-minded firm tries to create value-satisfying goods and services that consumers will want to buy. What it offers for sale includes not only the generic product or service, but also how it is made available to the customer – in what form, when, under what conditions, and at what terms of trade. Most important, what it offers for sale is determined not by the seller but by the buyer. The seller takes his cues from the buyer in such a way that the product becomes a consequence of the marketing effort, not vice versa.[7]

Stanton brings us back to the importance of definition, as he points out that the 'difference between marketing and selling is more than semantic'. Yet many of the criticisms aimed supposedly at marketing are really meant for some of the excesses of hard selling – shifting the goods on to the consumer at all costs.

It is difficult to see how much criticism could attach to marketing's aim of establishing customers' needs and setting out to satisfy them. There are still *some* criticisms, however. Consider the following:

1 The 'limited resources' argument, which suggests that it will not prove possible in the long run to satisfy everyone's needs. There is increasing doubt whether the whole world can ever live at the average level of present-day American families.
2 However well conducted most of it is, *some* marketing activity is bound to misfire and attract justified criticism. It is important to disentangle such situations from criticism of marketing as a whole.
3 Since marketing is concerned with satisfying customers' needs, there will always be concern over to what extent it is right or desirable that those needs should be satisfied. One man's necessity is another's totally undesirable luxury. A legitimate aim for one person seems to another a perversion of human existence.

Add to this the fact that (in the quotation at the head of the chapter), marketing is concerned with *anticipating* customer requirements. This is bound to lead on occasions to the charge that marketing creates needs and in the process causes people to buy things they could be perfectly happy without. During the 1970s and 1980s vociferous minorities emerged in strong support of consuming less rather than more and writers such as Schumacher in *Small is Beautiful*[8] questioned the whole concept of constant large-scale development (see Section 10.5).

It is better for our purposes perhaps to avoid this philosophical minefield and to concentrate on a rather narrower view. We happen to have in the U.K. (and many other countries) at the present time an economic system that allocates resources largely on the basis of a series of purchasing decisions made by individuals, followed by action taken by businesses to satisfy the demand thus created. While some people are happy with this system and many others feel that it is not totally satisfactory, it remains true that to the majority it still seems the best system on offer. Certainly, it is the one we currently have to work with.

This being the case, it seems undoubtedly best that businesses should devise their policies and carry them out with the customers' needs, not the needs of the business, as their central concern. Indeed any business that does not follow this course is likely to be unsuccessful in the long run, if not in the short, since, ultimately, it is the customer who decides whether to buy or not to buy.

It is this crucial role of the customer, the buyer, the consumer, which is the essence of the marketing concept. While our present economic system prevails, any business ignores consumer needs at its peril.

In our present economic system, for most businesses – even many of those in the public sector – profit is the measure of their success. For those in the private sector, profit is indeed essential for long-term survival. Since profit comes only from winning sufficient revenue at a sufficient margin over costs, profit ultimately depends on support from customers. Thus the whole future success and even continuation of the business depends on offering customers what they want at prices they will pay. This is the essence of the reasons why the marketing concept is so vital to a business. Increasingly, in the 1980s, it is being realized that even publicly-funded services cannot be sustained unless the investment in them produces worthwhile returns, i.e. they have to be 'profitable' in a sense.

1.5 Social Marketing and the Concept of Value – a Wider View of Marketing

It is becoming increasingly recognized that the marketing concept is just as applicable in non-commercial situations, where profit at least in the strict sense (but see above) is not one of the objectives, as in commercial situations. The term 'social marketing' is often used in this context. Government departments, the police, trade unions and trade associations, environmental groups and churches can all be said in a sense to have 'customers' and to be offering 'products' and 'services'.

Philip Kotler, a Montgomery Ward Professor of Marketing at the Graduate School of Management, North Western University, Evanston, Illinois, has examined this idea in depth. From it he has developed a wider concept of marketing than one that deals only with profit-making commercial organizations. The central theme of his argument runs as follows:

> What then is the disciplinary focus of marketing? The core concept of marketing is the transaction. A transaction is the exchange of values between two parties. The things-of-value need not be limited to goods, services, and money; they include other resources such as time, energy, and feelings. Transactions occur not only between buyers and sellers, and organisations and clients, but also between any two parties. A transaction takes place, for example, when a person decides to watch a television programme; he is exchanging his time for entertainment. A transaction takes place when a person votes for a particular candidate; he is exchanging his time and support for expectations of better government. A transaction takes place when a person gives money to a charity; he is exchanging money for a good conscience. Marketing is specifically concerned with how transactions are created, stimulated, facilitated and valued. This is the generic concept of marketing . . .
>
> Marketing is an approach to producing desired responses in another party that lies midway between coercion on the one hand and brainwashing on the other.
>
> The core concern of marketing is that of producing desired responses in free individuals by the judicious creation and offering of values. The marketer is attempting to get value from the market through offering value to it. The marketer's problem is to create attractive values. Value is completely subjective and exists in the eyes of the beholding market. Marketers must understand the market in order to be effective in creating value. This is the essential meaning of the marketing concept.
>
> The marketer seeks to create value in four ways. He can try to design the social object more attractively (configuration); he can put attractive terms on the social object (valuation); he can add symbolic significance in the social object (symbolisation); and he can make it easier for the market to obtain the social object (facilitation). He may use these activities in reverse if he wants the social object to be avoided. These four activities have a rough correspondence to more conventional statements of marketing purpose, such as the use of product, price, promotion, and place to stimulate exchange (*see* p. 33 for reference).

This brings us back to the commercial profit-making world again, where it is common to talk of 'added value': for example, Douglas W. Foster says, 'Basically, marketing is concerned with adding maximum value to a product or service to make it attractive and desirable to consumers while keeping costs at a minimum'.[9]

Value can be added, for example, in the following ways:

1 By converting raw materials into components or finished goods (steelmaking, car manufacture).
2 By breaking bulk, packing or processing products (wholesaling, takeaway meals).
3 By transporting goods from one place to another (importing tropical fruits).
4 By making goods available at a more convenient time (canned or frozen foods).

1.6 Customers and Their Behaviour

Since the customer is the focal point of all business activity, we must be clear about how customers behave. Because marketing is concerned with satisfying people's needs, we must understand what those needs are and the ways in which people go about getting them satisfied.

Any individual has a whole range of needs that he must or would like to satisfy, from the purely physical necessity of food and drink, through the emotional wish to be loved and appreciated to the desire to develop his personality – through education, a leisure activity or a fulfilling occupation. An American psychologist, A. L. Maslow, has expressed these varying levels of need in a way that is useful in the marketing context. He has written of the 'hierarchy of needs', the following five-stage progression:[10]

1 Basic physiological needs (food, sleep, temperature).
2 Safety needs (protection from danger).
3 The need for recognition (love, belonging).
4 Ego needs (self-esteem, respect from others).
5 Self-fulfilment (realization of one's total being, creativity).

It is clear that, as we progress through these stages, we are dealing first with needs that all people at all times have to some extent or other and have to satisfy in order to live. At the other end of the scale we have needs that few will ever satisfy, mainly because the majority of people are preoccupied with the more pressing needs at the lower levels. On the other hand, once a pressing need is satisfied, it is no longer felt. This is why people with sufficient income to keep them well fed, safe and warm become more and more aware of other, less basic, needs such as ego-satisfaction. 'Keeping up with the Joneses' may or may not be laudable but it does become a strong need for many people once they are fed, housed and clothed to a reasonable level.

Thus individuals will vary widely in the needs that at present pre-occupy them. Some will be mainly concerned with acquiring the bare necessities (you will fail to interest them in fancy furnishings), whereas others will be seeking exciting leisure pursuits (no good talking to them about buying their first suit – they already have four).

We also need to be aware of how people satisfy their needs. There is a multi-stage process, which can be expressed as follows:

1 *Need.* A need is felt. This may be a vague or general need (I am feeling jaded and need a bit of excitement) or specific (I want to go to the cinema today).

2 *Search*. Ways of satisfying the need are actively or passively sought. The newspapers and magazines may be scanned for offers that may satisfy the need (e.g. the lists of 'What's on' in entertainment); or I may merely keep my eyes and ears open and register more keenly than usual any possible solutions to my need.

In more complex situations the search process may be long and deliberate. The family seeking new kitchen equipment will read magazines, talk to friends, go to showrooms and exhibitions. The industrial buyer may ask for samples, demonstrations, competitive tenders or carry out extensive cost-benefit analysis.

3 *Decision*. When sufficient information has been gathered and suitable alternatives examined, a decision will be taken and the purchase made.

4 *Post-purchase feelings*. For the customer-oriented company the process does not end when the purchase is made. The customer's need is only satisfied if the product or service does perform in the expected fashion and does indeed meet his need, not only initially but, where appropriate, over a longer period. It must perform in the expected way, and after-sales service must be adequate.

The precise way in which this process works needs to be understood. It will vary from one group of consumers to another, in particular in its time-scale: for a snack bought to satisfy a sudden pang of hunger the whole process may be over in a few minutes, but for a power station or a new military aircraft it will take many years. The domestic appliance industry in the U.K. wasted vast sums on advertising at one stage because it did not clearly appreciate that only when people are in the 'search' stage will they be receptive to advertising of this kind of product. (See Sections 10.1–10.3 for further discussion of these aspects.)

1.7 The Competitive Situation

Marketing is not carried out in a vacuum but usually in a highly competitive situation. Classical economics talks of the state of perfect competition, where the following conditions apply:

1 Many suppliers none of whom dominates the market.
2 Many purchasers, again unable individually to exert pressure on suppliers.
3 One supplier's product or service is no different from another's.
4 There is free entry to the market.
5 There is 'perfect knowledge', i.e. everyone knows what is being offered and at what price.

In this situation the outcome is that prices and profits are pushed down to the minimum, since new suppliers will be attracted to the industry if prices rise, and the extra amount available over what is demanded by customers will force the price down. On the other hand, if prices fall too low, some suppliers will leave the industry, and the drop in quantity will make prices rise. So there is an 'equilibrium price', which anyone trading in the market has to take; firms are 'price-takers'.

This is, of course, the real-life situation in some specialized markets – commodities, fresh farm produce, the Stock Exchange. But, typically, this simple model does not fit the facts of the real world – as economists have realized in developing the concept of imperfect competition.

One of the main factors in imperfect competition is that all products are not the same. Indeed, since firms generally do not wish to be price-takers, with no control over their level of profit and, hence, whether or not they can stay in business, they will do all they can to develop ways in which they can satisfy customers' needs in a better way than can their competitors.

This has given rise to the concept of 'competitive differential advantage'. Firms will try to outdo their competitors by offering customers a clear-cut difference in the products and/or services they offer, in the hope, naturally, that customers will find the difference an improvement on what competitors are offering. The difference may be created in a number of different areas, as follows:

1 *Product*. The product or service itself may be different. The soup may have a richer flavour or take less time to prepare; the car may have better performance or use less fuel.
2 *Cost*. There may be a cost advantage to the customer, because the initial price is lower, because maintenance will cost less, because better credit terms are available.
3 *Services*. As well as the basic performance the product or service gives, there can be a whole range of services offered as part of the marketing process, including:
   Pre-sale. A civil engineering company may do a free feasibility study, a television rental firm may offer a week's free trial, a car dealer a test run.
   Post-sale. Free maintenance for a period, training of operators, a supply of 'up-dating' material (*Encyclopaedia Britannica*, for example).
4 *Distribution*. The sheer availability of a product may be a very attractive feature. Car-hire firms will meet customers at the station or airport, Coca-Cola is available in lean-to shops in African bush villages as well as in big city centres.
5 *Promotion*. The way a product is presented may enhance its appeal to the consumer. Perfume attractively packaged and exotically advertised, bakery products with an 'olde-worlde' presentation ('like those mother made').

One of the reasons why the idea of the marketing mix is so important (Section 3.2) is that from the elements of the mix we can develop a strong competitive differential advantage to offer to our customers. (See Section 19.4 for further development of this theme.)

1.8 A Dynamic Activity

A firm with a marketing policy (and all firms have, whether they recognize it or not) is dealing all the time with a whole series of variables. Among them are the following:

1 *The General Economic Situation*. Boom or recession, growth or stagnation, a developed or an under-developed economy, will have a profound effect on what is possible and on how marketing can operate.
2 *Customer Needs*. The social climate will affect the needs customers feel to be important, as will the level of development of a society.
3 *Competition*. What competitors are doing will profoundly affect what is possible.

4 *Technology*. The introduction of a new technology, such as plastics or electronics, will completely change the existing situation.

5 *Legislation*. Governments are increasingly intervening in the operation of the market place and hence changing the commercial environment.

These and other factors change all the time, both independently of each other and in reaction to each other. Collectively, they have a kaleidoscopic effect, which means that the total marketing environment constantly changes. Companies must be aware of these changes and react to them. Going on doing as we have always done must lead sooner or later to a situation where we apply yesterday's answers to today's problems, and disaster must follow.

Because marketing is concerned with what people will do tomorrow, it is always subject to risk and uncertainty. (Risk means that we know that certain actions may have a number of different outcomes, and we have to calculate the odds in favour of the outcome we desire; there are other areas where we just do not know – that is uncertainty.) There can never be total knowledge about the future; we can, however, make sure that we do know what the present situation is, and where events appear to be leading. Information is a precious commodity in all business activity, and nowhere more so than in marketing.

The factors listed here are often referred to as the non-controllable variables – those which companies and individuals cannot control but have to build into their marketing planning. The marketing mix (Section 3.2) contains the controllable variables which can be changed to provide us with the appropriate response.

1.9 The Marketing Process

We can view marketing as a constant series of actions and reactions between the customers in the market and the marketing organizations trying to satisfy their needs. The customers make their needs known, the firms make it their business to receive the information. The firms use their resources (money, materials, skills, ingenuity) to develop ways of satisfying the needs. Firms must then communicate the existence of the 'solutions' back to the customers, whose needs created the 'problems' (Figure 1.1).

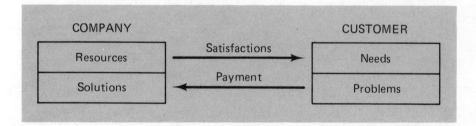

Figure 1.1 Marketing process

The remainder of the first half of this book is devoted to examining this process in more detail. It is in providing the necessary information that marketing research is all-important (Chapter 2). On the other side of that 'loop', satisfactions are provided by offering the correct marketing mix (Chapter 3) – the right product, at the right price, available in the right places and promoted in the right way. The provision of satisfactions by developing the correct marketing mix depends on the full exploitation of all the possibilities of developing differential advantages, through product (Chapters 4 and 5), pricing policies (Chapter 6), distribution (Chapter 7), and promotion (Chapter 8).

1.10 Special Marketing Situations

There is a natural tendency for people to see their own particular industry, market or type of operation as being quite different from every other. Thus seminars are held and books written on e.g. the marketing of financial services (banking, insurance, etc.) or on industrial marketing. Clearly the type of customers one is dealing with and the nature of the needs they are trying to satisfy or the problems to which they seek solutions has a strong influence on the way marketing companies respond. This book however supports the approach of most serious marketing thinkers – there is no fundamental difference in the marketing process. The same analysis has to be done, the same questions asked. The marketing answer will be different, but there are few if any clear lines along which these differences split. Marketing pop records to teenagers is different from marketing

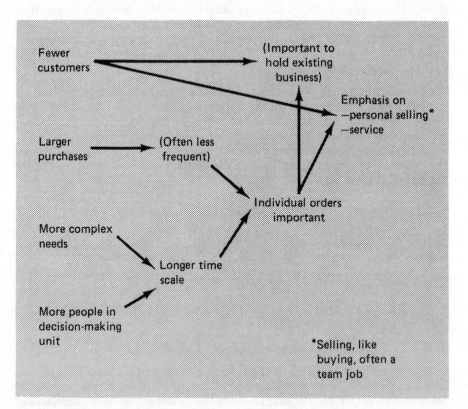

Figure 1.2 Industrial marketing characteristics

pharmaceuticals to doctors. Banks however may find themselves offering their services to students using techniques very similar to those used to promote clothes or electronic equipment to the same market.

If there is a clear distinction it is probably between purchases made for personal satisfaction (which we may refer to as consumer purchases) and purchases made on behalf of an organization (loosely called *industrial* or *business to business marketing*) (See Section 4.24).

1.101 *Industrial Marketing* (Business to Business Marketing)

There are some differences here which mainly consist in:

1 A rather more rational, deliberative and scientific approach. This should not be exaggerated. 'Industrial consumables' (stationery etc.) are sometimes bought with very little thought; expensive consumer purchases (cars, houses, etc.) may sometimes be approached very scientifically.
2 A more complex decision-making unit (see Section 13.5) although again in some major domestic purchases the whole family may be involved.
3 Because there are frequently a small number of very large companies, holding existing business may be very important indeed.
4 The complexities of technological products mean that a great deal of service is required.

For these last two reasons, the personal sales force may carry a much higher weight of responsibility than other promotional techniques such as advertising in the promotional mix (see Section 8.2).

1.102 *Marketing Services*

Great play is often made of the difference between goods (tangible products) and services (intangible products). This distinction has little value when it comes to marketing considerations, since what customers buy in any case is the 'satisfactions' delivered by either a tangible or an intangible product (see Section 4.2).

1.11 Summary

1 Marketing is the term used to describe the following:
   (a) A part of the company or a particular job within the company.
   (b) A series of activities, such as sales, advertising, or market research, which are more particularly concerned with the company's customers.
   (c) A business philosophy – the marketing concept.

2 The marketing concept puts customers at the centre of the company's activities. The business is then concerned with satisfying customers' needs at a profit. 'What the customer thinks he is buying, what he considers value, is decisive – it determines what a business is, what it produces and whether it will prosper.'[11]

3 The marketing concept has become more and more necessary with the growth of mass production and mass distribution, with the consequent lengthening

and complication of the chain of communication between manufacturer and customer.

4 The marketing approach is of value not only in commercial situations but in any 'transaction' (exchange of values between two parties), including 'social marketing'.

5 The marketing process starts with a customer's need, for which he seeks a satisfaction. The search leads ultimately to a decision – but the marketer is also concerned with the customer's post-purchase feelings as to whether his need has been adequately met.

6 The marketing process operates in conditions of imperfect competition, and a key aspect of it is the identification of the competitive differential advantage.

7 Marketing is a dynamic activity, which must constantly respond to changes in a whole series of variables, including the economic situation, customers' needs, competition and the development of technology.

8 Marketing is best viewed as a process in which companies deliver solutions to customers' problems (hence satisfaction of customers' needs) in return for payment.

References

1 Statement by the Institute of Marketing and Sales Management, forerunner of the Institute of Marketing.

2 In *The Fundamentals of Marketing*, 3rd ed. (McGraw-Hill, 1971).

3 In 'Marketing Myopia', *Harvard Business Review* (July–August 1960). For the full implications of the marketing concept, Theodore Levitt's paper is a 'must'. Most college libraries with a management studies department will have back copies of the *H.B.R.* in which it appeared. It was also printed as one of a series of articles in *Modern Marketing Strategy*, edited by Bursk and Chapman, and published in paperback by the New English Library (Mentor Books, 1965). Some of the other articles are well worth reading, too.

4 In *Management: Tasks, Responsibilities, Practices* (Peter Drucker).

5 *Wealth of Nations* (1776).

6 *In The Fundamentals of Marketing*, op. cit.

7 ibid.

8 Schumacher, E. M. *Small is Beautiful* (Abacus, 1974).

9 In *Planning for Products and Markets* (Longman, 1972).

10 All Maslow's discussions of consumer needs appear in his *Motivation and Personality* (Harper & Row, 1954).

11 In *Management: Tasks, Responsibilities, Practices*, op. cit.

Further Reading

Donaldson, Peter. *Economics of the Real World* (Pelican, 1973). This originally accompanied a series of programmes on BBC TV. It is intended for the general reader, and gives a no-nonsense explanation of the way supply and demand operate and examines critically (but without jargon) economic theories of perfect and imperfect competition. A good layman's introduction to economics.

Drucker, Peter. *Managing for Results* (Pan, 1967). Marketing in relation to business management is dealt with superbly in Chapter 6, 'The Customer is the Business'.

Foxall, Gordon R. *Consumer Behaviour – A Practical Guide* (Croom Helm, 1980). An excellent summary of consumer behaviour theory.

Rodger, Leslie W. *Marketing in a Competitive Economy* (Hutchinson, 1965), p. 60. A good analysis of the differences between production-oriented and marketing-oriented companies.

Questions for Discussion

1 How is the marketing concept relevant in the following situations? In each case discuss what would be the 'product', who the 'customer', what form distribution would take and how 'promotion' would be carried out.

   (a) A 'population control' programme by the government of an under-developed country.
   (b) A 'stately home' open to the public.
   (c) A new inexpensive method of insulating houses against heat loss.

2 (IM, Nov. 1982) Why has marketing only fairly recently become an important aspect of management?

3 Can marketing be justified in an era when we are becoming more and more conscious of the finite resources of 'Planet Earth'?

4 Write briefly about three firms which appear to you to be very customer-oriented, saying on what basis you make this judgement.

5 Outline two examples of firms who seem to you to be production-oriented and indicate any disadvantages you think this situation offers

   (a) to the firms,
   (b) to their customers.

6 How would you define the 'value added' by the following?

   (a) An airline.
   (b) Your local college of further education.
   (c) A shopping precinct or covered shopping centre.
   (d) A frozen food company.

7 Peter Drucker claims that 'the business enterprise has only two basic functions: marketing and innovation. Marketing and innovation produce results; all the rest are "costs".' How would you justify this statement to

   (a) a production man,
   (b) an accountant?

8 What customer needs are satisfied by the following?

   (a) The Royal Opera House, Covent Garden.
   (b) Chinese take-away restaurants.
   (c) Marketing textbooks.
   (d) Canned pet food.
   (e) Electric typewriters.

2. *Gathering Facts for Marketing*

(Market Research is) the gathering, recording, analysing and reporting of all facts relating to the transfer and sale of goods and services, from producer to consumer. It is usually, but not necessarily, based on statistical probability theory and always uses the scientific method.

Max K. Adler. *Lectures in Market Research*

2.1 Why Marketing Research is Necessary

We saw in Section 1.8 that all business is conducted under conditions of risk and uncertainty. The success or failure of any business is dependent on a whole complex of factors; the economic situation, the changing tastes of consumers, the extent and nature of competitive activity are just a few of them.

Business decisions, and especially marketing decisions, are decisions about the future. Marketing has been described as 'making the future happen'. Since the future cannot be totally known, the uncertainty cannot be completely removed,

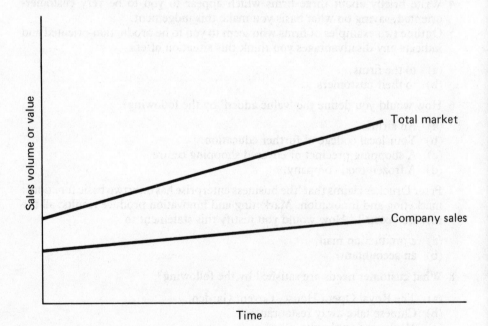

Figure 2.1 Rising sales with falling market share

16

or the risks be precisely calculated. However, it is asking for trouble not to use whatever information is available. Many facts can be known and unnecessary risk can thus be avoided.

For example, while a firm can very easily know how its own sales are progressing, this information is relatively meaningless without knowledge of the total size of the market and whether that is increasing or decreasing. A company may be confident in the knowledge of a rising sales curve but unaware of the fact that the total market is increasing at an even greater rate, so that really it is losing ground, with a reducing market share (Figure 2.1).

Often information on the total market for a product is freely available – from government statistics, trade associations or similar sources. If it is not freely available in this way, market research techniques can be used to get it. But, as we shall see later, this is just one example of the vital necessity for information about the market situation.

2.2 What Marketing Research Is

'Research' is defined in the *Concise Oxford Dictionary* as 'Careful search or inquiry; endeavour to discover new facts etc., by scientific study of a subject, course of critical investigation; and 'scientific' as 'According to rules laid down in science for testing soundness of conclusions, systematic, accurate'. The *Dictionary*'s use of such words as 'careful', 'systematic', 'accurate', 'new facts', and 'investigation' indicates what kind of activity market research is. We can go further and say that if it is objective (not subjective) and unbiased, its investigations will be systematic, orderly and exhaustive.

Note, incidentally, that marketing research is the preferred term used by the Institute of Marketing and in this book, because it is all-embracing. It covers all research activities carried out in connection with any aspect of marketing work. Thus it includes audience and readership research, product testing and many other kinds of research. Strictly speaking, 'market research', on the other hand, means research into 'markets' – their size, composition etc. – but in practice the two terms are used synonymously. The professional body is the Market Research Society, and many of the standard books (including the one quoted in the heading to this chapter) have the words 'market research' in their titles.

The range of activities covered by marketing research is enormous. We examine them more fully in Chapter 11, but here is a summary of some of the main ones.

2.21 *Markets*

1 What is the size of the market (in terms of volume and/or value) and is it decreasing or increasing?
2 What are the market shares of ourselves and our competitors and are these changing?
3 How is the size and trend of the market influenced by various factors (economic, social, seasonal)?
4 What is the composition of the market in terms of age groups, income groups, size of company or geographical area?

5 What are the main distribution channels and how do they function?

2.22 *Competitors*

1 What competitors are there and how do their product ranges, prices etc., compare?
2 What are their marketing strategies?
3 How are their products distributed, advertised, packaged?
4 How does their sales force operate?
5 Are any new competitors likely to enter the market?

2.23 *Products*

1 Which products do consumers prefer and why?
2 Are proposed new products acceptable?
3 Do consumers have complaints about products presently on the market which could indicate a possible new product opportunity?

2.24 *Advertising*

1 Who reads which publications; who watches/listens to which TV/radio channels?
2 Are existing or proposed advertising campaigns communicating effectively?
3 What are the motivations that activate consumers and is our advertising correctly interpreting them?

2.3 The Origins of Marketing Research

Marketing research seems to have developed in America during a period from the late nineteenth century up to and into the 1920s. Charles Coolidge Parkin, who seems to be acknowledged as the outstanding figure in this development, is said to have founded the first commercial research company in the 1920s. Names which also stem from this era and which are still going strong are Daniel Starch (advertising effectiveness research) and George Gallup (opinion polls).

Although marketing research developed originally in the United States, Great Britain soon followed. Unilever was conducting market research among consumers during 1920–24. For many years the best known company in the field here was Mass Observation Limited, founded in 1937. Not until 1947, however, was the Market Research Society founded, and this was a reflection of the fact that the business was now firmly established.

2.4 How Marketing Research Is Organized

Marketing research is a specialized job. While in principle it can be carried out by anyone, there are serious potential pitfalls, as follows:

1 The necessary objective unbiased approach needs to be acquired or 'trained into' people. Salesmen, for example, are usually not suitable for obtaining research information, because their training and instincts are such that they are

enthusiasts for a particular point of view – partisan for their own product. If not, they might well be less effective as salesmen.

2 Some of the techniques employed demand skills and disciplines that have to be learned.

Usually therefore, marketing research is a task for the specialist. These specialists are found in three main groups.

2.41 *'In-company' Departments*

Many companies have their own marketing research departments. This has the advantage that the people concerned can specialize, and over the years acquire great knowledge of the fields in which they operate and the best techniques for gathering information for their particular purposes. It can thus be a very economic way of providing the necessary information. The disadvantages are a possible tendency to bias, which can, of course, be guarded against and resisted; and the fact that it may be difficult to give them a full workload at all times, so that the operation may become uneconomic. But they do provide additional security of information.

2.42 *Advertising Agencies*

Advertising agencies need to prepare advertising campaigns within a total marketing plan and in the light of the fullest possible knowledge about markets. They also need much detailed information on readership and audiences, on motivation and on reactions to advertising themes. For these reasons many agencies employ their own marketing research specialists, who work for the agency and its clients. Indeed, the agencies had much to do with the whole development of market research in this country.

The trend over many years now has been for these market research units to be operated as quite distinct departments or completely separate companies. They work for a whole range of clients, in addition to those of the advertising agency, and normally charge for their services in the same way as would a market research agency (which is what many eventually become).

2.43 *Market Research Agencies*

There are many individuals and companies offering their services as market research agencies. Some offer a very wide range of services, whereas others are highly specialized. The Market Research Society publishes a list of these with an indication of their capability in its annual Yearbook.

Among the specialist services available are (a) retail audits and panels, (b) motivation research, and (c) audience measurement. Some organizations specialize in one stage of the research process, such as interviewing or the processing and analysis of data.

2.5 Sources of Marketing Research Data

The items of information gathered as the basis of marketing research are usually referred to as data and we speak of *primary* data and *secondary* data. The former is information collected by means of a research programme carried out for a specific purpose. The latter is information that already exists, because it was collected as part of a previous research operation or for some different purpose.

Secondary data can be found inside a company, in sales records in particular. When used for marketing research, such data probably need reorganizing. For example, sales of a particular product will often be listed customer by customer, whereas the research might call for a geographical breakdown. Alternatively, many external sources of secondary data are available, in government departments, trade associations, professional bodies, the press, specialist research agencies and many other sources. The increasing availability, power and flexibility of computers makes it increasingly easy for this information to be made immediately available to decision-makers.

Some research agencies operate syndicated research programmes in special fields. These are research programmes set up on a co-operative basis and paid for by contributions from each of the companies taking part. Usually it is possible to 'buy into' such a programme and thus gain access to data already collected. Alternatively, agencies sometimes themselves mount a programme of research and offer the results for sale to anyone interested. Trade associations often make certain information freely available to their members but sell it to 'outsiders'.

Increasingly all this kind of information is built into a total 'Marketing Information System' which is constantly up-dated.

2.51 *The Collection of Primary Data*

If the information required for a particular marketing research project does not already exist as secondary data, we have to determine the best way of collecting it. There are three fundamental approaches to the collection of primary data – observation, experiment, and survey. It is the third approach that most people normally associate with market research, and later sections deal with it at length. The first two, however, also have an important role to play in certain circumstances.

Observation. It is sometimes better to watch what people do rather than to ask them what they do. This has the advantage that it eliminates any problem of interviewer-bias and avoids the difficulty that people do not always remember their actions – especially trivial ones – very clearly. For example, a hidden camera may be the best way of establishing how customers move through a shop, and a tape recorder the best method of establishing the sales approach used by salesmen. Similarly a physical count is normally used to establish the volume of traffic on key roads and the volume of different brands sold by important retail outlets.

Experiment. Simulation of a real situation may often be a better way of assessing likely future behaviour than asking people hypothetical questions. It is notoriously difficult to get reliable answers about possible future behaviour; but, if for example, we want to know which of two possible packages housewives would prefer, we can put them side by side in a real or dummy shop, give a group of housewives a shopping list and money to spend and see which pack they choose.

Similarly, a way of assessing children's preference for one toy as against another is to give a group of children a selection of toys to play with and see what happens (the way in which they play can also yield valuable insights). Test marketing is of course an example of experiment as a means of obtaining marketing research data.

2.6 Basic Types of Survey

If it is necessary to obtain primary data by survey, three methods are available. They are (a) personal interviews, (b) telephone interviews, and (c) postal questionnaires. In general, the cost decreases as we go down this list, but so does the reliability and the extent of the information that can be obtained.

Personal interviewing is the most versatile and can fairly readily be carried out on the basis of a properly selected sample (see Chapter 11). A large number of detailed questions can be asked, and the answers can be supplemented by the interviewer's personal observations if required. But the cost per interviewer is high, and the degree of planning and supervision required adds further to the cost.

Telephone interviewing enables many people to be reached quickly over a wide geographical area. For this reason it is widely used in industrial marketing research. Its drawbacks are that, generally speaking, only short interviews of an impersonal nature can be carried out; and since, in the UK at any rate, telephones in the home are by no means universal, an inevitable bias is likely to be introduced where most consumer marketing situations are concerned. This situation is changing rapidly however as telephones are installed in more and more households – around 70 per cent and rising fast in 1983.

Postal questionnaires are relatively very cheap and do not have the built-in bias which obtains when telephones are used. However, the response rate (number of people who return properly completed questionnaires) is usually very low, which introduces its own form of bias.

2.7 Further Survey Methods

For particular purposes, variations of the following surveying techniques have proved valuable.

2.71 Panels

When continuing research is required, the panel method is often used. This differs from the *ad hoc* enquiry (see Section 11.2) in that the same group (or panel) of informants is used to provide a series of answers over a period of time. This arrangement is particularly valuable when the need is to establish trends. Disadvantages are that it is difficult to maintain over a long period a panel that is truly representative; panel members may gradually become self-conscious and the information they provide no longer a spontaneous expression of their personal views.

Panels are used extensively in listener/viewer research and the retail shop audit panel is a well established source of information.

2.72 *Discussion Groups*

A small and carefully selected group of people are brought together to discuss a particular topic. The interviewer does not normally pose specific questions but intervenes only to ensure that the discussion stays on subject and that all important aspects are discussed. Because interpretation of results can be difficult, interviewers (or more correctly discussion leaders) are frequently qualified psychologists.

Discussion groups cannot be regarded as properly representative and statistical analysis is normally impossible. However, they have the advantage that (a) they are relatively inexpensive, and (b) that the dynamic group situation may bring out information that would not have been foreseen by someone constructing a questionnaire. The technique is particularly valuable in obtaining information rapidly and inexpensively, e.g. as a guide to copywriters and product development groups and as an aid in constructing questionnaires for pilot surveys.

2.73 *Motivational Research*

This had a strong vogue some years ago but is now much less popular. It uses methods adapted from clinical psychology in an attempt to establish motives for behaviour and opinions. The methods used include word association, ink-blot tests, and sentence completion tests.

While in theory such methods can give deep insight into human attitudes, in practice much doubt has been cast on the validity of the results. Certainly, to carry out such tests thoroughly is very expensive of highly trained manpower, since interviews must be individually conducted and each can last several hours.

2.8 How Marketing Research is Conducted

A great deal of time and money can be wasted unless marketing research is conducted in a carefully planned manner. Some kind of logical sequence, such as the following, should always be observed.

2.81 *Identify the Problem*

It is vital at the outset to be quite clear what information is needed and for what purpose. Usually it will be required to provide a basis for a management decision. The nature of that decision and the precise way in which the additional information will help in taking it will dictate the kind of information required. Without such definition marketing research is liable to be used to gather a vast quantity of information at great cost but with low utility.

2.82 *Agree Terms of Reference*

At what time is the information needed, how much is it worth spending to obtain it, precisely what areas are to be studied and what is their relative importance?

2.83 *Plan the Survey*

Factors to be decided upon at this stage include the following:

1 Define the market in which we shall be interested; this is the 'universe', the total number of people from whom the sample will be selected.
2 Decide on the sampling technique. More will be said about sampling in Chapter 12 – sufficient here to say that marketing research uses extensively the technique of assessing the response of the many by studying that of a carefully selected few, just as a farmer judges the ripeness and quality of his wheat crop by examining a few grains from different parts of the field.
3 Decide on the survey method to be used.
4 Draft the questionnaire. Most surveys use a series of questions (the questionnaire), which must be constructed with great care to elicit suitable responses from those being interviewed. The principles are discussed in Chapter 12.

Planning the survey will also include working out a detailed timetable and allocating manpower and such other resources as computer time. It will also have to be decided whether a single- or multi-stage survey is necessary, and whether there is need for a 'pilot' survey in advance of the survey proper.

2.84 *Execute the Survey*

The survey has now to be carried out.

2.85 *Analyse the Results*

This is normally done by computer, the questionnaire being constructed whenever possible so that results can be entered in tabular form and easily transferred on to punched card or tape (or even entered in magnetic ink, which can be electronically 'read'). With the rapid development of 'microchip technology' it becomes increasingly easy – and hence inexpensive – to feed results straight into the system for analysis.

2.86 *Report to Management*

Market researchers differ as to whether they should merely report results, go further and interpret them, or go further still and offer recommendations. While one can disagree about whose job it is, ultimately the results of marketing research must be translated into management decisions. There is thus an intermediate and vital stage between delivery of the 'raw' facts and management coming to a decision, which means interpreting the facts and assessing their importance.

2.9 The Limitations of Marketing Research

It is tempting to think that all management decisions would be easier if only there was more information, and that marketing research is the key to better marketing management. There is some truth in this but marketing research does have severe limitations. First, it can be very costly. This can mean that obtaining the information on which to base a 'better' decision would absorb any profit the decision might produce. Second, it can be time-consuming. Time is often all-important in marketing decisions. A good guess at the right time may be better than precise knowledge two months too late. Third, it solves nothing by itself. All over the world there are shelves full of market research reports that have not been acted upon. Marketing research is only valuable if it helps in making effective decisions. This takes us right back to the beginning and the vital importance of being quite clear at the outset why we need further information.

2.10 Summary

1 Marketing research is the careful systematic search for facts about markets and about all aspects of the marketing process.
2 Marketing research is an important aid to management because it can improve decisions by providing a greater quantity of more reliable information than would otherwise be available.
3 Information consists of *secondary data* from existing sources, and of *primary data*, which is obtained by (a) observation (b) experiment, or (c) survey.
4 The three types of survey are (a) personal interview, (b) telephone interview, and (c) postal questionnaire; they are listed in order of decreasing cost but also of decreasing yield and reliability.
5 Marketing research must be conducted according to a carefully conceived plan and in the light of a clear understanding of how the information to be obtained will contribute to improved management decision-making.
6 The limitations of marketing research are cost, time and that it is of no value in itself – only if acted upon.

Further Reading

Adler, Max K. *Lectures in Market Research* (Crosby Lockwood, 1969). A very good summary of all aspects of the subject.
Crouch, Sunny. *Marketing Research for Managers* (Heinemann, 1984).
Journal of the Market Research Society (July 1974). Two papers, which won the 1973 Gold Medals for marketing and advertising research, deal interestingly with the origins and development of marketing research, and throw a great deal of light on its uses.

Questions for Discussion

1 What sources of secondary data would you consider if you were seeking information on the following markets:
    (a) Snack foods (peanuts, crisps, etc.).
    (b) Combine harvesters.
    (c) Dishwashers.
    (d) Word processors.
2 Give three examples of business situations where an experimental research technique could yield valuable information.
3 Similarly, give three examples where observational techniques might be the best approach.
4 (IM, June 1983) 'Although an up-to-date knowledge of the market is essential for successful marketing, research seldom provides all the answers and is never a substitute for executive decision-making'. Comment on this statement

indicating the scope, value and limitations of marketing research.
5 Which of the three main survey methods (personal interview, telephone, postal) might be most appropriate to each of the following situations:

(a) An electronics journal aimed at technical people in industry and with a world-wide controlled circulation wishes to gain knowledge of the job function and seniority pattern of its readers.
(b) A manufacturer of highly specialized machine tools wishes to know how they are rated by customers and non-customers in comparison with competitors' products.
(c) A manufacturer of knitting wools finds sales of his products falling, although the quality and price compare favourably with those of competitors.
(d) A brewery wishes to know whether a proposed new beer will be preferred to existing beers.
(e) A food company wishes to gain some insight into the probable acceptance and likely market segments for a meat-flavoured man-made protein.

6 (CAM, Nov. 1982) Charles Revson is quoted as saying 'In the factory we make cosmetics. In the Drug Store we sell hope'. Explain what is meant by this statement.
7 (IM, June 1982) What are the main activities of your own company and your competitors on which marketing research can provide information?

3. *The Right Mixture and the Vital Spark*

'Marketing mixes have to be changed from time to time in response to new factors in the marketing picture. The firm can react to environmental changes in an expedient or a systematic fashion.'

Philip Kotler. *Marketing Management*

3.1 Satisfying Customer's Needs

In Chapters 4 and 5 we shall go on to see what are the characteristics products have to have in order to meet customers' needs, and then look at how best to develop suitable products. But, first, we must put products into perspective and recognize that, in order to satisfy customers' needs, we have to consider not merely the product as such but other things as well.

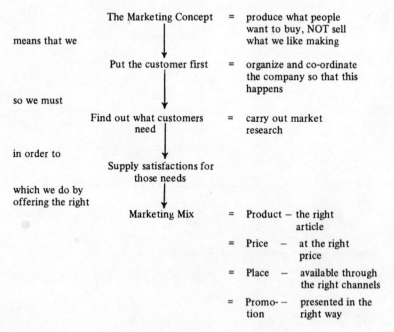

Figure 3.1 The marketing concept

26

We saw in Section 1.7 that the competitive climate within which marketing operates gives rise to the need to seek a competitive differential advantage. It is naive to assume that competition can be met only by producing a 'better' product. (In any case, what is 'better' for some customers may be 'less good' for others – the man whose pocket will only support a Mini may recognize that a Rolls is 'better' in some respects, but the Mini is 'better' for him.) We have to take into account the whole range of customer requirements. These will include not merely product performance, but also price, convenience of purchase and the way the product or service is presented. We describe the marketing process very simply in Figure 3.1.

3.2 The Marketing Mix

The 'marketing mix' is the term used to describe the appropriate combination, in a particular set of circumstances, of the four key elements that are at the heart of a company's marketing programme. It is easy to see why if any one of these elements is wrong, the marketing programme will fail, and the company will not profit from the operation as it should.

3.21 *Product*

If the product or service (see Section 4.2) offered does not perform in the required way, customers will not buy a second time, and the word will get round to prospective customers so that they will not buy even once. A car with poor performance or excessive breakdowns, a 'tasty snack' that does not seem very tasty to its consumers, a magazine that does not interest its readers, or a laundrette that is never open when customers want to use it, are all examples of faulty products. (Clearly, to some extent, other items in the marketing mix can act to compensate for shortcomings in this area. I may decide to accept more breakdowns in a car if it is cheap enough, or buy the snack I do not like too well if my usual shops stock it rather than the one I prefer.)

3.22 *Price*

No matter how good the product, some people will be unable to pay more than a certain price. Others may be able to afford it but believe that another way of spending that sum of money would give them greater satisfaction. Conversely, as we have just seen, simply being cheap is not enough – the product must come up to some level of expected performance. In some situations (luxury goods, etc.) a high price may even make the product more desirable than a lower one. The likely response of demand to a change in price ('elasticity' in economic terms) will affect our decisions on pricing policy (see Chapter 6).

3.23 *Place*

We must not expect customers to shop around too much in order to find our particular product. It should be available at the place convenient to them. In some cases their attachment (brand loyalty) to a particular manufacturer's product may be so strong that they will go miles to find it and refuse to accept alternatives; but this is unusual. If one type of beer is not available, many people will take another, or if one evening newspaper is sold out, will buy its rival. The biggest single factor in deciding which brand of petrol people buy is which garage is most convenient for them to stop at. Coca-Cola is the world's best-selling soft drink largely because it is readily available virtually everywhere. Sometimes the best way of making the product easily available is to give people easy access direct to the producer (mail-order, freephone ordering using credit-cards, Prestel, etc.).

3.24 *Promotion*

The term is used here to include personal selling as well as all forms of advertising and sales promotion, packaging and display.

A well presented product will score over one that is badly presented. Men would be unlikely to buy as a present for their wives a perfume, however good, which was offered in a cheap plastic bottle inside a grubby brown box. In the case of gifts, presentation can be all-important. Easter-egg packaging may well cost more than the chocolate it contains. The way some kinds of consumer product are spoken of by salesmen or in advertising may give them the aura customers seek, whereas an oil rig or a machine tool must above all else carry out its function, and its presentation is relatively unimportant. Note 'relatively' unimportant, because even in the extreme case it is likely that promotion will have some part to play.

So far we have established the point that a failure in any one of these four factors may damage the chances of success in the market place no matter how good the others are. The opposite point needs to be made also. Getting any one of them right adds to the total chances of success. Getting them all right will have a synergistic effect. In other words, the total combined effect will be greater than we might expect by adding up the individual effects – the whole is greater than the sum of the parts.

There is, however, a complication: what we do to one element in the marketing mix can have an effect on one or more of the others, especially the price. Thus, if we want to improve the product's performance, we may have to build in features that will add to its price. On the other hand, the fact that the product performs better may make it more acceptable to more people; this in turn will lead to higher sales, bigger production runs and lower unit costs and prices.

Price and promotion are linked in this way also. Promotion can cost a great deal of money and, for example, heavy advertising expenditure can be justified only if *either* the advertising convinces customers that the higher price (necessary to cover advertising costs) is justified by the benefits the product offers them; *or* advertising leads to higher sales and therefore lower unit costs. The savings thus achieved pay for the advertising without an increase in price. Both these situations can apply at the same time, of course, so we may have an and/or rather than an either/or alternative here.

3.3 Marketing Mix Decisions

We have seen that being able to satisfy customers' needs profitably depends on making right decisions in the four main areas of product, price, place, and promotion (the four Ps). In practice, this will mean answering a whole series of key questions. Again, we have to bear in mind that the questions cannot be answered in isolation, but that each may have a bearing on the others. The questions to be answered will vary from situation to situation but will commonly include the following:

3.31 *What Should the Product Range Be?*

Should we standardize on a few items, offer a wide selection or make to customers' requirements? How much stock should we carry? How many variations should we make available?

3.32 *What Is Our Pricing Policy?*

Shall we offer products that are 'expensive' or those that are 'economical'? Shall prices be standard or subject to negotiation in view of customers' special requirements? What about wholesaler/retailer margins, and quantity discounts?

3.33 *How Shall We Sell?*

Shall we sell direct to customers or through wholesalers/agents/retailers? Which retailers? What kind of salesmen, and how many? What after-sales service shall we offer?

3.34 *How Shall We Distribute the Product?*

Shall we use our own transport? Or send by road/rail/air/sea? Shall we despatch direct from the factory or do we need regional depots (build our own or rent)? How important is speedy delivery and how shall we achieve it?

An example of how these questions interact with each other is the physical distribution decision. There is a whole complex of interlinking factors. If customers do not expect quick delivery, the problems may be relatively small. Deliveries can be made from a stock held at the factory or even delayed until a new batch of the product is made. Already, though, we are having to balance the cost of holding stock so as to meet orders fairly quickly against possible problems arising from cutting costs by not holding stock. Thus, if we hold no stock, either customers must wait (and perhaps choose to buy elsewhere), or production schedules must be disrupted (adding to costs) in order to meet an acceptable delivery date.

If delivery time is really important, we shall certainly have to carry stocks, and they may have to be held near our customers. Supermarkets have a high turnover, and carry small stocks, which need replenishing regularly and at short intervals. This leads many major food packagers to establish regional warehouses from which the appropriate mixed loads can be taken for delivery to supermarkets and other customers over a relatively small radius. The decision must be taken on whether this system (where goods must be handled twice) is cheaper than direct deliveries from the factory or perhaps several different factories. Clearly, there is no standard answer, and the 'right' answer may well change with circumstances (see Section 7.6).

The kind of product will have a great bearing on the kind of selling and the distribution channels used. Some standard household goods – nylon sheets, for example – can be sold direct to customers through the post. The purchasing decision is an uncomplicated one – cost is low, quality is not difficult to establish, styles are standard, colour range limited. Cars, on the other hand, represent a very difficult and complicated purchasing decision by the customer, for a great deal of money changes hands (after their house it is the biggest single outlay most people make). There is a wide choice of prices, styles, and performance, and generally a used car is being sold as well as a new one bought. After the purchase is made, it will need servicing. All this points to the need for personal selling as a key element in the marketing mix; and clearly it is logical to link after-sales servicing with this part of the process. So we have a need for each main centre of population to have a sales/servicing point. The decision still has to be made whether the company marketing the cars sets up units of its own to do this or whether it employs independent distributors to do so. This is partly a matter of cost – either the manufacturer must find the capital to operate these distribution points or, through substantial discounts on the retail price, make it attractive for others to do so. In most cases, in Great Britain anyway, the latter system is used.

3.4 Examples of Mixes

Three examples may help to illustrate the different marketing mix that emerges from differing situations. They are 'typical' cases, but it must be remembered that within the categories referred to there will still be considerable individual differences. One company may spend less on its sales force and more on advertising than another one will.

3.41 *Fast-moving Consumer Packaged Goods*

The typical food and confectionery products fall into this category. There is a mass market that can be economically reached through advertising, which therefore plays a big part in the marketing mix. Pricing may be very critical, since many retail outlets are used. The sales force may be very large (although in some cases the fact that a very high proportion of customers can be served through a few large supermarket chains may change this picture). The product is likely to have a low unit price and 'impulse' buying may play an important part, so that packaging and point-of-sale activity are important. Advertising budgets are commonly about 10 per cent of retail turnover and sales force costs about 5 per cent, but both may be even higher.

3.42 *Consumer Durables*

Cars, washing machines, freezers and similar goods present a different picture. Impulse buying is unlikely, and frequency of purchase is much less. Price, while still important, may not be so critical, although 'discounting' is common as a means of competition between retailers. The ability to inspect the product may be important, and the availability of after-sales service certainly is. A smaller number of distributors than with fast-moving consumer goods is therefore common, but they are much more than the simple purchasing points they are with the fast-moving goods. Advertising and sales force costs may represent 5 per cent and 2 per cent of sales respectively, but retailers' margins will be higher.

3.43 *Industrial Capital Goods*

Heavy capital equipment for industry is likely to be supplied to order rather than from stock. Technical performance of the product is all-important and price may well be a secondary consideration. There are probably a small number of customers and therefore a small (though highly trained and specialized) sales force. Because of the specialist role and the lengthy selling process, sales costs can be high. Advertising is likely to play a very minor role (advertising costs may be 0.5 per cent or less, but sales costs may vary from 2 per cent to 10 per cent, although there is really no norm). Distribution is almost certain to be direct to customer, while installation and after-sales services may call for a large engineering division quite apart from manufacturing. Similarly, Research and Development (R. & D.), drawing office, and such commitments will be high.

3.44 *Financial Services*

Until fairly recently financial organizations such as banks and building societies relied heavily on people seeking them out and then being sufficiently satisfied with their services not to move their business elsewhere. During the 1960s and 1970s the market developed rapidly and competition was on the basis of a wider and wider network of branches supported by increasing promotional expenditures. In the 1980s more attention was paid to developing different products (offering higher interest rates, 24-hour cash-tills and, more recently, computerized instant access banking through Prestel or similar data transmission systems.

3.5 S for Service

We have talked of the marketing mix as the '4 P's'. Some authorities add 'and the S'. Service can be a vital ingredient, especially with costly items – industrial equipment, cars, household appliances. Important decisions, then, have to be made about how service is to be provided, and how far it makes sense to increase production costs in order to produce greater reliability. The alternative may be to accept a higher need for servicing, with more breakdowns, repairs and replacements. The first approach adds to the initial price, whereas the latter costs more over the years and may well cause considerable 'backlash' from customers in the long run.

3.6 The Importance of Timing

Another important factor, which runs through all marketing decisions, is timing. The best product in the world will fail if it is launched before there is a ready market for it (the dishwasher market in Great Britain has, in 1984, yet to 'take off', although several efforts have been made to set it going). To be too late may give competitors a chance to establish themselves in the market.

A product launch for an expensive new product that coincides with a recession, and hence low consumer expenditure, will encounter far more difficulty than if it is timed to meet an upswing in the economy. To get into the shops by Christmas, a new toy must be 'sold in' to retailers by August, and probably needs to be shown at the Toy Fair in the previous January.

3.7 The Vital Spark

There is a grave danger inherent in the writing of books about marketing, and indeed in the whole idea of marketing as a course of study, that by analysing each aspect of it and trying to understand the mechanics and thought processes behind it, we begin to believe that marketing is the fact-finding, the analysis, the careful weighing of one alternative against another. It is not. To study all these processes may be an aid to successful marketing, just as the study of strategy may help a successful general, but marketing, like war, is about activity. It is doing, not merely thinking. To be successful at it, one must be creative as well as analytical, aggressive as well as meticulous.

As J. H. Davidson[1] puts it:

> Many companies mistakenly regard marketing as an amalgam of specialist activities rather than as a total approach to business which should permeate the whole organisation. The pressure of detailed routine has turned most marketing people today into maintenance men.
> All this is the very opposite of offensive marketing, which is a set of attitudes and techniques designed to exploit the marketing situation fully. It requires a company to innovate every major new development in its markets and to respond to competitive moves by counter-attack, not by imitation.[1]

Davidson also speaks of the need for developing marketing 'from a limp theory into a dynamic practice'. Students should grasp this necessity from the outset. Marketing is about winning votes from customers in the marketplace, it is about beating competitors to the punch, it is about making optimum profits.

Above all marketing is about spotting customers' needs faster than anyone else, satisfying them better than anyone else and in the process making better profits than anyone else. It is about exploiting opportunities more than about avoiding problems.

The study, the analysis, the weighing of facts and alternatives are all important, but the creative aggressive competitive spirit is equally necessary. The right marketing mix is the fuel, but it needs igniting by this vital spark.

3.8 Summary

1 We have seen that the success of a product is dependent on a whole number of factors: the product itself, the price structure, the method of distribution, and the promotional policy. In the next five chapters we examine each of these areas in more depth. It is important to recognize from the start, however, that we need to consider them all at one time and in relation to each other.
2 It is not sound to deal in isolation with such questions as the following:

What should our prices be?
How much should we spend on advertising?
What kind of sales force should we have?

How wide and how varied should our product range be?
What is the best method of delivery?
What kind of retail outlets do we need and how many?

3 The answer to each of these questions is related to all the others and must be considered in the light of the total market situation, taking into account such things as the following:

(a) The type of product and how it is bought (impulse or considered, consumer or industrial, frequently or infrequently).
(b) Size of market and complexity of distribution and service required.
(c) Competitive activity, and whether the market is relatively static or fast-changing.
(d) Capital/cost flow implications and sales/production required to produce acceptable break-even points.

4 It must be recognized that the marketing mix represents only those factors over which management has control. Decisions must be taken in the light of all the many other factors that are not controllable, such as the social, political and economic climate, which influence available spending power and consumer choices as well as the level and type of industrial investment.

5 Getting the marketing mix right is not merely a question of passively evaluating all the factors and 'getting the sums right', important though that is. Elements of creativity, aggression and competitiveness provide the vital spark that leads to higher profits through satisfying customers' needs better and faster than anyone else.

Reference

1 In *Offensive Marketing* (Pelican, 1975).
Davidson's book conveys the nature of successful marketing excellently. All students should dip into it regularly as a useful supplement to periods of academic study. At the same time, the book contains numerous practical examples, many of which illuminate the way the elements of the marketing mix can be used in varying patterns to achieve successful results in different situations.

Further Reading

Kotler, P. *Marketing Management* (Prentice Hall, 1977)

Questions for Discussion

1 What kind of emphasis would you expect in the marketing mix for the following?
(a) Water skis.
(b) Motor oil.
(c) Yoghourt.
(d) Management textbooks.

2 (CAM, Nov. 1982) How would you counter the argument that it is not reasonable, or a sound use of taxpayers' money, to have a Marketing Department in the nationalized, and therefore monopolistic industries, such as gas/coal/electricity?

3 On what basis would you decide whether to spend more money on promotion when that would mean increasing the price of the product?

4 How important is efficient after-sales service for the following?
   (a) Cheap watches.
   (b) Bicycles.
   (c) Sewing machines.
   (d) Dishwashers.
   (e) Colour TV sets.

5 (IM, June 1982) Choose a manufacturing or service company and say what factors determine its product or service unit.

4. *The Ever-changing Product*

'Change is the only permanent element in the complex problems that face business managers in a developed economy.'

Roderick White. *Consumer Product Development*

4.1 The Management of Products

Every company has to make decisions about the products it sells – how many products, of what kind, at what price levels, suitable for which markets. These decisions will have a profound influence on the company's long-term success or failure. They have to be taken in relation to the best use of the company's financial and manpower resources, the kinds of market opportunity that exist, the economic climate, the changing technological situation, and the activities of competitors.

H. I. Ansoff[1] has defined four main product-market strategies for a company seeking increased business, as follows:

1 *Market penetration.* The company seeks increased sales for its present products in its present markets through more aggressive promotion and distribution.
2 *Market development.* The company seeks increased sales by taking its present products into new markets.
3 *Product development.* The company seeks increased sales by developing improved products for its present markets.
4 *Diversification.* The company seeks increased sales by developing new products for new markets.

4.2 What is a Product?

It is not the product as such that customers are interested in, but what it will do for them. What the customer buys is a set of satisfactions, and those satisfactions *are* the product. Products must be evolved not purely in terms of engineering or techniques, but in terms of design, presentation, packaging, brand-image and all the attributes which, together, give the customer the satisfactions he is paying for. A box of high-quality chocolates, an expensive perfume, or a fashion shirt, cannot be divorced from its packaging, its presentation and the atmosphere created around it by advertising and other forms of display. All these things together make up the product. It is in relation to 'products' in this sense that we consider in this chapter the background against which policy questions concerning products have to be decided.

The word 'product' is used here as a piece of convenient shorthand. It is not used to mean only tangible 'things', but includes services (the intangibles) as well

35

as things that can be touched and seen and tasted. Thus, a hairdressing, car hire or business consultancy service is just as much a product as a washing machine or fish fingers. Professor Kotler defines a product as 'A bundle of physical, service, and symbolic particulars expected to yield satisfactions or benefits to the buyer'.[2]

Products are often referred to under the three main categories of durables, consumables, and services.

4.21 *Durables*

Tangible goods that are used many times over a long period are durables. Cars, domestic appliances, hi-fi equipment, and cameras would all fall into this category.

4.22 *Consumables* (or non-durables)

These are goods normally consumed over a short period. Foodstuffs are typical examples, as are drinks, tobacco and confectionery; but also stationery items, heating oil, sewing cotton and many other goods are consumables.

4.23 *Services* (intangible products)

Services comprise intangible 'activities', benefits or satisfactions offered for sale. Insurance, travel, and entertainment are typical examples.

4.24 *Further Classification* (industrial purchases)

We also distinguish between consumer products bought for the use of the purchaser and his family, and industrial products bought for use by an organization. Sometimes the goods can be the same ones used in a different situation (ball-pens, chairs, light bulbs, are random examples of goods with consumer and industrial uses). We can go on further to distinguish between industrial durables (machinery and equipment) and industrial consumables (such as raw materials, stationery, fuel).

4.3 Reasons for Changes in Customers' Needs

Since the sole purpose of a product is to provide satisfactions for customers, every marketing organization is in a highly dynamic situation. This is because customers' needs are constantly changing. Their incomes, their life-styles, their customs, their fashion sense, are dynamic and not static. Therefore our marketing policies must be dynamic not static, and the products we offer must come constantly under review and must frequently change.

Here are some of the reasons why customers demand new satisfactions.

4.31 *Rising Incomes and Expectations*

In the developing industrialized western world in particular we have been living in a phase of increasing affluence, which in turn has led to an atmosphere in which expectations constantly change. Thirty years ago the British were renowned for their cold houses; now even people with relatively modest incomes would expect to live in centrally heated homes. It was exceptional a few years back to own a car; now there are two cars for every ten people. Not so long ago things like television sets, tape-recorders, and hi-fi equipment were very unusual pieces of equipment to find in a home; now the former is almost universal and the others such as video tape-recorders and home computers are spreading rapidly. Changes like this are made possible by technology but stimulated by the fact that, once the basic necessities of life are satisfied, rising incomes make a whole range of other satisfactions possible.

4.32 *Increasing Education and Sophistication*

Universal education to an increasingly high level, new social trends like the wide-spread custom of holidaying abroad, and the fact that virtually everybody sees a wide range of different life-styles and activities on television, all lead to a much greater readiness to accept and demand new things. Coupled with this demand for new things is a rising expectation in the standard of performance of existing things. Cars are not new, but cars with efficient heating, reclining seats and many other comforts and safety devices are still relatively new. Universal viewing of television has developed an appetite for knowledge, which is being met by providing new distribution methods for low-priced, well produced paperback books.

4.33 *Change in Social Habits and Customs*

Rising incomes, more education, and foreign travel, have all led to a much more fluid social situation, where habits and customs change rapidly. This leads to ready acceptance of new forms of entertainment, new styles of dress, new eating habits. Instead of formal dinners or 'high teas', family television has led to informal easy-to-prepare meals. At the same time, a much wider range of tastes and eating experiences has evolved. Baked beans and sardines on toast have been joined by pizza, paella and many other dishes that would have been unknown to most British televiewers only a short time ago. There has been a phenomenal growth of 'Fast foods' and 'takeaway meals'.

4.34 *Fashion*

Traditionally, fashion changes started at the top end of a fairly well defined social scale and gradually worked their way down. Nowadays the social pattern is much more difficult to define, and fashion changes take place much more rapidly. This is partly due to the fluid social situation, but even more to the much greater range of communication systems now available. Television and radio stations, together with an ever-increasing variety of specialist magazines and books, feed avid social appetites.

All these influences lead to the demand for constantly changing products to meet the developing needs of consumers. Other factors at the same time make these changes possible and also reinforce the rate of change.

4.35 *Technological Change*

It is a well documented fact that the pace of technological change is increasing very rapidly. New materials and processes make the satisfaction of old needs possible in new and cheaper ways. As more and more simple tasks can be carried out more efficiently by computer controlled equipment, robots, etc. the whole pattern of employment is changing – often referred to as de-industrialization as many of the older industries decline or even disappear. At the same time many new jobs appear in fields such as leisure facilities and information technology.

4.36 *Business Factors*

Because customers are becoming increasingly receptive to changes, so industry and commerce are responding to these changes. This is especially true in retailing. Thus the commercial situation itself is becoming increasingly dynamic as companies vie with each other in being the first to offer a new or revised product for which a demand is anticipated. This itself leads to marketing management tasks, since many of the new products meet a rapid death. Chapter 5 deals with the management of new product development

Unfortunately many people prefer to think and behave as though we were in a static environment whereas a highly dynamic one is the reality.

4.4 The Product Life-Cycle Concept

Because we live and work in this dynamic situation, managers must accept as the

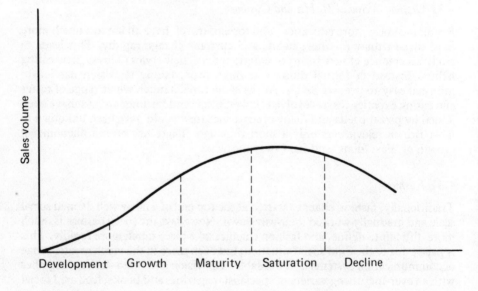

Figure 4.1 Product life-cycle

normal state of affairs that all products have a limited life. This fact is commonly expressed in the form of the product life-cycle curve (Figure 4.1). Products during their existence go through the phases indicated on the curve, as follows:

1 Before, sometimes long before, a product reaches the marketplace, there is a development phase. Market research must be undertaken, the product designed, prototypes built, plant laid down. While costs can be very high, income will initially be nil and will probably grow only slowly. Profits are a long way off yet. Many products are slow to 'catch on' and this part of the curve typically does not rise steeply.
2 During the growth phase the product reaches general acceptance, and sales increase steeply. Profits mount as development costs are recovered and unit costs decrease with greater volume of production.
3 As the product reaches maturity, initial demand is beginning to be satisfied, competitors may have arrived on the scene, and there will be greater reliance on replacement sales. Sales increase more slowly, and profits come under pressure and may start to decline.
4 When the market is fully saturated, sales will 'peak off' and profits decline still further.
5 Finally, sales will go into definite decline and margins come under very severe pressure as it becomes increasingly costly to maintain sales at a reasonable level.

The curve as illustrated is of course a generalization. The curve for any particular product may be steeper or flatter, the time-scale may be longer or shorter. Some products seem to go on for a very long time indeed (Guinness and Bovril, to name but two). For this reason the pattern must be applied with care. In addition, we must be careful what we mean by a product in this context: for example, the market for glass has risen steadily over the past 50 years, but within this period the sale of lamp glasses has declined and that of milk bottles has risen steeply (to decline again in some countries in face of competition from waxed cartons or plastic).

In the U.K. total consumption of bread has declined steadily since World War II. In that time sliced wrapped bread was introduced, became very popular and is now in decline. Many different types of bread are being eaten in its place.

Nonetheless the typical pattern stands as a warning that it is dangerous to rely too heavily for too long on one product, so that, as profit from one declines, profit from its successor rises to fill the gap. Ideally this will give a steadily rising profit for the company as a whole, even though some products have entered the 'decline' phase of the product life-cycle.

It must be emphasized that the product life-cycle diagram is not a rigid description of exactly how all products always behave. Rather it is an idealized indication of the pattern most products can be expected to follow.

There is nothing fixed about the length of the cycle or the lengths of its various stages. It has been suggested that the length of the cycle is governed by the rate of technical change, the rate of market acceptance and the ease of competitive entry. Thus, each year numerous new fashion styles are introduced, many of them to last only a few months. At the other extreme, a new aircraft must have many years of life if it is to be commercially worthwhile.

The main importance of the life-cycle concept is to remind us constantly of the three following facts:

1 Products have a limited life.
2 Profit levels are not constant but change throughout a product's life in a way that is to some extent predictable.
3 Products require a different marketing programme at each stage of their life-cycle.

4.5 Implications of the Product Life-cycle

If we have to accept that no product will go on earning profits indefinitely, then we must plan so as to have a whole succession of new products coming 'through the pipeline'. Figure 4.2 shows the implications of the product life-cycle.

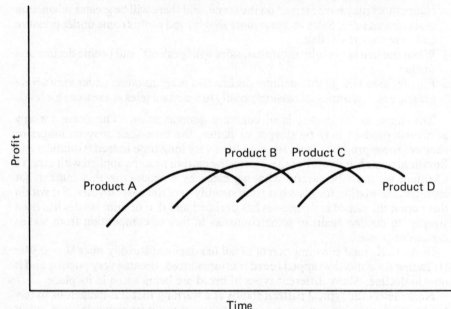

Figure 4.2 Effect on total profit of a succession of products

Peter Drucker[3] has drawn attention to the need to keep all products under review to ensure that not too high a proportion are at the end of their life-cycle. He describes the following six categories:

1 Tomorrow's breadwinners – new products or today's breadwinners modified and improved.
2 Today's breadwinners – the innovations of yesterday.
3 Products capable of becoming net contributors if something drastic is done.
4 Yesterday's breadwinners – generally products with high volume, but badly fragmented into 'specials', small orders and the like.
5 The 'also rans' – generally the high hopes of yesterday that, while they did not

	Introduction	Growth	Maturity	Decline
CHARACTERISTICS				
SALES	Low	Fast growth	Slow growth	Decline
PROFITS	Negligible	Peak levels	Declining	Low or zero
CASH FLOW	Negative	Moderate	High	Low
CUSTOMERS	Innovative	Mass market	Mass market	Laggards
COMPETITORS	Few	Growing	Many rivals	Declining number
RESPONSES				
STRATEGIC FOCUS	Expand market	Market penetration	Defend share	Productivity
MKG. EXPENDITURES	High	High (declining %)	Falling	Low
MKG. EMPHASIS	Product awareness	Brand preference	Brand loyalty	Selective
DISTRIBUTION	Patchy	Intensive	Intensive	Selective
PRICE	High	Lower	Lowest	Rising
PRODUCT	Basic	Improved	Differentiated	Rationalized

Figure 4.3 Implications of the product life-cycle (source Professor P. Doyle *The Realities of the Product Life-Cycle*)

work out well, nevertheless did not become outright failures.
6 The failures.

4.51 *Product Elimination*

From the product life-cycle concept and Drucker's analysis of product categories, it follows that all products must be kept under review to assess their present and likely future contribution to profits. A common mistake of marketing management is to keep in the range products that have little or no prospect of contributing to profits. Products are kept in the range until they fade away, meanwhile consuming valuable resources, which could be more profitably employed elsewhere. These marginal products lower the company's profitability, and it is essential to control them. The Hunt Canning Company in the U.S.A. reduced its range of products from over thirty to only three, and, as a result of this concentration of effort, increased its sales from $15 million in 1947 to $120 million in 1958.

4.52 *The Product Portfolio Matrix*

Figure 4.3 illustrates a useful device for considering the implications of the various products within the portfolio, the matrix developed by the Boston Consulting Group[4]. This positions products into four categories with 'star' products being those with a big share of a high growth market. 'Cash cows' generate funds which can be used to support the stars or, possibly, turn problem children into stars if the circumstances allow. 'Dogs' are clear candidates for product elimination.

| | | MARKET GROWTH | |
		High	Low
MARKET SHARE	High	STAR	CASH COW
	Low	PROBLEM CHILD	DOG

4.6 The Product Mix

A further outcome of the product life-cycle is that few companies can rely on only one product. Most need to offer a series of products forming a product range. (American textbooks and some British ones that follow American terminology use the term 'Product Line', but 'Range' is still the more common term in most British organizations.) In some situations, in any case, a marketing organization will be forced to have a range of products rather than just a single one. For example, it is almost inconceivable that a shirt manufacturer would offer only one type of shirt. He is almost bound, in the nature of things, to offer various collar sizes and a selection of different patterns and colours. If we carry this process too far, we shall have an almost impossible and highly uneconomic task. Financing and controlling stock is just one of the problems that follows from a very wide product range, so decisions have to be made as to where to draw the line.

Continuing the shirt example, we have to decide how many different patterns of cloth to use, and, for each pattern, how many different colourways. Are we going to offer collar sizes in centimetre steps or two-centimetre steps? Are we to offer slim-line styles as well as the full-cut style? Are we to offer different collar styles as well as different patterns? Each time we add one element of difference, we may add twenty or thirty additional products to our range.

On the other hand, a manufacturer who decides to economize on research and development, on manufacturing costs, storage and distribution costs, may find himself in trouble for other reasons. For example, electrical appliance dealers often prefer to buy a range of different products from one supplier rather than having to deal with many. One advantage is that they can gain better quantity discounts. The supplier with a narrow range of products is then at a disadvantage. An example of a product range in depth would be a car manufacturer offering one model of car using the same body shape and basic engineering, but offering a wide range of powerpacks, colours and finishes, and optional extras. A car manufacturer with a wide range would offer a larger number of models, but each would have a much more limited choice of colours and options. There is no fundamental reason why a product mix should not have both breadth and depth, except of course that we then become enmeshed in the rather alarming complexities referred to above. Generally, compromises have to be made.

There are, of course, a number of product attributes which have to be decided upon as part of the product mix decision. Here are some of them.

4.61 *Product Size*

In the case of a household detergent, for example, or a packaged food or a garden fertilizer, how many sizes will be available and what choice of sizes should be made? In some continental countries housewives buy many of their household goods in 1- or 2-kilo packs, whereas in the U.K. much smaller packs are standard. Should a manufacturer offer these larger family packs in addition to those he already carries?

4.62 *Packaging*

The style of pack has to be decided upon. Are we to have cardboard cartons, plastic drums, glass jars or a choice of two or more? A package may have a number of quite different functions to perform, including the following:

1 *Protection.* Fragile products (glassware, delicate equipment, many foodstuffs) need packaging that will resist crushing during transit or withstand shocks during handling. Others need protection against contamination, dust, light, heat and many other conditions.
2 *Indentification.* Distributors and retail customers need to be able to identify the product readily, especially if there are many competitors (e.g. cigarettes) or many varieties (e.g. car accessories).

3 *Display*. Both individual packs and 'outers' may have to contribute to distinctive displays in shops or in cash-and-carry warehouses. Increasingly, there is little room available for display items as such, and packs often have to do the job. At the same time, the pack can carry through the brand-image in a compelling way.

These requirements may carry different emphases in different parts of the country, or in different types of outlet. Which factors then are to have top priority and how many different packs will be necessary to meet the minimum requirement?

4.63 *Presentation*

Is the product to be packed and presented in stark simplicity or with frills and elaborations? What will this do to the price and are we to choose one of the options available or offer customers a choice? In some fields manufacturers offer a wide range of brands presenting slight variations on the same basic product (see Sections 4.7 and 4.8).

Cigarettes are a case in point. Each manufacturer has a wide variety of brands, which will vary in flavour, size, tipped or untipped, coupons or no coupons, style of packaging and other ways. Each one of these changes represents an additional item in the product range, and the product mix has to be carefully worked out to appeal to the maximum number of customers with the minimum of manufacturing, marketing and distribution complications.

4.7 Product Differentiation

One of the problems confronting marketing organizations is that very rarely do they have sole rights to a particular product. On the other hand, it is obviously desirable to be able to offer customers something that is unique, clearly different from anything else on the market. How does one do this with a product that is fundamentally exactly the same as everybody else's?

The answers are many, but brand-image, packaging and all the variables listed above represent ways in which this differentiation of product can be achieved. It is important to note that these are often key elements in the competitive fight. We may expect competition to take place mainly through price, but there are two strong reasons why this is not the case.

First, to compete mainly through price could lead either to all competitors in a particular market eventually arriving once more at the same price (i.e., once again with no choice offered to customers), or to price competition, leading to damaging results for some, or perhaps all, of the competing companies. Second, price is only one of the factors influencing customer choice. It is not always the case by any means that customers will look for the cheapest article that will meet their needs. They may be perfectly happy to pay a little more, even sometimes a lot more, for the product so packaged and presented that it appeals to their sense of visual appeal or just sense of fun. (The British housewives who preferred a plastic daffodil to 3p off a packet of detergent have gone into the history books.)

Thus, research and development goes into finding slight product differences, which may give one product an 'edge' over the others. Cigarettes with tips, more tobacco or coupons; seeds in 'harvest fresh' packaging or made into pellets for easier sowing; chocolates ready-packed with gift wrapping; all these are examples of product differentiation. At the same time advertising and presentation can achieve similar results by creating a different brand-image, one that has greater appeal for more people.

4.8 Market Segmentation

A further choice to be made by companies deciding on their product mix is whether to attempt to provide a product or range of products that appeals to the maximum number of people or whether to select a small group or groups of people in the marketplace and concentrate on pleasing them. The process of selecting carefully analysed 'segments' of the market and designing products to meet the requirements of that particular group of people is known as market segmentation. There are various ways in which markets can be segmented, among which are the following.

4.81 Demographic Segmentation

This means by age or sex. For example, a shoe manufacturer might concentrate (as some have) on children's shoes, on high-fashion shoes for women or on men's safety shoes for industrial use, rather than attempt to provide shoes that will be reasonably satisfactory for everybody in all situations.

4.82 Segmentation by Personal Taste

With products such as food, not everybody's tastes are the same, and a product that satisfies most people will leave others not completely satisfied. People less than completely satisfied by the 'standard' product form a ready market for a product formulated rather differently to meet their particular requirement. The attempt to meet these differing tastes is seen, for example, in the instant coffee market, which now offers a range of special blends in addition to the 'standard brew'. Taste may also be a factor of course in terms of design, styling, colour etc.

4.83 Geographical Segmentation

Concentration of effort can be achieved by aiming products only at those regions or countries containing a high proportion of customers for a particular product.

4.84 Segmentation by Ethnic Groups

In societies where there are different ethnic groups, it will often be necessary and profitable to produce distinct product ranges to suit their different tastes and requirements.

4.85 Psychographic Segmentation

With many simple consumer products, such as cigarettes, drinks and toiletries, people may have strong brand preferences, even though the measurable physical performance of the various brands may be virtually indistinguishable. Brand name, packaging, promotion, etc. are used to give the brand an 'image' which enables individual psychological and emotional preferences to be expressed (see Section 10.22). Table 4.1 shows how this might work in the case of automobiles. A related approach is segmentation by lifestyles.

Table 4.1
A Short Psychographic Output for Two Segments in the Automobile Market

A dependent driver group	An active driver group
What they are like	
Know little about cars	Know a lot about cars
Uninvolved in cars, driving, maintenance	Involved in cars and maintenance
Apprehensive about cars	Enjoy driving
Need reassurance that car will run well	Are power-oriented in driving
Car make and dealer important	Want to be in control when driving
Get pleasure from appearance of car	Believe in differences between makes
What they want	
Trust in manufacturer and dealer	Powerful cars for driving control
Dependable car	Top engine performance
Good engine performance	Good handling qualities
Good handling qualities	Cars made by major companies
Good styling	
Minimum maintenance	
Who they are	
Older	Younger
Well educated	Middle class in income and education
Higher incomes	
What they do	
More own Chevrolets, Pontiacs, Oldsmobiles	More own Fords, fewer Chevrolets and American Motors cars
Choose on trust in make and on styling	Drive more powerful cars
Own more cars; recent models	Choose on engine performance and on styling

Adapted from Ruth Ziff 'The Role of Psychographics in the Development of Advertising Strategy and Copy' in William D. Wells (ed.) *Life Style and Psychographics* (Chicago: American Marketing Association, 1974) pp. 145–6.

DeLozier[5] quotes the following as the kind of information lifestyle analysis might provide about 'the heavy beer drinker':

'Demographically, he is in the middle-income group and is a blue-collar worker who is young and has at least a high school education. Moreover, he is a "risk taker" and "a pleasure seeker", prefers a "physical and male-oriented existence", and is a "hero worshipper". "He is a dreamer, a wisher, a limited edition of Walter Mitty". With this profile of the heavy beer drinker, the Joseph Schlitz Brewing Company developed its "full of gusto" advertising campaign.'

4.9 Summary

1 A product is a whole collection of physical and other attributes offered to customers to satisfy a need.
2 The product life-cycle concept expresses the fact that products exist in a constantly changing situation. Product management is a dynamic, not a static, process.
3 A company's product range and product mix must be kept constantly under review. New products must be developed and old ones eliminated on a regular basis to ensure that the company can satisfy current customer needs.
4 It will rarely be possible to please all the people all of the time. The techniques of product differentiation and market segmentation can help to ensure that a company's products have a specific appeal to selected groups of people.

References

1 Ansoff, H. I. *Corporate Strategy* (Pelican, 1975).
2 Kotler, P. *Marketing Management* (Prentice Hall, 1977).
3 Drucker, P. F. *Managing for Results* (Pan Piper, 1964).
4 Boston Consulting Group, *The Product Portfolio* (Perspectives, August 1970).
5 DeLozier M. Wayne, *The Marketing Communications Process* (McGraw-Hill Kogakusha Ltd, 1976).

Further Reading

White, Roderick. *Consumer Product Development* (Longman, 1973).
Willsmer, Ray L. *Directing the Marketing Effort* (Pan, 1975). Chapters 7 and 8 deal briefly but well with the subjects of this chapter and Chapter 5.

Questions for Discussion

1 How would you describe the 'product' as perceived by the customers for the following?

(a) Easter eggs.
(b) Expensive lingerie.
(c) Trailer caravans.
(d) Numerically-controlled machine tools.

2 (CAM, Nov. 1982) What is the Product Life Cycle? How does the position of a product on its Life Cycle affect marketing planning?
3 List six examples (other than those in the text) of

(a) Industrial consumables,
(b) Consumer durables.

4 What changes in customer needs do you anticipate might arise from a

continuing increase in the cost of fossil fuels coupled with a period of economic stringency?

5 Suggest three products that at first sight do not fit in with the product life-cycle concept. Then discuss whether these are 'exceptions to the rule' or whether there is some other explanation.

6 What types of product would tend to demand (a) a wide product range and (b) a narrow product range?

7 Suggest ways of differentiating products in the following fields:

(a) Beer.
(b) Shoes.
(c) Motorcycles.
(d) Airlines.

5. The Search for New Products

'New Products are the lifeblood of business.'

Ray L. Willsmer. *Directing the Marketing Effort*

5.1 The Need for Innovation

Developing new products and launching them in the marketplace can be a difficult, costly and even dangerous business, as we see later in this chapter. So why do it? Why not leave well alone and be content with profit from existing products, concentrating effort on expanding sales of these products and finding new markets for them?

One reason is that seizing new opportunities as they emerge is a way to increase profits. (To be first in the field with a successful new product gives one the chance of creaming off large profits before effective competition develops.) But the main reason, as we saw in the previous chapter, is that it is dangerous to assume that profits from existing products will continue at present levels for ever. The product life-cycle concept tells us that they will certainly not continue for ever. At different rates, over varying time-scales, all products eventually achieve market saturation and then start to decline. Even while sales volume holds up, profits may well not; and retaining sales volume and profits may call for regular updating of existing products.

For most companies, therefore, a programme of product review and development is essential; and, for all companies, to ignore this area of activity is highly dangerous. A McGraw Hill study[1] in the United States showed that in 1963 the percentage of sales accounted for by products introduced since 1959 was 28 per cent for transportation, 18 per cent for electrical machinery, and so on, through a whole list of categories. In the consumer goods field instant coffee, ready-mix mashed potato, colour TV and aerosol-packed touch-up paint for cars are just a few standard examples of recently introduced products with a high turnover.

More recently still, video tape recorders and home computers in the consumer durables field together with microcomputers and software in industrial/commercial application show the same pattern.

There are three methods of obtaining new products: (a) modifying an existing product, (b) acquiring a new product, and (c) developing a new product. We now briefly examine the first two of these before looking in more detail at the business of product development.

5.2 New Products from Old

We first need to be clear what is a new product. Stanton[2] distinguishes three clear kinds of new product, as follows:

49

1 *Innovative*. These are unique products for which there is a real need, not being met satisfactorily by an existing product. Penicillin when first introduced fell into this category, as did the telephone, the internal combustion engine, and chloroform. We can also describe as innovative those products which, while replacing existing goods that have been satisfying existing markets quite well, offer totally different solutions. Examples would be television partially replacing the cinema and the radio, the zip fastener and later Velcro instead of strings or buttons, and solar power for other energy sources.

2 *Adaptive*. These offer significantly different variations on existing products: they include such items as instant coffee, freeze-dried foods, self-adhesive wallpaper, and typewriters with a memory. Another kind of variation is represented by package changes, styling modifications, new designs and colours.

3 *Imitative* ('me-too'). These products are already being sold by someone else but further sales opportunities exist for an additional brand, with or without minor modifications.

The divisions between these categories are obviously very fuzzy. Indeed, some authors have distinguished as many as a dozen different ways in which a product can be 'new'.

The truly innovative product is rare. Adaptive new products can sometimes necessitate a great deal of new technology and extensive research and development, though a 'new' product can often be produced by changes to an existing one. These may range from relatively minor changes, which effectively extend the life-cycle of a product, to much more extensive improvements.

An example quoted by Peter Drucker[3] that covers both is nylon, which was introduced in the U.S.A. by Du Pont and fairly rapidly became the dominant fibre in women's hosiery. However, once this market was saturated, the growth curve flattened. Du Pont had anticipated this and had developed strategies for providing further increases in sales of nylon stockings by such tactics as the following:

1 Introducing a wider range of colours, leading to an increase in the number of stockings bought by each user and a tendency to wear different colours with different outer garments.

2 Developing new uses, such as stretch stockings and socks; and moving into other fields, such as tyre cord and carpets. In this way nylon sales showed an overlapping series of life-cycle curves, giving a continuing upward trend.

The nylon success story depended both upon changing the product for existing users and making it suitable for whole new markets. Changing products for existing markets can be done in a number of ways, in particular by improvements in quality, features, and/or style.

In 1983, car manufacturers in the U.K. were engaged in a fight for the lucrative 'fleet' market (companies buying large numbers of cars for salesmen and other executives or for hiring out). Ford, Vauxhall (General Motors U.K. subsidiary) and the Austin Rover division of B.L. with the Sierra, Cavalier and Maestro respectively, all claimed the 'best' car for the task. The claims included lower maintenance costs and more corrosion resistance (quality); more features such as built in radio, better information clearly displayed (and available in computer-generated voice synthesizer form in the case of B.L.'s Maestro); easy, comfortable driving and pleasing design style.

5.3 Acquiring new products

There are various ways in which new products can be 'bought'. A company needs to decide whether it will 'make or buy', i.e. whether it will itself manufacture the products it markets or whether it will simply be a marketing organization, leaving the manufacturing to specialists in that part of the operation. Marks & Spencer's is an outstanding case of a very successful organization which develops detailed specifications for a wide range of products and exercises strict quality control, but does not itself manufacture, preferring to buy in from numerous manufacturing companies (which in turn are prepared to leave M. & S. to do the marketing end of the job for them). A company must similarly decide whether it is better to do its own product development or to 'buy in' this particular expertise. Thus new products can be acquired by the following ways:

1 Buying patent rights.
2 Acquiring manufacturing rights.
3 Arranging to act as a marketing organization for a company wishing to concentrate on manufacturing.
4 Acting as marketing agent in one country for a company manufacturing and marketing in another.

5.4 The Criteria New Products Must Meet

What we have said so far should not be taken as an indication that all new products are worthwhile, and that they all make a contribution to company profit. The majority do not (see Section 5.6), so that great caution must be exercised in devoting time and money to their development and launching.

Fortunately, some clear-cut criteria can be applied, and if they are observed, the chances of success are likely to be greatly increased. (It should be noted, however, that there is no way of totally avoiding the risk inherent in launching a product of which consumers have no previous experience.) These are the criteria:

1 *There must be an adequate demand.* It is quite pointless to produce a product that is unlikely to be bought in sufficient quantity for the revenue to cover development, production, marketing, and distribution costs, and also to make a contribution to profit.
2 *The product should be compatible with the company's marketing experience and resources.* A washing machine manufacturer could add a dishwasher to his range and market it successfully with his existing organization and through the same distribution channels. Customers' motivations and purchasing habits could be expected to be familiar. But a similar manufacturer deciding to sell paint or biscuits would be entering a totally new marketing area and would somehow have to acquire a completely new body of expertise. He would need different retailers and an appropriate pricing structure, he would be faced with quite new physical distribution problems, and his advertising approach and way of thinking would have to change.

3 *The product should fit fairly easily into the company's present production pattern.* The plant and machinery, technical expertise, servicing facilities may all be quite different for a new product field.
4 *The financial implications of launching the new product must be carefully thought through and appropriate arrangements made.* For example, if the new product needs high stock levels, the extra finance must be available; and if its sales are seasonal, the cash-flow fluctuations must be provided for. Developing and launching a new product generally means very heavy costs, so that a long time may elapse before it reaches break-even point. The cash to sustain this period of heavy 'losses' must be available.
5 *Adequate management time must be devoted to a new product.* Without such attention it will wilt and die.

In addition, any necessary legal and other procedural clearances must be obtained well in advance.

Finally, there is no point in trying to launch a new product unless it has some clear marketing advantage that can form the basis of a unique selling proposition to be featured in promotion and it can reasonably be expected to make a profit contribution in line with the management time and other resources it will absorb.

5.5 Why New Products Fail

Having established in the previous section what criteria new products should meet, we can see that any not meeting these criteria are likely to fail. Many new products do fail. Booz, Allen and Hamilton in a famous study[4] stated that 50 per cent of all new products fail after the marketing stage, and that fifty-eight new product ideas must be screened to find one good one. Other authorities put the failure rate much higher. It is impossible to reach an agreed figure because definitions of what constitutes success or failure will vary. So too will the definition of a new product. Does a new surface design for the pack and a change in price and advertising image give us a new product or just a revamp of an existing one? Where to draw the line between revision and new product is impossible to say. However, no one disputes that the failure rate of new products is extremely high.

In July 1983 however 'Marketing'[5] quoted some recent U.K. research based on 111 replies from 'important consumer goods companies' nearly three-quarters of which had launched from two to seven new products in the last three years. Over half the launches were said to have met the objectives set for them and the failure rate was said to be falling. Even so however, only one idea in 500–600 survived the 'long, laborious development process' to be actually successfully in the market-place.

A favourite occupation of researchers and authors is listing the reasons why new products fail. Many of them will, of course, fail because they do not meet the criteria for success listed in Section 5.4. These are, briefly, the following:

1 Ensuring an adequate demand exists.
2 Ensuring the product 'fits' the company's marketing capability.
3 Ensuring it fits the existing production capability.
4 Ensuring suitable finance is available.
5 Allocating adequate management time.

Most authorities would add (6) lack of a coherent policy for new product development and (7) lack of a suitable organization for developing new products. The most important reason by far is probably that quoted by McIver: 'The biggest single reason for failure of new products is the natural enthusiasm of all concerned to take a product forward even on the slimmest possibility of ultimate profit.'[6]

The answer to this is a rigorous procedure for 'screening' new products so as to counteract as far as possible any natural tendency for over-enthusiasm. This we consider in Section 5.6.

If we do take steps to screen products in order to ensure that only the likely ones reach the marketplace, then something like the pattern in Figure 5.1 will emerge.

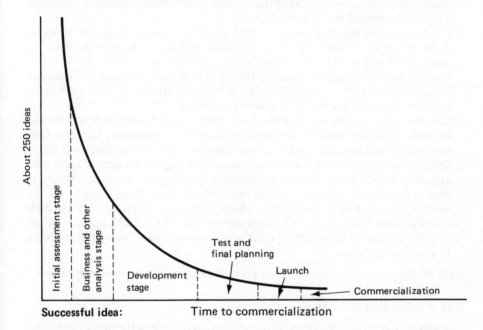

Figure 5.1 Mortality rate of new products (from: D. W. Foster, *Planning for Products and Markets* (Longman, 1972) p.138)

As we go from generation of ideas towards commercial development, the cost generally rises sharply. Thus it is important to have well defined procedures to ensure rigorous control over how far along the sequence any given product is allowed to proceed. This is in order to counteract the tendency, pinpointed by McIver, for the 'natural enthusiasm of all concerned' to carry through the sequence products with little chance of ultimate commercial success.

As Figure 5.1 indicates, many bright ideas for new products are available or can be stimulated, but very few are ever going to produce the 'crock of gold' at the end of the rainbow in the marketplace. The road thither is long, hard, dusty and very costly.

In the following sections we look at each in turn of the stages indicated in Figure 5.1.

5.6 The Generation and Screening of New Product Ideas

New products can come from many sources and through many kinds of individual with widely differing backgrounds. We can, however, think in terms of three main categories, as follows:

1 *Products developed to fill a known 'gap'* in the range of existing products available to meet a known need. An example would be the considerable development currently going on to produce an acceptable battery-operated car, to overcome the pollution problem created by the internal combustion engine and to achieve a more economical use of fossil fuels.
2 *Products arising out of scientific research* possibly devoted originally to quite different ends, or from 'pure' research in pursuit of knowledge with no commercial end at all in view. One famous example is penicillin, whose effect was first noticed by accident during a study of many different moulds. Another is teflon-coating of cooking utensils, a 'spin-off' from research into heat-resistant materials for the U.S. space programme.
3 *Creative ideas with no very logical origin.* These range from a technical break-through departing from the orthodox approach (the jet engine, hovercraft) to more trivial and less technical but nonetheless useful ideas, such as oven-ready french fries, ready-planted flowering shrubs for 'instant gardening', and self-assembly 'knock down' furniture. Generally speaking, of course, it is products that are developments of existing ones which arise from a study of the marketplace and new technology which gives rise to products with high novelty. Viewdata information displayed on home TV screens remains in the mid-80s a 'product in search of a need' and there are many 'high-tech' products in a similar situation.

Each of these ways of originating new products has its own method of approach.

5.61 *Finding gaps in the Market*

The aim here is to identify a need in the market and then find the product to fill it. There are three main approaches, as follows:

1 *Examine other markets.* For many years it has been commonplace for British companies to keep a close eye on international markets, the United States' in particular. If a product is selling well there, it has a fair chance of also succeeding in Great Britain. Indeed, many of the products now established in the market here were first developed in the United States, including ball-point pens, aerosol sprays, credit cards and 'finger-lickin' good' Kentucky Fried Chicken. The U.S.A. is, of course, not the only source, nor is it a one-way traffic only (as Schweppes and others have demonstrated by taking established British products to the U.S.A. and elsewhere).
2 *Segment the market.* Since people do not have identical preferences, it is unlikely that one product will completely satisfy everyone. A new product that gains a large market share may therefore suggest the possibility of a number of market

segments. Thus instant coffee was originally marketed with a single flavour, which was reasonably acceptable to most people; now we see the development of special blends – mild, bitter and so on – to suit smaller groups of people prepared to pay a premium price to obtain something that suits their personal taste more closely than the 'standard' flavour. 'Ribena' blackcurrant drink is available in standard 'dilute with water' form, as 'Baby Ribena' and as 'Ready-to-drink Ribena' already diluted in a one-portion container complete with straw.

3 *Gap analysis.* This is a rather complex technique of examining products on the basis of how people view them – what people 'think' they are. For example, if people viewed all existing chocolate bars as crunchy, but said they preferred a soft bar, then a gap might exist for a new chocolate bar brand promoted as 'the soft one'.

This 'fictional' suggestion in the first edition of this book became almost totally real a year or two later when research showed that customers were less than totally satisfied with existing chocolate bars. Cadbury Schweppes and Mars (with their Galaxy brand) had responded to rapidly increasing raw materials costs partly by increasing prices and partly by reducing the thickness of the bars whilst keeping the other dimensions the same. Thin chocolate tastes different from thick and has a different 'bite'. Responding to the research indications Rowntree-Mackintosh developed, tested and launched 'Yorkie' a premium-priced chocolate bar with a narrowed but thicker shape. It won them a very large share of a market in which they were previously barely represented.

5.62 *Scientific Development*

Achieving new products this way is a question either of a company maintaining its own research and development team or of it keeping closely in touch with development teams in universities, government establishments (such as Packaging and Allied Trades Research Association) and worldwide publications carrying reports of technological development. The former method is much the more expensive, but can be more directly applied to the areas in which the company is interested.

5.63 *Producing Creative Ideas*

The previous two categories both rely on some kind of systematic search. But the creative approach is almost by definition not systematic. Here we are looking for a new departure rather than a logical development from what already exists. The main technique used to achieve this is known as 'brainstorming'. The essence of this approach is to assemble a group of people, preferably with widely different attitudes and backgrounds, and then encourage them to 'spark off' and produce a stream of ideas. In order to encourage the maximum number of new thoughts the following 'rules of the game' are applied:

1 All ideas are written down.
2 Negatives are ruled out; even obviously idiotic ideas must be allowed to stand, because they may suggest others.

3 No critical analysis is applied until after the brainstorming session.

Once the ideas are all recorded, they can be sorted critically and further consideration given to those that look promising.

5.7 The Business Analysis of New Product Ideas

Far too many ideas have money spent on their development simply because they do seem to be good ideas, that is to say they appeal to someone, who then becomes committed to them. Roderick White points out two main reasons, for a vast proportion of new product failures:

1 Reluctance to terminate a project once a relatively early stage has been passed, and
2 Corporate arrogance – either simply about the product's quality or about the company's ability to use its 'marketing power' to sell an inferior product.[7]

The best way to avoid this temptation is to ask at a very early stage what is the likelihood of adequate profits accruing if the product is successfully developed and launched? Crucial questions will include the following:

1 What is the likely demand and at what price?
2 Can the product be manufactured and distributed at a cost that will fit the price/demand situation and also yield a suitable profit?
3 What will be the yield of capital and manpower invested in this way as against the comparable return from alternative ways of employing the resources? (In economic terms, what is the opportunity cost?)

5.8 Product Development

This is the process of technical development in the laboratory, on test-rigs in pilot plant, or whatever is necessary in the particular circumstances. Depending on the product, safety tests, quality tests, servicing and maintenance routines, and many other factors may need to be worked out. It is most important to keep clearly in the mind of everyone concerned the needs of the ultimate users, so as to avoid developing a product which either does not in one respect or another meet the requirements of the marketplace, or which does so superbly but at so high a cost that competition cannot be met or that profits cannot be made.

5.9 Test Marketing

This is dealt with at more length in Section 11.8. Here it is enough to recognize that a full launch on the national scale of a new product is (a) very costly, and (b) potentially dangerous.

As an interim stage, it is often sensible to launch the product initially in one carefully selected part of the country only. It is then often possible to check whether all aspects of the marketing mix are fully effective. If the optimum has not been struck, changes can be made in the national launch. In particular, if further product improvements need to be made in response to customer reactions, this can be done without too much damage to the company's reputation or too great a loss of future sales. A national launch of what turns out to be an imperfect product (or a wrongly priced or promoted one) can be an irrevocable and disastrously costly affair.

5.10 Launch and Commercialization

Only when all signals are green so far does it normally make sense to launch the product fully, although there may well be situations where it is wise to skip the test-market stage. A reference back to the product life-cycle (Figure 4.1) will quickly show that up to now each stage has produced a larger and larger loss. Only at some time, possibly a very long time, after the launch does revenue, and eventually profit (if all goes well), begin to be generated.

A further significant point is that even after the launch we may well still need to think in terms of a series of stages. The life-cycle concept suggests this, and a useful further concept is that of 'adopter categories'. Especially with innovative products, some people will adopt the new ideas quickly and eagerly, whereas others will be slower to take to them. Stanton[8] identifies five distinct groups, as follows:

1 *Innovators.* The venturesome 3 per cent who are willing to take the risk of trying something out first. They tend to be younger, of higher social status and more affluent than the other categories.
2 *Early adopters.* About 13 per cent of the market, including more opinion leaders than the other groups. They tend to be younger, more creative, more mobile than the groups below.
3 *Early majority.* About 34 per cent of the total market. A bit above average in social and economic standing.
4 *Late majority.* Another 34 per cent, more sceptical than the previous group. Adopt only under economic necessity or pressure from their peers. Older, worse educated, below average in social and economic status.
5 *Laggards.* The tradition-bound 16 per cent. Suspicious of innovation. They tend to be older than the rest and at the lower end of the social and economic scales.

While the innovators and early adopters are considerably influenced by promotion and by the apparent advantages of a new product, the later groups will tend to wait for the situation to develop until they feel virtually forced to follow suit. This is one reason for the slow and gradual development of the product life-cycle, and why a long-term, carefully monitored development plan with financial targets is essential.

5.11 A New Product Case History

The following case history is one of three outlined by Mr Riddles of Birds Eye Ltd.[9]

5.111 *Oven Crispy Cod Steaks*

We had long been aware of the trend away from frying towards the grilling of many food products for reasons of health, economy, convenience and safety. We had already modified a number of our products to make them more suitable for grilling. Existing batter technology, however, did not permit such a change. Yet it was clear that we needed to find some means of delivering that 'chip shop' taste without the inconvenience of frying and so a technical brief was issued to achieve this objective. It took 18 months to develop a new batter and it was when we had our first prototype samples that our research programme began. In the event the new batter meant that the product could be cooked either in the oven or under the grill (in the base of a grill pan). A first, qualitative stage of research was undertaken to assess consumer reactions to the concept and to gain guidance on the most relevant aspects of the product's appeal, particularly the cooking method. Four group discussions were undertaken amongst frozen fish in batter users. In two of the groups, current users of oven chips were recruited for we felt that they could provide us with some useful pointers (this product was gaining momentum at about the same time as our technical brief was issued).

It was clear from this research that there was no apparent dissatisfaction with the battered fish products currently marketed. Consumers' criticisms of existing products were really quite minor, with a slight feeling that the batter absorbed fat and that there was too big a gap between the fish and the batter resulting in the fish portion appearing small. The fact of frying battered fish was regarded as inevitable.

In contrast when the new Birds Eye concept was revealed reactions were very positive. It promised an easier cleaner, less smelly, less demanding method of preparation. Furthermore, oven cooking was indeed more reliable (it cooks the fish right through). There were some reservations – would an oven-cooked batter be crisped-up?; would it have a soggy inner layer?; perhaps the fish would dry out; it may be too time-consuming and perhaps too costly. Nevertheless, the concept was very well received. Both cooking methods were appreciated, grilling being considered the more appropriate for single-serving occasions. For family meals oven cooking was more likely and oven chip users were overall the more enthusiastic. When respondents came to consider a number of product names, those including 'oven' and 'grill' were both seen to be appropriate descriptors. However, while 'oven' conveyed the idea that the product might also be grillable the reverse was not true. The oven positioning was clearly the better option.

On trial of the product both within the group discussions and subsequently, it was deemed to live up to its promise – it looked golden, crisp, and appetising; it tasted fried with a very crispy batter and was moist. It was at least as good as the usual fried product, with the batter felt to be lighter and less greasy, and the fish firmer and fleshier.

From this small scale qualitative research it appeared that Oven Crispy fish should be of high consumer interest. Among light users of battered fish there was clear potential for expanding the market with the introduction of this product. The positioning also seemed clear – titled Oven Crispy, stressing the traditional delicious taste, and the modern, simple preparation.

We were not satisfied with the quality of the prototype product, the qualitative research as well as our own judgement suggesting that there was still room for improvement. Following further development effort, we undertook a quantitative study of the new Oven Crispy formulation alongside our existing Crispy

Cod Steaks and two competitive products. This research showed the two Birds Eye products to be equally highly esteemed. However, the oven product was clearly preferred by Southern housewives, probably due to a greater appreciation of the oven cooking method, while the more traditional housewives in the North favoured the original Crispy Cod Steaks. The difference in reactions in the two parts of the country strongly suggested that there may be two separate markets. Thus, our traditional product was not to be withdrawn, the two products being left to find their own levels in the market.

Research was also undertaken with regard to the advertising strategy, including a qualitative study of an animatic version of the 'Millie' commercial used at launch, as well as a quantitative check of awareness and recall of the advertising within the Midlands test area. The advertising strategy emerged extremely well from the research, communication of the product name, its convenience benefit and 'traditional deliciousness' achieving very satisfactory levels.

The success of this new product is now history but even we were surprised at the net additional business generated. Our market share increaseed by 9 points to more than 65 per cent and the total market grew by 30 per cent within the first few weeks of the Midlands test. Substitution with the traditional Crispy Cod Steaks was surprisingly low. This pattern of sales more than confirmed our belief that Oven Crispy would satisfy a gap in a battered fish market, rather than become a replacement. Although many consumers enjoyed traditional battered fish, it was not a regular purchase because of the less convenient cooking method. Oven Crispy was, therefore, satisfying the needs of new consumers for convenience, while, as repeat sales indicated, gaining high scores for product quality performance.

The extremely successful test market encouraged an earlier than planned national extension in February 1982. The television campaign was exactly as for the test market, supplemented by colour advertising in selected women's magazines. Due to the introduction of Oven Crispy, the total fish in batter market grew to £38 million in the last year. Sales of Birds Eye Oven Crispy Cod Steaks in 1983 should exceed £12 million.

5.12 Summary

1 It is important for all companies to be aware of the need for new products if profits are to be maintained.
2 New products can be obtained by modifying existing products, by acquiring new products, or by developing new products.
3 A new product development plan must ensure that products are only taken to an advanced stage if they fit the criteria of

   (a) an adequate demand,
   (b) compatibility with existing marketing capability,
   (c) compatibility with existing production capability,
   (d) adequate financial resources,
   (e) adequate manpower resources.

4 New products fail for a variety of reasons, but notably through over-enthusiasm.

5 New product ideas can come from (a) analysing market gaps, (b) new technology, and/or (c) creative thinking.

6 New products take time to find their way right through to the marketplace, because buyers vary from innovators and early adopters to late adopters and laggards.

References

1 Reported in *Printers Ink* (1 February 1963).
2 In *The Fundamentals of Marketing*, 35rd ed. (McGraw-Hill, 1971).
3 From 'Exploit the Product Life-Cycle', *Harvard Business Review*, Vol. 43, No. 6 (1965); included in *Modern Marketing Management* (Penguin, 1971).
4 In *The Management of New Products* (Booz, Allen and Hamilton, 1968).
5 In *Marketing* Vol. 14 No. 1 July 1983. 'Comment. Are we learning the innovation lesson?'
6 In *Marketing* (Pan, 1959), p. 190.
7 In *Consumer Product Development* (Longman, 1973), p. 69. A good easy-to-read summary with many case histories.
8 In *The Fundamentals of Marketing*, op. cit., p. 206.
9 In *Successful New Product Development* (Survey, June 1983).

Further Reading

Willsmer, Ray L. *Directing the Marketing Effort* (Pan, 1975). For a short review of the whole area of product range and new product development, see Chapters 7 and 8.

Advertising Works (IPA, 1980) and *Advertising Works 2* (IPA, 1982). Both contain good examples of new product launches.

Questions for Discussion

1 Suggest examples (other than those quoted in the text) of new products that are
   (a) innovative,
   (b) adaptive,
   (c) imitative.

2 Suggest examples of products that have recently been improved in terms of
   (a) quality,
   (b) features,
   (c) style.

3 (IM, June 1982) Suggest some basic criteria which need to be met if a new product is to prove successful.

4 On what bases could you suggest segmenting the markets for
   (a) shoes,
   (b) paint,
   (c) typewriters,
   (d) microcomputers

with a view to developing suitable new products for those market segments?
5 (IM, June 1981) In what circumstances might it be unwise for a company to pursue a policy of innovation?

6. *Where Price Comes In*

'But if you have a good product, don't spoil it by trying to sell it too cheaply. In other words, give the consumer the price which he wants and remember that it is not necessarily the cheapest price which will give him the greatest satisfaction.'

A. Gabor. 'Pricing in Theory and Practice.'

6.1 What is Price?

Price means something quite different to those on one side of the deal and those on the other. Price tells the manufacturer or retailer, if his accounting methods are good enough, how much profit he will make; and it tells the purchaser what the cost will be to him, though cost is not necessarily reckoned purely in terms of immediate cash payment.

A large proportion of individuals, when they buy a car, do so through a hire-purchase agreement. The important factor then becomes the size of the weekly or monthly payment. An industrial purchaser may actually be expecting to save costs by installing a particular piece of equipment. In both cases they may well be comparing the value or benefit they will get from this purchase with that from spending the same money in some other way.

Both personal and industrial buyers see price to some extent as a signal of quality. A. Gabor, in the article quoted at the head of this chapter,[1] gives some examples of products that failed to sell because they were priced too low. In one case oil with an unusual specification could not be sold at a low price, but when re-offered as a special formulation at a high price, it sold very well. Ray Willsmer[2] quotes the case of a new range of pastry and pudding mixes, which, test marketing indicated, housewives bought in substantially greater quantities at 7p than at 6½p (the two prices were offered at the same time in different parts of the country). The housewives could not accept that the quality product they expected from the packaging and promotion could only cost 6½p. At 7p all elements were in harmony and the total offer became more believable.

It is easy to test that this is a commonplace kind of reaction. Ask any group of, say, a dozen people what they would expect to pay for a normal household appliance such as a refrigerator of a certain size and appearance. While they may be fairly vague about the price, after a little discussion most will agree on it falling within a band, such as £150–£200. Only a small number would be willing to pay more, and they would expect to obtain better quality in return. Usually no one will be willing to pay a price below the agreed range because of the danger of receiving a product of unacceptable quality. Thus prices are a signal to the buyer of both cost and quality.

6.11 *The Plateau Effect*

For many products there is a top limit above which few people are prepared to pay for a given level of quality. Thus, for many years, certain items, especially in the drapery and haberdashery trades, would carry prices (in the old British currency) like 1s 11¾d (one shilling and eleven pence, three farthings), 5s 11¾d, where 2 shillings and 6 shillings represented the top limit of the generally acceptable price for a pair of stockings of given quality or a yard of a certain type of cloth.

The lack of small fractions of currency units and a high rate of inflation obscure to some extent the fact that this approach to pricing is still commonly applied. However, a look in some clothing boutiques for example will still show skirts or slacks at prices such as £19.95, and many other examples can readily be found.

It is well established that when buying gifts people have a sum of money in mind. They go shopping for something costing 'about a couple of pounds' or 'somewhere around a fiver'. Sometimes it is important that a present is known by the receiver of the gift to have cost a lot of money. Some perfumes, jewellery, and certain brands of chocolates illustrate the point. Offering these products at a lower price might well make them less, not more, attractive to the buyers.

Companies selling items intended to be given as gifts produce them at prices that fit into one of the categories in which customers themselves rank gifts. Thus one company produced a range of birthday cards incorporating a game or a 'cut-out' to meet the need of mothers whose children have been invited to a school friend's party; an ordinary birthday card costing, say, 20p would be 'too little', and a gift costing, say £1 'too much', but a card also serving as a small gift and costing perhaps 50p is 'just right'. Similarly, Viner's of Sheffield, who make silver-plate articles for the gift market, operate a conscious policy of tailoring the products and their prices to fit into clear-cut 'brackets'.

Thus the price of a product is not seen by the purchaser simply in terms of 'what is the cheapest'. Price is rather one element in the total 'bundle of satisfactions' which, as we saw in Chapter 4, is what really constitutes a product in the customer's eyes.

But this is a very subjective approach. Let us now examine some of the other factors that enter into pricing decisions.

6.2 The Economist's View of Price – Market Pricing

In classical economics, as we find it in the basic textbooks, the view of price stems from the theory of supply and demand. Simply put, this states that

Demand will fall as price increases.
Supply will rise as price increases.

This is logical and in agreement with commonsense to a large degree. It is obvious that, all things being equal, the rise in price of a product will cause fewer people to want to buy it, and the demand will fall off ('demand' in economics means the quantity that will be bought at a particular price); and it is equally obvious that if manufacturers are supplying a limited quantity of goods at a given price, then the unsatisfied demand will tend to force up the price, and as the price rises, more manufacturers will be inclined to produce similar goods, so that the supply will increase.

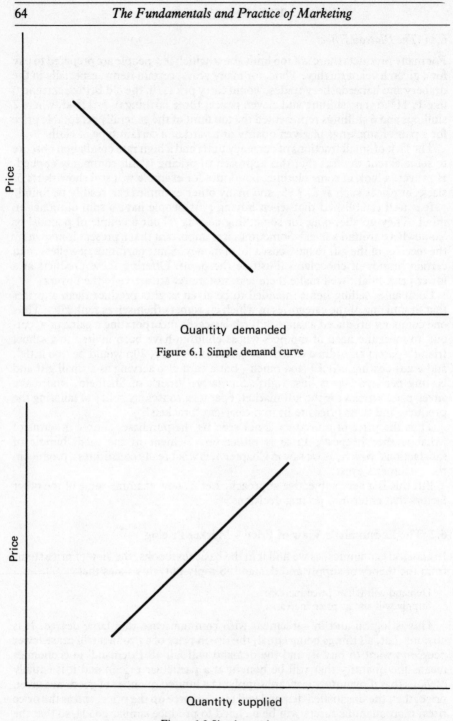

Figure 6.1 Simple demand curve

Figure 6.2 Simple supply curve

In a situation where demand is high and supplies low manufacturers may be able to price very high or 'charge what the market will bear' as it is often expressed.

Economists are accustomed to indicating these relations graphically, as in Figures 6.1 and 6.2.

When these two graphs are superimposed we get the position of a point of equilibrium at E (Figure 6.3), where the amount supplied Q is equal to the amount demanded at price P.

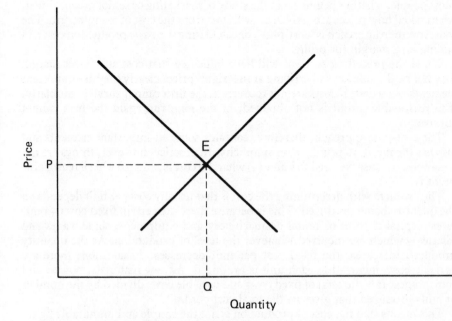

Figure 6.3 Demand and supply curves superimposed

Now, while it is true that in real life there will be a tendency for things to reach equilibrium in this way, in practice it is usually not quite so simple. The reason lies in the phrase 'all things being equal'. In real life all things are not equal.

For 'laws' of supply and demand to be true, economists have to assume a state of perfect competition, i.e., a market in which all suppliers and buyers are fully aware of the prices at which goods are available and where each type of goods is homogeneous. This is true in certain markets, such as primary commodities (metals, grain, cotton), currencies and stocks and shares. But in most markets in real life buyers and sellers do not have complete knowledge of the prices at which goods are on offer. Much more important, goods are certainly not homogeneous, but widely differing in performance, quality and in many other respects. Indeed, in a competitive economy, the seller's aim will normally be to bring about a situation where his product or service is clearly different from other people's – to establish, as we saw in Chapter 1, a 'competitive differential advantage'.

Thus, although total demand for a particular category of goods is an important factor determining the price people will pay, it is by no means the only factor and is frequently not even the most important factor. For example, the total demand for confectionery may well have virtually no bearing on the price that can be obtained by a manufacturer of very expensive, high quality liqueur chocolates mainly bought as Christmas gifts. What then are the other factors affecting pricing decisions?

6.3 The Importance of Manufacturing Costs – Cost-plus Pricing

Most people, whether beginners in the study of marketing or senior businessmen, when asked how prices are arrived at, will start from the cost of manufacture. The most common approach is 'cost-plus', or calculating the basic production cost and adding on a margin for profit.

While the preceding sections will have indicated that cost and profit margin may not be the sole keys to arriving at the 'right' price, clearly they are important elements. At worst, if costs are not recovered, the firm cannot survive. Similarly, if a 'reasonable' profit is not obtained, in the long run again the firm cannot survive.

The cost-plus approach, therefore, contains some all-important elements and also has the merit, in principle, of simplicity. In practice, however, things are not so simple, because we need to know (a) what the cost is, and (b) what a reasonable profit is.

The problem with determining the cost is that usually cost per unit depends on the quantity being produced. This is because there are certain fixed costs – rent, rates, capital charges or rental on machinery and equipment, some wages and salaries – which are incurred whatever the level of production. As the quantity produced increases, the fixed cost per unit decreases. In addition, there are variable costs incurred as each unit is produced, for raw materials, power, and some wages. It is the total of fixed costs and variable costs divided by the number of units produced that gives us the total cost per unit.

This means that the cost of production is not the simple and immutable figure that it is sometimes assumed to be. Worse still, the number of units produced will depend on demand, and demand, as we have seen, is influenced by price. So now we have the situation where we are trying to arrive at price with cost as the main determinant, yet cost is itself determined by price.

It must be remembered too that it is *total* cost we must work with (including marketing and distribution costs) not the simple 'Factory gate' cost of manufacture alone.

6.31 *Break-even Analysis*

A way of approaching the complexities we are now concerned with is the use of break-even charts, of which Figure 6.4 is a simple example.

We plot fixed costs and total (fixed plus variable) costs and the number of units being sold. We then plot the revenue against the number of units sold (revenue = number of units times price per unit). Where total revenue equals total cost we have the break-even point, but only at that price.

We can go on to plot a series of break-even charts at different prices, to establish

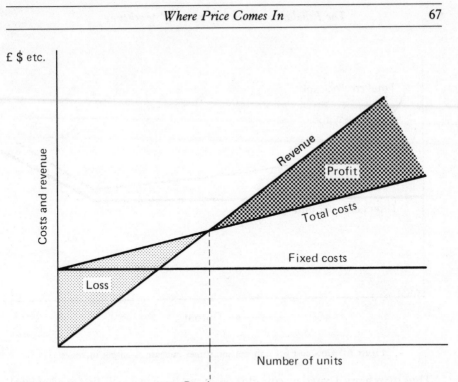

Figure 6.4 The basis of break-even calculations

how many units we would need to sell in order to break even at each price in turn. At the same time we can do a similar series of calculations (or they might have to be 'intelligent guesses') to find what the level of demand is likely to be at each price. We can then say, 'At price level X, demand is likely to be Y units and at Y units we do or do not break even'.

The 'Break-even Volume' can be calculated using the formula:

$$\text{BE Volume} = \frac{\text{Fixed Costs}}{(\text{Sales revenue} - \text{Variable Costs}) (\text{Units Sold})}$$

Thus if a firm has fixed costs of £10,000, variable costs of £15,000 and sells 5000 units for £30,000, the Break-even volume is:

$$\frac{10,000}{(30,000 - 15,000) \, 5000} = 3,333 \text{ units}$$

We see, then, that the cost per unit changes as the number of units changes. Generally speaking, the cost per unit decreases as the total number of units increases. However, it is possible to reach a situation, as depicted in Figure 6.5, where, beyond point C, overtime rates or shiftwork, coupled with fully utilized equipment lead to a sharp increase in cost per unit.

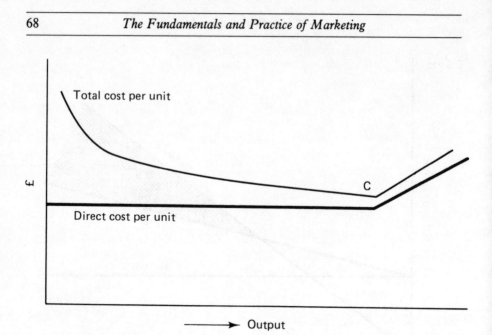

Figure 6.5 How cost per unit can sometimes increase as output increases

Thus to fix a price based on cost plus profit, we have to decide first at what level of production cost is to be calculated. If in fact that level is not reached, profit may be much less than anticipated or there could even be a loss. Even greatly exceeding the anticipated level of production may bring higher costs in some cases – with the same result.

In any case our price must be related to what customers expect to pay. Cost represents the level below which the price cannot go. In situations where manufacture is on a contract basis – in civil engineering for example – the level of output is exactly known in advance. The desired margin of profit can be added to produce a price that is then either above or below the competition's, and acceptable to the customer or not acceptable. But in the majority of situations, where cost per unit depends on the (as yet unknown) quantity to be produced, other factors have to be taken into account. (See Sections 6.4, 6.7 and 6.8.)

6.32 *Standard Cost Pricing*

A development of the cost-plus approach to setting prices is to use cost 'standards' based on management accounting systems. Variable costs of production (materials, labour, bought-in components, etc.) are added up and divided by the number of units intended to be produced to give a variable cost per unit. Similarly running costs of the organization (rent, rates, energy, maintenance, together with management and administrative costs) are totalled and divided by the number of units to be sold to provide the fixed cost per unit. Finally the profit required is added in on a per unit basis.

Adding together the variable cost, fixed cost and profit per unit gives the selling price. This approach is much used by companies producing a large range of products because it allows a complex situation to be subjected to disciplined control using standard accounting methods.

As Winkler[3] suggests 'Nothing could be simpler . . .' However, rightly, Winkler goes on to say . . . 'except that it is an inferior method of setting prices'.

'The first problem is that it assumes that costs are the thing which cause people to buy. But the market is not the least bit interested in cost. It is interested in getting what it wants at a competitive price . . .'

'Using the standard cost system, full cost accounting, full cost pricing, call it what you will, if your fixed costs are treated on a percentage basis, then if you manage to get your fixed costs down then your selling prices go down . . . As your selling price goes down, so will your actual profit per unit (but not your magic percentage).'

In other words, using costs as a basis for calculating prices needs tempering by consideration of what customers want and what they are prepared to pay if maximum profit is to be achieved (and sometimes if the company is even to be perceived as a high-quality supplier – See Section 6.1).

6.4 Pricing to Achieve Target Profits

The assumption made in simple economics theory is that in a situation of imperfect competition companies will be 'profit maximizers', that is, they will aim to make the highest profit the situation allows. A simple approach to achieving this is to charge 'what the market will bear' – the highest price that customers are prepared to pay (although once again we have the difficulty that in many situations price will affect the quantity sold). In practice, however, most companies seem rather to aim at a satisfactory level of profit – in economics language they are 'satisficers'. But this brings us back to the question introduced at the beginning of Section 6.3 – What is a satisfactory level of profit?

Clearly it is not enough to aim purely at the greatest amount of total profit, regardless of all other considerations. For example, suppose a business with £10,000 invested in it earns profits of £2,000. Then suppose that profits could be increased by a further £200 per annum but only by using further capital of £10,000. Clearly, this would not be a good use of the additional £10,000 which would earn more in the bank.

We have to look then at maximization of the percentage of profit in relation to the capital used in the business (usually referred to as 'return on capital employed'). There is a slight complication, since capital employed can be calculated in a number of different ways, but only the principle need concern us here.

A company can set as its objective a return of 10 per cent, 20 per cent or whatever on the capital employed in the business. The break-even approach can be used to establish whether a given project is likely to achieve this result and, if not, the project will not be taken up.

6.5 Marginal-cost Pricing

In a highly competitive situation companies may have the opportunity to gain business if they can offer a sufficiently low price. This is especially the case where individual contracts are negotiated such as large construction projects but is also increasingly evident in markets such as electrical appliances, where electricity boards, discount houses and other large retail chains are often in a position to 'shop around' for the best bulk discounts.

The question may then arise, 'What is the lowest level at which it makes sense to take the business?' One approach to this is to carry out a marginal costing calculation. In economics, marginal cost is the cost of producing one more unit. Usually in practice this means that fixed costs are already being recovered by a sufficient level of sales of units priced as discussed in the previous sections. The cost of producing extra units then affects the variable costs only, so that even if a very small profit per unit can be added, the business is worth taking.

We can go on from there and argue that even at no profit the business would be worth taking, because it may use resources (including people) that would otherwise stand idle. The danger here is that success in selling at these price levels may lead to additional orders and perhaps the situation indicated towards the end of Section 6.3, where additional business actually eats into existing profits.

For this reason Gabor does not regard marginal costing as a method of pricing but 'purely as a way of deciding whether certain orders should be accepted or not'.[4]

6.6 Competitors and Pricing

Clearly, what competitors are doing cannot be ignored when setting prices. For example, a company with a small share of the market will probably find the general price level already set for him. This does not of course rule out the possibility of finding a differential advantage, which will enable a price well above the general level to be charged, especially if only a small segment of the market is being attacked. For example, the fact that ball-point pens are widely available for a few pence does not prevent Parker's doing good business with very expensive (and top quality) pens for the gift market.

Very often it will be wise to accept competitive prices as the starting point for any development of a marketing strategy. It does assume, however, and possibly wrongly, that competitors have got their sums right. Against this, in an established market consumers will probably have come to accept this level as the 'going rate', and will need a lot of convincing if they are to accept something different. Traditionally the concept of the 'just price' has been talked of in some quarters. This was supposed to be the price acceptable to both buyers and sellers. Normally, of course, this will be the price level that has obtained in the market over recent times – in other words, what the major competitors in the field are currently charging.

Where the 'going rate' is set in this way by competitors, it is often useful to do backward costing, i.e. start with the price at which the product must be sold and then work backwards to the price at which it has to be produced if profit targets are to be met.

6.7 Pricing Strategies

We have already indicated that, rather than a single price that is right for a particular product, it is more likely that buyers will be thinking in terms of an acceptable price range with a 'ceiling' price above which demand might be expected to fall off significantly and a 'floor' price below which costs would not be recovered. It is even possible, by changing the attributes of the product (e.g. by giving it additional features or promoting its exclusive qualities), to gain acceptance for a price well above the normal range.

Even within the generally acceptable price range, however, the company must make a decision about where in the range to pitch its prices. In making such decisions there is often a strategic element, depending partly on what the company's objectives are. Stanton[5] lists the five following common price objectives:

1 Achieve target return on investment or net sales.
2 Stabilize prices.
3 Maintain or improve target share of market.
4 Match or undercut competition.
5 Maximize profits.

In a situation where the aim is to stabilize prices, i.e. avoid price-cutting, price wars and consequent lowering of profits, then clearly a follow-my-leader pricing policy is likely to be adopted. There are, however, a whole range of pricing strategies that may be adopted, and here we focus attention on the two extremes, normally referred to as 'skim-the-cream' and 'penetration pricing'.

6.71 *Skim-the-cream Pricing*

This means setting a price high in the acceptable range of prices, sometimes for a short period only, often for longer. It is largely, though not exclusively, associated with new products, for the following reasons:

1 In the early stages of a product's life (because there are few direct alternatives) demand is likely to be less elastic, i.e. less price-sensitive.
2 A high price may segment the market. Exclusivity can be used to appeal to certain income groups. At a later stage lowering the price can widen the appeal.
3 If a mistake is made, it is easier to lower the price subsequently than to raise it.
4 High initial prices can be used to recoup heavy research and development expenditure (a reason why this policy is commonly followed by the pharmaceutical industry among others).
5 Since production capacity may well be limited initially, a relatively low level of demand can be an advantage.

6.72 *Penetration Pricing*

Here a relatively low price is set in order to gain maximum penetration of the market as quickly as possible. This has obvious advantages where large economies of scale can be gained from higher levels of production, and also to make the market less attractive to competitors. A necessary condition of successfully applying this approach is, of course, that reducing the price will substantially increase the demand i.e. the demand must be elastic.

Once a company has gained dominance of the market by penetration pricing, it can be very difficult for a competitor to enter successfully.

Typical of products where a 'skim the cream' policy is applied are newly discovered ethical pharmaceuticals. Here there is high investment on research and development to be recovered, a market virtually closed to competition by patent protection – at least in the short run – and a probable high demand if the new drug cures a disease previously hard to treat.

It is also often used for other kinds of high-technology products. Sinclair home computers for example were introduced at around £100 each then progressively reduced in price until the original model was selling at under £40 in 1983, by which time the second generation model (with larger memory capacity) was on the market at the original price level.

A penetration policy however is being applied by Sinclair with their new small screen TV priced so as to undercut severely the Sony 'Watchman' which was launched earlier.

6.8 Price Structures

So far we have talked of 'a price' or 'the price'. In practice, a whole structure of related prices has to be devised.

Only when the manufacturer sells direct to the user is there a simple one-price arrangement. Usually we need to ask 'The price to whom?' Where the goods pass through a distribution chain such as manufacturer to wholesaler to retailer to customer, there may be a whole series of prices appropriate to each stage of the process. Wholesalers and retailers each need revenue to cover their own operating costs and profit. Traditionally this was often achieved by the manufacturer fixing the end price to the ultimate customer and allowing a discount to the retailer and a further discount to the wholesaler.

The price structure would then look something like this:

Retail price		£5.00
Less retailer's discount 20 per cent		1.00
Price to retailer		£4.00
Less wholesaler's discount 10 per cent		0.40
Price to wholesaler		£3.60

The abolition of resale price maintenance meant that manufacturers could not enforce a fixed retail price. So, in the U.K. at least, the alternative system is now much more common in that the producer starts at the other end with a price 'ex factory' (i.e., for goods bought direct from the manufacturer) and dealers at each stage add their own 'mark-up' to cover costs and profit, as follows:

Ex-factory price		£3.00
Wholesale mark-up 10 per cent		0.30
Price to retailer		£3.30
Retail mark-up 20 per cent		£0.66
Retail price		£3.96

(e.g. if a retailer bought from a manufacturer at £80 and sold for £100 he would be adding a 25 per cent mark-up. If however, the manufacturer sets a 'recommended retail price' of £100 but sells to the retailer at £80 he is giving a 20 per cent discount off the higher price).

The difference between mark-up and discount is sometimes confused, and it is important to get the distinction clear. A 20 per cent discount is the same as a 25 per cent mark-up.

Frequently used in pricing are 'quantity discounts'. Here the price will vary according to the quantity bought (on the basis that transport costs, administration and so on will be proportionately higher on small deliveries than on large ones). Some manufacturers rely exclusively on quantity discounts and do not have separate wholesale or retail price lists. Anyone can buy direct and the price is determined solely by the quantity bought.

A further source of price differences is 'differential pricing'. Different price levels may be set, e.g., for delivery to different parts of the country (to reflect transport costs). Rail fares are commonly cheaper at times when fewer people travel (in an attempt to divert pressure from the overloaded trains to those with free capacity). Hotel rates are cheaper in the 'off-season' for the same kind of reason.

Clearly in all the calculations in Sections 6.3 to 6.8 close liaison with the accountants within the company is vital. They will need to supply many of the figures, and in return they will need to be advised of any pricing proposals, so that they can study their implications.

6.81 *The Importance of Negotiation*

In many business to business marketing situations, the price structure worked out by the marketing organization will often be merely a starting point for discussion. Large retail chains, industrial organizations and public authorities (such as county supplies departments, regional hospital authorities) normally place very large contracts. This gives them enormous buying power and makes their business highly desirable. So a dialogue has to take place between buyer and seller and this demands negotiating skill on both sides in order to arrive at the most advantageous 'deal'. Often the negotiations with large buyers will be handled by specialist salesmen often called key accounts executives or national accounts executives (see Section 14.11).

6.9 Price Changes

There can be a number of situations which cause companies to consider changing their prices:

1 Substantial changes in cost.
2 Holdups in output (e.g. strikes, raw material or component shortages).
3 Sharp increase in demand.
4 Change in competitors' behaviour (e.g. price increases, changes in output).
5 Changing economic situation.
6 Legislation or other pressures from government.
7 Changing price as a deliberate marketing strategy.

6.91 *Price-Cutting*

Firms can be 'pushed' into deliberate price-cutting because, e.g. (a) they must have immediate cash; (b) sales must be increased urgently; (c) management feel the need to do something.

Alternatively, price-cutting may be used as a deliberate 'pull' strategy in order to, e.g. (a) drive out marginal producers; (b) achieve lower costs by expanding sales; (c) to improve distributors' turnover and hence encourage support by them.

6.92 *Competitors and Price Changes*

Before deciding on price changes it is necessary to consider what is likely to be our competitors' response. This may be to: (a) match our new price; (b) cut the price still further (assuming our new price is lower); (c) offer alternative benefits (e.g. product quality, service, advertising or other forms of promotion); (d) offer better backup to resellers; (e) attempt to persuade the price-cutter to come back into line (by persuasion and/or threat of retaliation).

(N.B. When faced with price cuts by a competitor some action must be taken or the company's own volume will probably suffer.)

A company's attitude to price changing should be influenced by its relative positions in a particular market. Thus a brand leader can probably also be a 'price leader' whereas a company with a small market share may have to fix its prices very much in the light of the lead given by its larger competitors.

6.93 *How Customers react to Price Changes*

A price change may be seen by customers as meaning, for example: (a) the quality of the product has changed; (b) the product is about to be superseded; (c) the change will be followed by further changes in the same direction; (d) the seller is in financial difficulty.

A large increase in price for an item which represents an important purchase may affect customers in the following ways: (a) alters their financial resources and so changes their pattern of spending on other things; (b) makes it necessary for them to borrow; (c) increases their monthly repayments.

The effect of price-cutting on customers will vary, depending on:

1 Frequency of purchase.
2 Timing of the price cut.
3 Whether the product can be stored.

As with competitors, the likely reaction of customers to any price change must be very carefully considered before any action is taken and should be continuously monitored.

6.94 *Distributors and Price Changes*

Account must be taken also of the likely reaction of distributors who may be carrying stocks purchased at the old price. Consideration may have to be given to compensating them if the new price is lower.

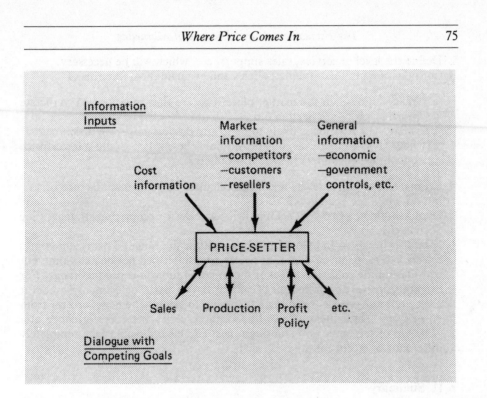

Figure 6.6 The price-setting process

6.10 The Price-setting Process

Figure 6.6 illustrates the complexity of the price-setting process. The person or group with the task of setting a price has first to deal with a mass of information and arrive at an acceptable price range based on an assessment of:

market
cost
customer expectations
competitive strategies
economic situation, etc.

But this will seldom lead to a clear cut, one and only 'right' price. The company's own policies and goals will have an influence. Typically (though over-simplifying) sales people tend to argue for a lower price to make their task easier; production people on the other hand would prefer not to be too straitened in their choice of production methods, materials, etc. so may tend to argue for a higher price; finance and general management will 'take a view' on the profit level that is desirable or essential.

The following is a suggested sequence to be followed in the price setting task:

1 Identify end customers and distribution channels. Establish any views and feelings they have about price.

2 Define the level of service, sales support, etc. which will be necessary.
3 Consider competitors' pricing policies and evaluate them in terms of:

    (a) relative power in the market place (e.g. are they in a position to dictate price levels? – see Section 6.6),

    (b) what their reaction is likely to be to any pricing moves we make,

    (c) how loyal are their customers and ours (how much would a lower price encourage customers to switch suppliers?).

4 Estimate likely sales levels and then calculate costs of manufacture, distribution, etc. (See Section 6.3.)
5 Establish 'floor' price and 'ceiling' price and decide on pricing strategy. (See Section 6.7.)
6 Establish prices of individual products within the range. This is sometimes referred to as 'team pricing', i.e. prices are established not one at a time but considering the collective effect of the prices of the whole product range. For example, one particular marque of car may have a 'basic' or 'economy' model at a very attractive price (enabling advertising to claim 'The new Sorcerer from only £4,000!') but other models with more accessories, better performance, etc. (The top of the range Sorcerer might cost £5,500 and would be a completely different car except for the body shell.)

6.11 Summary

1 In basic economics terms price reflects the level of demand, but practice is a much more complex matter.
2 Buyers have subjective views on what is an appropriate price and there is normally a range of prices for a given product which they find acceptable. They tend to shop within a certain price bracket.
3 Price is also a signal of quality to the buyer.
4 From the seller's point of view, cost is only one element in fixing the price. Cost is in any case not simple to arrive at, because cost per unit normally varies with output, which is itself influenced by the price.
5 Break-even analysis enables cost per unit to be calculated at various levels of demand and on different price assumptions.
6 Companies may be profit-maximizers but are more likely to see their objectives in terms of reaching an acceptable profit target, when they behave as 'satisficers'.
7 Competitors' pricing policies are an important factor, and may influence choice of pricing strategy between the two extremes of skim-the-cream and penetration pricing.
8 A company's price structure will probably take account of wholesale and retail profit margins. In addition, or as an alternative, it may include quantity discounts. In some situations a differential pricing policy may be adopted.
9 Prices have on different occasions to be adjusted and the impact of this on consumers and distributors will need to be accurately predicted as well as the likely reaction of competitors.

References

1 In *Management Decision* (Summer 1967); included in *Modern Marketing Management* (Penguin, 1971). A good summary of up-to-date thinking on pricing policies.
2 In *Directing the Marketing Effort* (Pan, 1975).
3 In *Pricing for Results* (Heinemann, 1983). An excellent 'how to do it' book on competitive pricing techniques.
4 In *Management Decision*, op. cit.
5 In *The Fundamentals of Marketing*, 3rd ed. (McGraw-Hill, 1971), p. 414. Chapters 18–21 give a good, fairly detailed outline of all important aspects of pricing.

Further Reading

Donaldson, Peter. *Economics of the Real World* (Pelican, 1973). *How British Industry Prices* (Industrial Marketing Research Ltd., 1975). An outline of current pricing practice.
Winkler, John. *Bargaining for Results* (Heinemann, 1982). A sound guide to negotiating skills.

Questions for Discussion

1 For each of the following products would you expect the seller to be more likely to adopt a skim-the-cream or a penetration pricing policy?

(a) A new software package enabling householders to use cheap home computers to reduce their energy consumption.
(b) A cigarette made from a new strain of tobacco containing a low level of carcinogens.
(c) Wall covering that can be applied like paint but gives a 'fabric' finish.
(d) A diesel-fuelled car with acceleration comparable with equivalent petrol-engined models (assuming diesel fuel is substantially cheaper than petrol).
(e) A lightweight portable colour TV with stereo sound.

2 How much account should be taken of competitors' prices in fixing the price of your own product?
3 Give six examples of prices that illustrate the plateau effect.
4 Under what circumstances does marginal costing become a sensible business policy?
5 Name three products that seem to you to have an elastic demand, and three that have an inelastic demand.
6 (CAM, Nov. 1981) Explain what is meant by differential pricing and give three examples.
7 The text gives railway fares and hotel tariffs as examples of differential pricing. Can you think of three others?
8 (IM, June 1983) In setting an original price on a product the marketing manager needs to consider more than manufacturing cost. What are some of the major marketing considerations in this type of pricing decision?

7. Getting the Goods to the Customers

'Stocks of a commodity piled high in a factory warehouse are about as useful to the customer or user as milk down on the farm is to a householder living in the middle of London or Manchester.'

Leslie W. Rodger. *Marketing in a Competitive Economy*

7.1 The Importance of Place

Place was one of the all-important 'four Ps' listed in Chapter 3 as elements in the marketing mix. Only when all four are right and correctly balanced with each other will the customer receive in full measure the satisfaction he is seeking.

So far we have considered in detail how the 'right' products are produced and how the 'right' price is arrived at. Now we need to consider how products can be brought to the 'right' place – where the customer wants them to be.

In some very simple situations there is no problem about this. The village baker baking his bread on the premises, with his customers all around him, simply makes the goods available and his customers come a few hundred yards to him or he takes his wares a few hundred yards to their homes. But there are not many such village bakers left, in the U.K. at any rate, nor many similar situations. The more usual case is that manufacture on a large scale is carried out at one location, and customers live in very many other widely separate locations hundreds or even thousands of miles away.

Generally speaking, customers are in no position to go to the manufacturer, and in any case, they want the goods or services to be provided where they are. Somehow the manufacturer must make it so.

Someone buying a car does not want to have to travel more than, say, 20 miles to view and test it, certainly not to have it serviced. People living in towns do not want to have to travel to the country for their milk or their fruit. Having his wants provided for at the place of his choosing is part of what the customer pays for when he buys a product.

It is sometimes feasible or even essential for the manufacturer to deal direct with his customer. The civil engineering contractor building a power station and the bespoke tailor making a suit will certainly need to. The manufacturer of chocolate bars, canned soups or refrigerators does not need to. So a company offering products or services has two basic decisions to make in this area:

1 Is there any vital need to deal direct with the customer?
2 If not, what is the best method of providing the product or service at the place where it is convenient to the customer?

7.2 The Channels of Distribution

A producer has the choice of dealing direct or of passing his goods through other organizations, including wholesalers and/or retailers sometimes collectively referred to as resellers. The route(s) followed by the products (or at least their ownership) as they travel to the ultimate customers by way of these other organizations are usually called the channels of distribution.

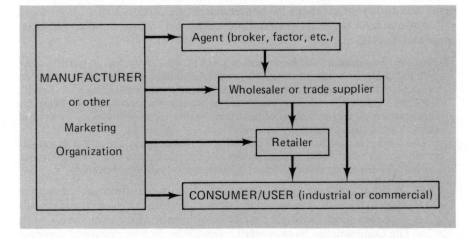

Figure 7.1 Some alternative routes to the customer

There are a number of choices available, as in Figure 7.1. The figure shows the five main variations which are possible. Avon Cosmetics and *Encyclopaedia Britannica* are examples of companies selling direct to the consumer. Many goods and services, from heavy machinery and raw materials to nuts and bolts and stationery, are also sold direct to industrial users. But a high proportion of goods such as groceries and services (such as travel) are purchased by consumers from resellers.

7.21 *The Middleman's Function*

Operating the channels of distribution are the middlemen – independent businesses standing between the producer and the household consumer or industrial user.

The first group listed – brokers, factors, agents – differ from the others in that they normally arrange sales transactions but do not take title to the goods. But there is widely differing usage of the various terms.

Retailers are people whose main business is to sell direct to the ultimate private user. In some cases (cars, TV, domestic appliances) they may also carry out servicing and maintenance after the sale, although this can sometimes be a quite separate function.

Wholesalers are concerned with selling to others (mainly retailers) who are buying in order to resell or to those who are buying for business use (i.e. not for personal consumption).

There is some overlap of function. Some retailers may sell on occasions a large quantity (at discount) to a company for business use – the wholesale function. Wholesalers may also do some retailing. It was usual, for example, for British builders' merchants to have a 'wholesale counter' (for purchase by builders and decorators) and a 'retail counter' (for purchases by individuals for their personal use). More recently many of them have become 'cash and carry' suppliers to the trade and do-it-yourself shops for householders (see Section 7.39).

Stanton defines the middleman's function as that of concentration, equalization and dispersion.

> Frequently the quantity and assortment of goods produced by a firm are out of balance with the variety and amounts wanted by consumer or industrial users. A businessman needs paper, pencils, typewriters and desks. A homeowner wants grass seed, topsoil, fertilizer, a rake and a roller and eventually he hopes to need a lawnmower. No single firm produces all the items either of these users' wants and no producer may sell any of them in the small quantity the user desires . . .
>
> The job to be done involves (1) collecting or concentrating the output of various producers, (2) subdividing these quantities into the amounts desired by the customers . . . and (3) dispersing this assortment to consumer or industrial buyers.[1]

Some producers may own part of their own distribution channels. Thus most public houses in the U.K. are owned by brewers: Burmah Oil owns the Halford's chain of accessory shops (which is a major outlet for their Castrol motor oil). The Marley Tile Company has its own retail shops under its own name and there are many other examples. Similarly, retailers like Boots and Marks & Spencer's also organize their own production and in the case of Boots also carry it out for a wide range of goods. But these examples of vertical integration do not in any way alter the distinct functions of production and retailing.

7.3 The Retail Scene

To understand fully the reasons behind the way in which distribution channel decisions are made it is important to be clear how the retail section of the marketing system is made up. The best and possibly only way to obtain this understanding is by observation and personal experience, whether in marketing or simply as a retail purchaser. Using the U.K. as an example what follows is meant to point out some landmarks and provides definitions of the more common expressions used in describing the retail scene. It should always be remembered in this context that distributors' marketing interests will not always precisely coincide with manufacturers' distributive objectives and that a bargaining situation exists always between the two parties, in which each will endeavour to secure the best possible terms of trading for itself. This partly explains the emergence of multiple groups and voluntary chains which are able to exert immense buying power in dealing with the bigger manufacturers.

7.31 *Direct Marketing*

This is carried out by producers in the following ways:

1 Door-to-door direct selling by companies like Avon. Salesmen of industrial products calling on company buyers are also 'direct selling', of course.
2 'Party plan' by Tupperware containers, Sarah Coventry jewellery, Oriflamme cosmetics and others. Both these categories use part-time representatives selling on commission to people in their homes.
3 Mail order through catalogues (e.g. Littlewoods), book clubs etc. Here there is no face-to-face contact and the whole transaction is carried out through the post. Although 'agents' sometimes hold a catalogue and earn a commission on any orders they take for their friends and relatives, it tends to be passive rather than active selling.
4 Selling 'off the page' through advertising direct to consumers (e.g. Sinclair personal computers, Damart thermal underwear – Damart also use catalogues).
5 Own retail outlets, such as Boots, Marley's, Marks & Spencer's, Burton tailoring.

7.32 *Independent Shops*

'The independents' account for the majority of shops but only a minority of the turnover, since they are smaller and have less capital and expertise than the multiples. They are losing ground to the multiples as a result.

7.33 *Chain Stores*

'The multiples', as they are called, are groups of retail stores (such as Burton's, Woolworth's, Sainsbury's) with common ownership and varying, but usually high, degrees of central direction and control. They normally have a common 'image' (range of goods, promotion, decor and so on) and specialize in a particular type of merchandise – although the 'variety chains' such as Woolworth's, Marks & Spencer's and the British Home Stores carry a diversity of goods.

7.34 *Department Stores*

These act as a collection of 'shops' or departments all under one roof, each with its own buyer and range of goods. There is central ownership of the whole operation, although sometimes parts of the store are rented out (e.g. to manufacturers of a branded range of cosmetics or clothing), when they are known as 'shops within a shop'.

7.35 *Co-operative Societies*

In many ways Co-ops resemble chain stores but traditionally were owned by their 'members', who, when they shopped regularly, were paid a 'dividend' out of the trading surplus – this dividend taking the place of profits to shareholders. Owing largely to their democratic structure, they suffered a little from poor management and have lost part of their share in the market. But they still account for a very substantial proportion of all retail sales, especially in the North of England. In recent times, in order to counter the growing strength of the supermarket chains, they have largely substituted cut-priced goods and trading stamps for the old-style dividend.

7.36 *Discount Stores*

These are large 'warehouse' type shops, saving on costs by (a) out-of-town locations (hence lower rents etc.), (b) minimum service and display, and (c) bulk purchase. Hence they are able to offer goods at substantially lower prices than conventional retailers. They are especially common in electrical goods and furniture (partly because of the traditionally high profit margins), where their large range of goods in stock is an added attraction.

7.37 *Franchising*

Combining the advantages of centralized management expertise with the vigour and flexibility of the independent, the franchiser supplies a name and 'image', products, services and general know-how, including advice on locations, loan capital facilities and methods of operation and control. The franchisee supplies all or a large part of the capital and agrees to purchase supplies from the franchiser. Particularly common in the catering field – e.g. Wimpy Bars (operated by J. Lyons & Co. Ltd), Kentucky Fried Chicken – but also in many other fields – e.g., Dyno-rod drain cleaning service. Coca-Cola operates a franchise system, with area distributors buying special syrup from the company, diluting and bottling, then distributing in their area.

7.38 *Supermarkets and Hypermarkets*

Usually operated by multiples, though not always, supermarkets are self-service shops with a sales area of over 4,000 sq. ft. They are especially common in the grocery field, but are spreading, particularly into hardware. Originally in town centres, more recently many have been sited out of town to ease customers' traffic and parking problems – and incidentally to take advantage of lower rent, rates, etc., and easier unloading for delivery vans.

Still few in Britain, although very common in other E.E.C. countries, hypermarkets are defined as self-service shops on one floor with at least 25,000 sq. ft. of selling area. Usually they are out of town and have very large free parking areas. They normally carry a wide range of merchandise, and in a sense are self-service department stores all on one floor, although there is a much lower degree of self-sufficiency by each department. They offer customers the full advantage of 'one stop shopping' at attractive prices. 'Superstores' are a variant on these.

7.39 *Voluntary Chains*

When grocery distribution was transformed by the rapid growth of super-markets, wholesalers lost a great deal of their traditional business because many of their retailer customers lost business or closed. Some wholesalers themselves closed. Many of the remainder had to change their methods.

One outcome of this is 'cash-and-carry' where, instead of a regular call from the wholesaler to take orders from the retailers, followed by delivery of the goods ordered, retailers now frequently go to the wholesaler's warehouse and collect their own goods – on a self-service basis – and pay cash. This reduces the wholesaler's costs very considerably.

The term cash-and-carry is also used to describe a kind of retailing, especially in grocery, where private consumers have access to a similar kind of warehouse and can buy foods etc. 'by the case' at bulk prices.

A further development is that some wholesalers have led their retail customers into the formation of *voluntary chains* (Mace, Spar, Vivo are examples). This enables the 'independents' to stay independently owned but to gain some of the advantages enjoyed by the multiples – a common image, a central pool of management expertise, better access to capital, joint promotions and some degree of bulk purchasing.

7.4 Selecting Distribution Channels

Middlemen have a number of very important functions, which may be summarized as follows:

1 Assembling products at the place most convenient to the purchasers, in the 'mix' and variety they desire (men like to buy their cigarettes at the same time as their newspaper; housewives their butter, jam and dried fruits all at once; and manufacturers of electronic equipment a wide range of components from one source).
2 Making it easy for potential customers to see and examine products and to compare alternatives (electrical appliances and furniture, for example).
3 Offering a range of pre-sale and post-sale services, such as technical advice (e.g. what power an electric heater should have for a particular size of room); delivery and/or installation and fitting (e.g. carpets); after-sales service (central heating, cars, business machines).
4 Making it easy for customers to buy in the quantity they need: the butcher can supply ½-kilo of beef, but the farmer is not geared to it; the grocer will supply one small can of baked beans, but the Heinz factory despatches them by the van-load.

All these functions could in theory be carried out by the producer, and sometimes they are – many farmers have a wayside stall selling seasonal fruits such as strawberries and many will supply meat ready for the home freezer. Any producer has to decide who will carry out these functions – himself, a middleman, a series of middlemen. A number of factors influence the decision; they are related to the kind of market, the kind of product and the kind of company concerned, as follows:

1 *The Market*. Industrial products will need different channels from consumer ones. A market with very many potential customers will more likely need middlemen to service it than one with only few customers. Conversely, a compact market is easier to serve direct than one that is widely dispersed. Products bought frequently in small quantities at low cost are more likely to need middlemen than high-cost items bought infrequently.
2 *The Product*. Generally speaking, items of low unit value are likely to have larger chains of distribution. Heavy and bulky items are likely to be delivered

direct from producer to user (even if the selling is carried out by an intermediary). Perishable goods need special channels of distribution equipped either with appropriate storage facilities or geared for a quick turn-round. The range of products may have a bearing – for example, electrical retailers are reluctant to deal with too many suppliers, and a producer with only one or two products might have to deal through wholesalers. Products whose customers are not clearly aware of their need (such as life insurance) or which are custom-built (civil engineering or tailored suits) are more likely to be sold direct.

3 *The Company*. Dealing direct with customers and providing all the facilities that go with it (storage depots, delivery vans, servicing arrangements etc.) can be very expensive. So smaller or under-capitalized companies tend to have to use middlemen. Companies entering a market with which they are unfamiliar may also need the expertise of middlemen accustomed to dealing in that market.

The factors discussed above influence mainly whether or not middlemen will be used, but another decision has also to be made. Which channels of distribution are to be used.

This decision will be influenced in the main by (1) Customer contact (which channels are best in touch with the target market for the product concerned); (2) Facilities (which channels have the facilities for display, servicing, special storage, or whatever the particular product might need); and (3) Control and motivation (whether the producer will be able to exercise control over the way the wholesalers/retailers handle his product). Will he be in a strong or weak bargaining position? Is the product likely to be of sufficient interest for the dealer to give it active support? As an example of the kind of question arising here, a small manufacturer might, from some points of view, be glad to sell his entire output to Marks & Spencer's or Halford's, for it would relieve him of many problems; but it would also leave him very little room for manoeuvre, and make him vulnerable. A producer whose product represents only a small profit potential for his retailers will find it difficult to get them to give it the strong promotional support it might need.

7.41 *Overlapping and Split Channels of Distribution*

We have spoken so far as though a producer needs to choose one single channel of distribution. In fact, very frequently a multiplicity of channels will be used. Mars bars and cigarettes are not only sold in C.T.N. (confectionery, tobacconist and newsagent) outlets, but also in supermarkets, on garage forecourts and in cinemas.

Often different channels are used to reach different segments of the market. Engine oil is sold when garages use it in carrying out oil changes for customers. But more than half the car owners put in their own oil, which they buy mainly from such other outlets as accessory shops (Halford's), supermarkets (Tesco), and chain stores (Woolworth's).

Even something with a clear-cut and obvious distribution channel of its own will have other subsidiary ones as well. Greengrocers are the traditional channel for fresh fruit and vegetables, but these can also be bought from general stores, supermarkets and garden centres.

Distribution patterns are constantly changing, with new types of retailer developing and old ones disappearing. The old-style drapers have gone, boutiques have taken some of the traditional business from department stores, and do-it-yourself stores have blossomed everywhere. And how many people under 60 have even heard of an oil chandler?

7.42 *A Dynamic Situation*

J. H. Davidson[2] compares the pattern of distribution to the hour hand of a clock. It is actually moving all the time, although at a given moment it looks static. Producers must therefore keep their distribution channels always under review to ensure that they are not relying on obsolescent ones, while their competitors' products are flowing towards outlets that are in a phase of rapid growth.

One final point. The 'obvious' channels are not always the most effective. For example, garages look like the best outlets for replacement car tyres, yet a whole new business has developed in stocking and fitting tyres. The reason? Customers only buy a replacement tyre when they must. Then they want quick 'while-you-wait' service with the right tyre in stock. Traditionally, each garage fitted just a few – it was a slow-moving business and skilled fitters were taken off a repair job to (grudgingly) fit tyres. The profit margins were high to reflect the high stock value, low turnover and cost of fitting. The specialist companies get high turnover, have lower costs and so can 'give away' part of the profit margin in lower prices. The sale of paperback books shot up when they ceased to be sold only in bookshops and became available as 'impulse buys' for people at airports, railway stations, in hotels and shops or just walking along the street.

7.5 Distribution Channels Decisions

The decision as to the distribution channels a marketing organization is to use is a vitally important one for two key reasons:

1 The decision affects all other aspects of the marketing operation. For example, the pricing structure will depend on the number and types of intermediaries being used. The sales force structure and management will vary enormously if the choice is between direct sales to user and dealers as intermediaries.
2 It normally presages long-term commitments. For example, a manufacturer of cars, farm machinery or earth-moving equipment needs outlets to sell and service his products. Setting up a channel of dealers to carry out these tasks means their investing in stocks and equipment. This means that these arrangements do not lend themselves to short-term changes.

7.51 *Some Key Aspects of Distribution Channel Decisions*

There are several aspects to be considered when deciding on the distribution arrangements for any particular marketing operation. They include the following:

1 The types of intermediaries to be used and the number of stages, e.g. retailers or retailers/wholesalers (see Section 7.4).

2 The number of each type of intermediary to be used.
3 The tasks and responsibilities to be carried out (a) by the marketing organization, and (b) by the organizations forming the distribution chain.

7.52 *Decisions on Numbers of Intermediaries*

The second of the above aspects is often a specially important one, and is closely linked with other crucial decisions concerning market share, sales volume and profitability targets. It is customary to distinguish three levels of 'market exposure', as follows:

1 *Intensive distribution*, where efforts are made to get every possible suitable outlet to stock the product (torch batteries, ice-cream).
2 *Exclusive distribution*, where the number of outlets is deliberately limited (top quality fashion goods). Some of the objectives that might lead to this approach are:

    (a) Enhancing the 'image' of the product and hence achieving higher mark-ups.

    (b) Encouraging dealers to support the product more strongly and sell it more aggressively.

3 In between these extremes come varying degrees of selective distribution. Here the marketing organization seeks to find the optimum number of outlets that will on the one hand give adequate coverage of the market but on the other will not lead to the expense of dealing with large numbers of outlets yielding only small sales volume (domestic appliances, microcomputers, tyres and car batteries).

7.53 *The All-Important Cost and Profitability Factors*

This brings us on to what in essence is the crux of all decisions regarding distribution channels. The aim must always be to choose the distribution pattern that will in the long term yield the desired sales volume at the lowest cost.

While it may often be very difficult to do in practice (although that does not mean it should not be attempted), in theory it is possible to compare alternative distribution channels by means of the following calculation:

$$\text{Rate of return} = \frac{(\text{Estimated sales revenue}) - (\text{Cost of channel})}{\text{Costs of channel}}$$

Then that channel, or set of channels, which gives the highest rate of return will be chosen.

7.6 **Physical Distribution**

As well as deciding through which channels goods will move or selling will proceed, one must consider another whole aspect of distribution. This is the business of physically moving products from factory to customer – the logistics.

Until fairly recently this was often taken for granted, and frequently allowed to happen rather haphazardly. But with rising costs of transport, labour and buildings, transport and storage can become a very significant part of the total end cost of the product.

A new study of Physical Distribution Management (P.D.M.) is developing to deal with this part of the business in the most cost-effective manner. Essentially, this deals with every aspect of getting goods from the end of the production line safely and economically to the user. It means approaching the whole business on a 'system' basis, not as a series of separate fragments. Some of the many elements making up the system are transportation, warehousing (including location decisions), stock control, packing and materials handling, and order processing. The costs of each of these cannot be viewed in isolation, nor can their efficiency in terms of ultimate satisfaction to the customer.

For example, looking purely at warehousing, it might appear that money could be saved by reducing the number of area depots from fifteen to twelve. However, some customers would then be farther from a delivery point and transport costs could well rise to an extent greater than the savings achieved by cutting out some depots.

Reducing stock levels would save interest on the capital tied up (or enable it to be employed more profitably elsewhere), but, at the same time, the risk of being out of stock would increase (unless other steps, also with costs attached, were taken to offset the risks), with the consequent chance of delays in delivery and ultimately loss of business through poor service to customers.

To decide between centralized stocks as against regional storage depots, one would have to balance the saving on building or renting of depots, coupled with double-handling and transport (factory to depot, depot to customer), against the cost of longer journeys (factory direct to customer) with half-empty vehicles and probably the need for a more expensive vehicle fleet. Similarly, using expensive forms of transport (such as air freight to overseas markets) may enable urgent delivery requests to be met at a lower total cost than holding stock at numerous points around the world and thus being able to cut transport costs.

7.7 Distribution for Industrial Markets

While we have talked mainly of consumer markets, the same kind of factors will apply in distribution for industrial markets. Industrial consumables indeed may follow a virtually identical pattern. Thus, stationery and similar goods are frequently sold through retail shops stocking a wide range of such materials, as well as direct to big users.

Only when we come to the heavier, less frequently bought, items do we find a totally different pattern. Here problems of weight, size, installation and servicing force the use of special techniques and tend to favour a direct sales approach, with delivery direct from factory to user. We then see a tendency to use specialists for some aspects of distribution – for example, transporting wide loads, packing for shipment by air or sea, or the making up of container loads.

7.8 International Distribution

All the factors discussed in connection with channel selection and physical distribution management became more complex if we are dealing with an international, not merely a national, situation and this aspect will be explored in Chapter 18. The basic concepts remain the same, however.

7.9 Summary

1 Producers have a wide range of distribution channels open to them when deciding how to sell and physically move their products from the factory to the customer.
2 Middlemen (agents/factors, wholesalers and retailers) exist to provide customers, at the point most convenient to them, with the desired choice of goods, to make goods available in convenient quantities and to offer the necessary pre-sale and post-sale supporting services.
3 The distribution system is complex and constantly changing. Producers must keep it under regular review. The present and 'obvious' channels are not necessarily the ones that will be most effective in the future.
4 The choice of channels is determined by the size and characteristics of the market, the type of product and the capabilities of the producer, as well as by the nature of the distribution channels available.
5 Very often a multiplicity of channels will be used, not just a single type of outlet.
6 Physical Distribution Management is becoming increasingly important as the relative costs of transport handling and storage continue to increase.
7 Distribution to industrial concerns and to customers in other countries involves an extension of the same principles.

References

1 In *The Fundamentals of Marketing*, 3rd ed. (McGraw-Hill, 1971).
2 In *Offensive Marketing* (Pelican, 1975).

Further Reading

Burton, Graham. *Effective Marketing Logistics* (Macmillan, 1975). A good up-to-date and comprehensive view of the physical distribution aspect.
Giles, G. B. *Marketing* (Macdonald & Evans, 1974). Chapter IX is a simple but very comprehensive guide to the choice of distribution channels, with good definitions of the various types of middlemen.

Questions for Discussion

1 Suggest suitable channels of distribution for

   (a) paper plates and cups,
   (b) hand-made chocolates,
   (c) folding garden chairs,
   (d) automobile components.

2 Describe in detail the distribution functions carried out by

(a) a cash-and-carry grocery wholesaler,
(b) a garden centre,
(c) a franchised supplier of domestic heating oil,
(d) a travel agent.

3 Evaluate the current status of 'out of town shopping centres' (such as Brent Cross in London) and of 'city centre' shopping precincts (such as the Arndale Centre in Luton and other cities).

4 The text gives books as an example of a product whose method of distribution has changed radically in recent years. What others can you suggest?

5 (CAM, Nov. 1982) Franchising is becoming more and more popular as a method of marketing. Explain what is meant by 'Franchising' and state what you consider to be the advantages and disadvantages of this method of trading. You must include in your answer examples of franchising, covering both goods and services.

6 In what ways could a 'traditional' High Street retailer of electrical goods react to competition from an out of town discount house recently opened a few miles away?

8. *The Message and the Medium*

'Basically, promotion is an exercise in information, persuasion, and influence.'
William J. Stanton. *The Fundamentals of Marketing*

8.1 What Promotion Means

The word 'promotion' might have been used by Humpty-Dumpty, the character in Lewis Carroll's *Through the Looking Glass* who asserted that words meant what he wanted them to mean. 'Promotion' is such a word, used by different people, in different ways, to mean different things.

In this book it is used mainly as an all-embracing term to describe an important part of the marketing mix. When the right product, at the optimum price, is available in all the right places, through the most cost-effective distribution channels, we still have a problem. The people who might want to buy the product have to be told about it.

Just occasionally they simply have to be told of its existence – 'Jaguars are now in stock at Bloggs' showroom' (after a period of short supply and high demand perhaps). More usually they need to be given information about the product – to be told what it will do for them; what shapes, sizes and colours it comes in; what its quality is and its price; perhaps whether credit terms are available.

Very frequently there will have to be a considerable element of persuasion. People do not always readily grasp the advantages of a new product, especially if its function is entirely novel and perhaps would cause a change in their habits. The acceptance of frozen foods was rapid but not immediate. Even in Great Britain in 1983 relatively few people had dishwashers. They knew of their existence, were aware of what they did, but remained unconvinced that buying one would bring them greater benefit than the same expenditure in other directions.

The other reason why both information and persuasion are necessary is the existence of competition. No product can afford to be 'invisible' – the situation where people are aware of competitive products but not of this one. People must be aware of the product before they can buy it. Similarly, they must be persuaded that Product A is worth testing against Product B, which they perhaps already use, and that Product A has some distinctive features.

The word promotion is used here, firstly, to describe the whole collection of methods by which the tasks of information and persuasion may be carried out. In the main these consist of the following:

1 Personal selling (see Chapter 13).
2 Advertising (Chapter 15).
3 Sales literature, films and demonstrations (Chapter 15).

4 Sales Promotion and Merchandising (Chapter 17).
5 Public Relations (Section 17.8).

Secondly, the word is used here in a more abstract sense. The point was made in Section 3.2 that the way in which the customer perceives the product becomes a part of the product, an important element in what that customer buys in order to satisfy his or her needs in the fullest possible way. The example was used of a perfume bought as a present. The chemical ingredients are an important but relatively small element in what is bought. Exactly the same ingredients could be used to provide a cheap 'popular' perfume and a moderately expensive 'exclusive' perfume. The difference between the 'popular' perfume and the 'exclusive' perfume lies not in the perfume itself but in how it is perceived. How it is perceived will be determined by such things as the following:

1 The price.
2 Packaging (materials used, the way they are constructed, the surface design and colour).
3 The name.
4 What is said about the perfume in sales literature, in advertising.
5 The way it is displayed in shops.

All these things we can describe collectively as 'the way the product is promoted'. Thus the word promotion is used to describe both the methods used to communicate with customers and the total effect of the communication. We may talk later of 'promotional methods' that go to make up the promotional mix – that is using the word in the first sense. We may also talk of the 'promotional aims' towards which the promotional mix is directed, which is using the word in the second sense.

8.2 The Promotional Mix

The word 'mix' is a particularly valuable and hard-worked one in marketing. We have already discussed the marketing mix (Chapter 3) and the product mix (Section 4.6). Now we must approach the concept of the promotional mix. The way in which the promotional methods listed above are used, and their weight and cost relative to each other and to the other ingredients of the marketing mix, will vary from one situation to another. The group of methods to be used in a given situation and the weighting attached to each method is referred to as the 'promotional mix'.

Arriving at the correct promotional mix is a very complex business, which we discuss in outline in this chapter and in more detail in Chapters 13, 15, 16 and 17. First we look at the kind of factors that influence the make-up of the promotional mix. We can see these clearly in relation to advertising and to personal selling, although similar considerations can be applied to other ingredients in the mix.

8.21 *Personal Selling*

This is an important element in the mix under the following circumstances:

1 There are relatively few customers and they are easily identified and not too scattered.

2 The product needs demonstrating or the benefits of its use need to be explained in relation to the customer's personal needs (e.g. life insurance).
3 The product has to be specially made or developed to fit the customer's needs (life insurance again; also many technical products and products or services with a design element, such as office furnishing).
4 There is a need to establish personal rapport (services such as business consultancy, advertising agencies).
5 The product has high unit value, so that time spent with an individual customer can be easily paid for by the occasional sale.
6 The salesman buys as well as sells (cars, for example, are normally sold against trade-ins). (N.B. Throughout this book, wherever any reference is made to salesman, marketing man, etc., it should be seen as referring equally to women.)

8.22 *Advertising*

This approach is favoured in such circumstances as the following:

1 Product of low unit cost selling to very many customers, widely scattered.
2 The need to inform many people very quickly – such as a new product launch, a bargain sale, a special offer.
3 Uncertainty as to who is likely to buy, or difficulty in locating potential customers.

Some products are easier to advertise than others. Products that can be strongly differentiated lend themselves well to advertising, as do those with an emotional appeal and those that are strongly branded. Advertising works better when a product is on the 'upswing' part of its life-cycle – it is more difficult to use advertising cost-effectively when the intention is to 'buck the trend'.

8.3 Deciding Promotional Aims

In theory it is possible to have a marketing mix that excludes promotion – where the right product at the right price, available through the right channels will 'sell itself'. In practice it is hard to think of examples, although 'commodities' – agricultural and mineral primary products – are often in that situation. Other products at first sight come near it – timber, plywood, hardboard for example. These products are undifferentiated ('homogeneous' is the economics term). One piece of softwood timber, say, is likely to be indistinguishable from another. But this impression is only true at first sight, for two reasons.

First, it overlooks the fact that distribution is a multi-stage affair and so is promotion. So in the case of hardboard, for example, it is true that customers are influenced almost entirely by availability and are not very concerned which hardboard they buy. But the distributors have to be persuaded to stock one manufacturer's product rather than another's. The fact that this may be done through price/delivery negotiations does not alter the fact that a selling job has to be done. It simply means that in this instance personal selling at dealer level (perhaps supported by some modest point-of-sale material) is the main element in the promotional mix.

Secondly, however, it may mean that marketing of a particular type of product is still at a fairly undeveloped and unsophisticated stage. In the same field 'Contiboard' gained a large share of the market by taking an equally homogeneous product – chipboard – and giving it a high degree of differentiation by adding a plastic surface. The added value thus provided, and the additional benefits to the customer, were promoted in colourful leaflets, point-of-sale displays and advertising. This is an example of the point made above that differentiated products lend themselves to advertising.

It also illustrates the fact that a different promotional mix can be used with very similar products in the same field. Arriving at the most effective mix must start from a properly constructed marketing plan, going through a stage-by-stage analysis, along the lines set out in Chapter 19. For the present it is sufficient to be aware that we must be able to answer the following questions:

1 Who are our customers?
2 Which of their needs are we trying to satisfy?
3 How does our product or service provide satisfaction?
4 In order to demonstrate this.
   (a) What facts do we have to supply (information)?
   (b) What emotional appeals do we need to express (persuasion)?
5 How can we best communicate these things to the ultimate customers?
6 What do we need to communicate to the various parts of the distribution chain and how best can we do it?

We should note that the distinction between 4(a) and 4(b) is more conceptual than practical, more apparent than real. The provision of the right facts is in itself a form of persuasion (we select the facts that will best make our case, just as a barrister, a lecturer or a journalist does). Also, for the customer, it is what he perceives and senses that is important. How he feels about, say, a car is to him a 'fact', and may be more important than some of the things an automobile engineer would regard as vital pieces of information.

In connection with 6 above, we must note that what needs to be said to distributors will be different from what is said to customers. Customers will want to know 'How will this product meet my needs, what benefit will I gain from it?' (economy, convenience, enjoyment). Distributors will want to know 'How will this product increase my profits?' (faster turnover, bigger discount, more customers in the shop). Different levels of the chain of distribution may well need to be told different things. Thus wholesalers will be concerned about warehouse space, ease of handling and transport, and minimal breakages; and retailers will want to know about advertising support, introductory discounts, estimated turnover, and profit margins.

Step-by-step analysis of this kind brings us to the point where we have established (a) a number of audiences to whom we have to communicate (ultimate customers, the various levels in the distribution chain, others able to exert an influence); and (b) the kind of messages we wish them to receive (which will have been based on an analysis of their needs and matching them with a product, existing or specially developed, which we believe will meet those needs). The purpose of the promotional mix is, therefore, to ensure that the messages are conveyed in the most cost-effective manner.

8.31 *Positioning and Branding*

Quite apart from the communication of specific messages, there is often a more general job to be done, although it is all part of the task of being sensitive to how the customers are likely to perceive the product. Thus we need to signal to customers whether the product is for the early adopters or for the majority (Section 5.10), for old or young, male or female or both, for the 'big spenders' or for those on low incomes, for families with young children or for sophisticated couples on their own.

Putting the product in its right 'slot' in this way is often referred to as 'positioning'. Thus we can position a product as 'up-market' (for the more sophisticated and the bigger spenders) or 'down-market' (for ordinary people with limited budgets). We can position it to appeal to older people rather than the young, or vice versa. The latter case can be an important one. All established products run the danger of finding themselves being bought entirely by older people. If nothing is done about it, all its regular customers will eventually die. Meanwhile younger people are reluctant to try a product that is thought of as what 'Mum and Dad' or even 'Grandma' buy. Some repositioning is necessary to ensure a continuing market for the product. Oxo started the 'Katie' campaign to present Oxo as a product used by bright young housewives in all kinds of dishes, not just by old people for mixing gravy.

In planning to market a new ball-point pen we would need to consider whether to position it as an expensive/exclusive gift, as a reasonably priced working tool or as a cheap 'expendable'.

Branding can also be an important factor in communication. A brand in its simplest form is a name – 'Embassy', 'After Eight', 'Penguin'. But other features, such as visual design, colour, typography and slogans, usually come into it. The use of a brand can bring a number of advantages, including the following:

1 The product is easily remembered and easily identified, e.g. on the super-market shelf.
2 It becomes easier to provide strong links between advertising and other forms of promotion.
3 New products can be more easily introduced under an existing, well established and well regarded brand name. Heinz do not have to start from scratch each time they add a new flavour of soup to their range or enter a new sector of the snack foods market.
4 Alternatively, a producer with a successful brand in one sector of the market can enter another sector with a different brand (such as Cadbury's with their food products). Companies like IBM in computers or British Aerospace in aircraft or space satellite systems similarly have a headstart with new products in the areas where they already have an established reputation.

These positioning and branding aspects will affect the messages we need to transmit to customers and potential customers. Perhaps even more important to realize is that they will affect the way in which the message is transmitted and will therefore have a strong influence on the promotional mix. If there is a need for branding, then there is a strong case for advertising. A manufacturer may of course supply more than one competitive brand (to gain maximum market share). A retail chain may supply lower priced own-label brands, selling in competition with manufacturers' advertised brands, to divert customer loyalty to themselves rather than to the manufacturer.

8.4 The Salesman's Role

By far the most important means of communication between producers and consumers is personal selling. For every person employed in advertising there are at least 100 others taking part in the face-to-face communication that contributes to the selling process, whether 'on the road' as travelling salesmen or 'behind the counter' of a shop or office or (increasingly) over the telephone.

Personal selling has the following two main advantages over the other forms of marketing communication, listed in Section 8.5:

1 It can carry out the whole of the sales process, which the others rarely if ever can.
2 It is flexible and can be tailored to the requirements and attitudes of individual customers. Similarly, it can be receptive to the reactions a particular message is creating and can modify it accordingly. With advertising, by contrast, one message has to be transmitted to a wide audience, and there is no way of altering or modifying it in the light of individual reactions.

8.41 *The Selling Process*

The total selling process can be said to consist of a number of stages, although not all of them are present, in this order, in every selling situation:

1 Making the initial contact with a customer.
2 Arousing interest in the product.
3 Creating a preference for the product as against competitors or alternative uses of the customer's money.
4 Making a specific proposal.
5 Closing the sale.
6 Ensuring post-purchase satisfaction and generating future sales.

A good salesman can do all these things, but only with a relatively small number of people, and therefore at high cost. Other forms of marketing communication can reach far more people, so that they deliver a much cheaper message, but usually they can only effectively carry out some parts of the total process.

Thus advertising can be very good at (1), (2) and (3) above, not usually good at (4) and (5), and sometimes moderately good at (6). At first sight we might rule out (5) entirely, as a task for advertising, but advertisements for unit trusts, for example, do sometimes deal with the whole process right to the point of 'send cheque with order'. Sinclair home computers established a dominant position in an expanding market entirely by 'selling off the page'.

In general, though, we can contrast the good salesman dealing at high cost with the whole process as against advertising dealing much more economically with some parts of it. Despite the contrast, however, each can be used to reinforce the other, and they will often be used together as important ingredients in the promotional mix.

8.42 *The Different Selling Jobs*

The term 'selling' embraces a wide range of different tasks in a variety of situations. Some sales people, such as the following, are basically order-takers:

1 The salesman who is really a delivery man (e.g. of milk or bread). He could in theory generate extra sales but in practice rarely does.
2 Retail counter salesmen, whose customers normally know what they want to buy in advance.
3 Travelling salesmen calling regularly on established retailers or other customers who normally re-order to bring their stock back to its desired level. In some cases the retailer is virtually obliged to stock the product because of high customer demand generated by advertising.

At the other end of the scale, some salesmen have to do a very 'creative' selling job, because the customer may not be aware of his need, or must have the fact that the particular product will satisfy his needs better than any alternative explained or demonstrated to him. Some writers have distinguished between selling tangible products and intangible products but the principles are not substantially different. In some cases the salesman will be primarily a technical expert, since he would not otherwise be able to show the customer how his needs can be met.

Not only does the selling situation differ, but the salesman's contribution to the total selling process outlined above will be different. Not every salesman is expected to take orders, for example. Some have the task of preparing the ground by introducing customers to new products, while the salesman who regularly calls will take orders for both new and existing products. Many companies employ people called merchandisers, whose task is to ensure that products are properly displayed in the main retail outlets, that special promotions are prominently featured and so on (although this is becoming less common as the more sophisticated retailers take on this responsibility themselves).

Thus, not only do we have to decide what emphasis should be given to personal selling in the marketing mix, but also what kind of salesman or salesmen needs to be employed and in what role or roles. It should be clear from other sections that salesmen often work with other promotional methods. For example, advertising can be used to produce 'leads' which the salesman follows up.

8.5 Marketing Communications

This term is often used as convenient shorthand to embrace all the methods available for communicating with customers other than personal selling. Just to confuse the issue, it is occasionally used to include that also, but not often, and it is useful to be able to draw the distinction. We do make the distinction here mainly on the basis that personal selling is a highly individual ('one-to-one') affair transmitting slightly different messages at each encounter, depending on the recipient. While it can be planned to some extent, how he conducts each interview must be left to the individual judgement of the salesman.

Marketing communications, on the other hand, are normally 'across the board' communications to mass audiences, carried out on a planned basis with a common message throughout.

The purpose of communication is to help move a potential customer from a state of ignorance towards a position of decision and action. We use marketing communications methods to convey messages that will aid in this process in the teeth of the forces operating in the opposite direction (Figure 8.1).

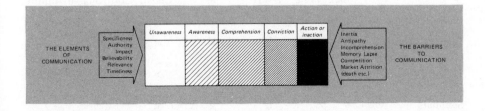

Figure 8.1 The communication process (Source: Rodger, Leslie W. *Marketing in a Competitive Economy* (Hutchinson, 1965), p. 184)

For each situation, we have to choose which selection of communications methods will help us. Some of them were listed in Section 8.4, and we deal with them in detail in later chapters.

A very important (perhaps the most important) means of communication, which is easy to overlook, is 'word of mouth'. People looking for ways of satisfying a need do not merely talk to salesmen and read advertisements and sales literature. They read relevant newspaper and magazine articles, listen to radio and watch TV, but, above all, they talk to each other. People contemplating buying a new car, or a new washing machine, talk to friends and relations and get their reactions. People who buy a new product and like it recommend it to their friends. If they dislike it, they warn off their friends. There are problems about using this as a method of marketing communications, however, for it takes a long time, its workings are not clearly understood, and it is almost impossible to control. On the other hand, since messages received in this way are seen to be without vested interest, they are perceived as being trustworthy. It is, therefore, well worth seriously setting up special events, projects and new product trials that have as their main aims simply getting people to talk. Conversely, every possible step should be taken to avoid adverse word-of-mouth criticism. The highly successful Oscar-winning British film 'Chariots of Fire' was launched in the U.S.A. on a wave of favourable word of mouth stimulated by a well-planned series of 'invitation-only' previews.

Very frequently, however, we shall find ourselves using more 'structured' methods of communication, because they are faster and their effects are more predictable and controllable.

8.6 Choosing Methods of Communication

There is no 'best' way of communicating with customers. To discuss whether advertising is 'better' than public relations or personal selling is meaningless. Each method has advantages and disadvantages, and, depending on the circumstances, one may be more cost-effective than another. Every marketing situation calls for its own special marketing mix and its own unique promotional mix. Valid generalizations are few, but Figure 8.2 gives a rough guide to the way some of the main methods of communicating with customers rate according to a few key criteria.

	Believable	2-way	Fast	Cheap	Controllable	Action
Word of mouth	✓	✗	✗	✓	✗	✓
Personal selling	✗	✓	✗	✗	✓	✓
Seminars	✓	✓	✗	✗	✓	✓
Advertising	✗	✗	✓	✓	✓	✗
Sales promotion	✗	✗	✓	✓	✓	✓
Public relations	✓	✗	✗	✓	✗	✗

Direct Mktg?

Notes:
1 In the table, a cross means 'No rather than yes', a tick 'Yes rather than No'. The judgements are subjective ones and simply illustrate the kinds of assessment that have to be made – based on facts if they are available or judgement if they are not.
2 The criteria used are the following:
    Believable. Do the receivers of the message tend to regard the source as believable?
    2-Way. Is there good communication back to the company?
    Fast. Does the message travel quickly from source to destination?
    Cheap. Is the cost per message received relatively cheap?
    Controllable. How much control does the company have over the message as received?
    Action. Is the message very likely to produce immediate action?
3 Seminars, in this context, are meetings to which prospective customers are invited to hear a technical presentation of new products or techniques. 'Hardsell' is kept to a minimum.

Figure 8.2 Promotional methods compared

8.7 Integrated Campaigns

It is important that the ingredients used in the marketing mix and the promotional mix, whatever they are, make a coherent whole. Each activity, each piece of promotional material (advertisement, leaflet, display stand or whatever) must be part of a well conceived plan. Often the term 'integrated campaign' is used to describe this carefully worked out scheme, where all the individual pieces fit together and support each other. If this is not done, a conflicting effect can result, with poor response from customers – who are confused rather than motivated by the varying messages they receive. An integrated campaign, on the other hand, can have a synergistic effect – that is, the total effect can be greater than the sum of the various individual activities. Outstanding examples, such as Esso's classic 'A tiger in your tank', Coca-Cola's 'The real thing' and Philips' 'Simply Years Ahead' benefit even further from the same message being stated in various languages – but in the same well recognized format – all over the world.

8.8 Summary

1 Promotion is the term used to describe all the methods available for communicating with customers and potential customers.
2 This communication normally contains both information and persuasion.
3 Promotion also means the way in which products are presented to customers so as to match their needs and their perceptions.
4 The correct promotional mix is arrived at by considering what has to be communicated to which groups of people and then selecting the most cost-effective media to carry that particular message.
5 As a generality, personal selling is favoured as an element in the marketing mix when dealing with a few people buying a product of high unit cost; advertising comes strongly into its own with low-cost items sold to a mass market.
6 But there are many other factors and many other promotional methods, each with its own strengths and weaknesses.
7 Normally a range of methods will be used, and it then becomes important that they are carefully planned to operate in support of each other in an integrated campaign.

Further Reading

Stanton, William J. *The Fundamentals of Marketing*, 3rd ed. (McGraw-Hill, 1971). Further references on particular aspects are given at the end of Chapters 15, 16 and 17.
Wilmshurst J. *The Fundamentals of Advertising* (Heinemann, 1984). This provides an overview of all forms of promotion.

Questions for Discussion

1 Suggest a suitable promotional mix for

   (a) wind-surfing boards,
   (b) pre-mixed cocktails sold in 'one-glass' sized bottles,
   (c) electric shavers,
   (d) a new range of expensive cosmetics,
   (e) fire extinguishers for use in factories and offices.

2 (IM, June 1983) Many salesmen argue that expenditure on advertising and sales promotion would be better spent on the sales force. Using examples explain how advertising and sales promotion can help the salesman in his task of selling.
3 Give three examples of products or services that seem to rely heavily on promotion for their success. What seem to be the reasons for this?
4 What is the function of a brand name in the marketing of a product or service?

Is there any difference in its value in consumer as opposed to industrial markets?

5 How do you reconcile the idea that the marketing concept is concerned with satisfying customers' needs with the existence of persuasive advertising designed to convince people that they need something they have not previously thought of buying?

9. *Where the Marketing Department Comes In*

'Marketing departments, like planning departments, personnel departments, management development departments, are usually camouflages designed to cover up for lazy or worn out chief executives. Marketing, in the fullest sense of the word, is the name of the game. So it had better be handled by the boss and his line, not by staff hecklers.'

Robert Townsend. *Up the Organisation*

9.1 Why Have a Marketing Department?

The point was made in Chapter 1 that if marketing means anything, it is an attitude of mind that must permeate the company from top to bottom; and Chapter 3 spoke of the 'total approach to business' and the need for a 'vital spark'. Yet many companies have a marketing *department*, probably headed by a marketing director, which seems to mean that they see marketing as just one of the functions that a business has to carry out. Which of these apparent opposites is the right approach? The answer is that both are right. It is perfectly true that a company cannot 'do' marketing by having a few people labelled 'The Marketing Department'. On the other hand, such a department can make sense, for three main reasons.

First, unless the chief executive is to do it personally, someone else has to be responsible for ensuring that the whole company does work to pursue its marketing aims, that everyone does understand what they are doing and why. In particular, there is a built-in tendency for each main specialist department to go its own way and pursue its own aims. It is not at all uncommon for sales department and production department, for example, to be at loggerheads over quality standards, over delivery times, over stock control policies. Since all these should be features of a detailed marketing policy, it can make sense for a marketing director to exercise a co-ordinating role – to ensure that everyone understands the company's marketing policy, subscribes to it and faithfully carries out their part of it.

Second, if everyone is to work to a detailed plan, someone must produce that plan. Again, if the chief executive is not to produce it personally, someone must do it for him. It is sensible to give that person the title of Marketing Manager or Marketing Director. Since it can be a big task – collecting marketing research information, preparing and assessing promotional plans, working out sales and profit forecasts and possibly specifying new product needs – we may have the beginning of a sizeable marketing department rather than an individual. This is the 'planning role' of the marketing department.

101

Third, while it is true that everyone in the company should be marketing-oriented, striving to provide customer satisfactions at a good profit, it is also true that some are more directly concerned with customers than others. The purchasing manager's main focus of attention will be on suppliers and their delivery dates, quality standards and negotiating the best price for his company. The production manager will have his eyes particularly on equipment and raw materials, on production schedules and machine allocation, on the recruitment, training and motivation of his skilled work-people. In many parts of the company, in fact, the customer is the distant horizon. On the other hand, there are other groups of people in the company who are mainly dealing with customers, and are much more immediately concerned with their needs. For sales, advertising, market research, and product development, customers are their main concern. Consequently, if often makes sense to group all these people and departments together, thus making it easier for them to work closely with each other, and easier to direct and co-ordinate their activities as a group of specialists. This is marketing in its 'functional role'.

So if we find a marketing department within a company, we should expect to find it carrying one or more of these three roles:

1 Co-ordinating.
2 Planning.
3 Specific functions.

We go on to examine each of these roles. But first a word of warning. The 'Marketing' title does not necessarily indicate that the company has embraced and understood the marketing concept. Marketing has been through a fashionable phase, and has become one of the 'in-words' of management. It is tempting for an ambitious sales manager or a would-be 'with it' chief executive to change the name on the organization chart and the office door so that the 'Sales Department' overnight becomes the 'Marketing Department'. Nothing has really changed.

Conversely, there are many companies which, consciously or not, have adopted the marketing concept but do not use the word 'marketing' at all. The chief executive or the sales director may be acting as a marketing director without calling it that or even recognizing that that is what it is.

This is particularly likely to be the case (1) in small companies which thrive because the entrepreneur (often a technical man) who starts them has been forced to grasp the need to satisfy customers in order to survive, make profits and develop his company; and (2) in companies producing technical products, where (a) the nature of the situation often means working closely with customers anyway, and (b) the term, 'marketing' does not carry the cachet it brings in the consumer products field. Indeed, industrial products companies are often deeply suspicious of the term, which they tend to associate with a rather slick approach to selling consumer products of dubious value. So we need to look beneath the surface when judging whether a company is or is not consumer-oriented and whether a marketing department is what it says it is.

9.2 The Marketing Department in Its Co-ordinating Role

It is an interesting exercise to draw up company organization charts showing the role of the marketing department in varying types and stages of organization. Predictably, the ultimate in organization charts usually winds up as showing the marketing department in charge of virtually everything, except perhaps preparing company accounts and arranging overdrafts (finance); finding staff, mainly for the marketing department (personnel); and operating the factory (production). This is unfortunate for the two following reasons:

1 It underrates the importance and relative weight of the other parts of the organization.
2 The use of organization charts, while having a value, is increasingly seen in management theory as a stultifying concept. Informal communications in a company are often more important than the 'chains of command' ones. A man's personal authority and influence can be much wider (or may be narrower) than is easily expressed in a set of boxes and lines on a chart.

In so far as the organization chart concept is of value in assessing the role of the marketing department, much of its responsibility would normally need to be expressed in 'dotted line' terms. That is to say, its direct authority may well be very limited but its responsibility for consulting, guiding and co-ordinating other departments very much wider.

Thus the simplest form of company structure looks something like Figure 9.1

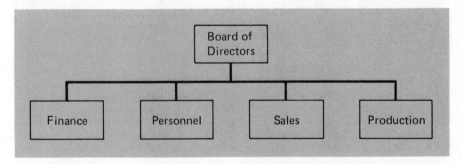

Figure 9.1: Basic company organization 'without marketing'

(to play the organization chart game for a minute), especially if the company is production-oriented.

As mentioned above, the chances of conflict between the various sections of the business, especially between sales and production, are infinite. They will only be resolved if (a) there is a clear company plan which all are aware of, and (b) the chief executive or someone on his behalf, but with authority over all departments, ensures that proper co-ordination is maintained.

There is a further problem with this type of organization as soon as moves are made towards a customer-oriented approach to business. The sales manager is probably a specialist, since his task will have been to sell what the factory is producing. What is to happen if, for example, market research or advertising are embarked upon. Either they will become the responsibility of the sales manager/

director, who will have no knowledge of (and perhaps little sympathy with) them, or they will have to report to the chief executive or other board member, or be put into one of the other departments – an anomalous situation.

The tendency is of course for one of three things to happen:

1 A separate department is created operating alongside sales – often named the marketing services department.
2 The sales manager/director takes on wider responsibilities and becomes the marketing director.
3 A new senior man is brought in to head both sales and marketing services, probably with the marketing director title.

If (1) is the choice, either both departments must be headed by a board member (in which case he is in effect the marketing director) or the situation quickly turns to option (3). Either way, we then have a situation where the company structure has become something like Figure 9.2.

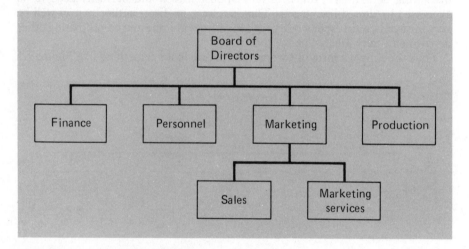

Figure 9.2 Basic company organization 'with marketing'

This partly resolves the problem, but does not get over the need to ensure that all departments work together to a common plan. Assuming that there is a marketing plan (see Section 9.3) the 'dotted line' responsibility of the marketing department now comes into play (Figure 9.3).

The dotted lines indicate the relations with other departments and marketing departments' responsibility for ensuring that they contribute to the development and the execution of the company marketing plan. For example, it is no good preparing a marketing plan for a product that cannot be economically produced on the existing equipment, unless finance can be made available for new equipment, and unless the necessary new staff can be recruited and trained at the appropriate time. Once the plan is agreed, then continuing co-ordination is necessary to ensure that agreed production schedules can be met (or the plan

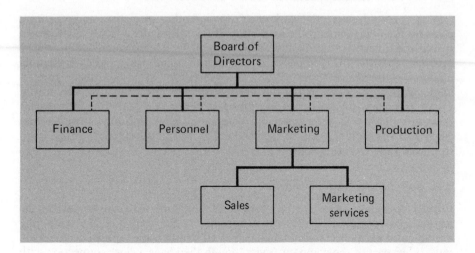

Figure 9.3 Company organization with marketing department in a co-ordinating role

modified accordingly), that the turnover and profit targets agreed with the finance department still look reasonable in the light of experience, and so on.

9.3 The Marketing Department in its Planning Role

The whole idea of marketing planning is dealt with in Chapter 19, so little will be said here about the details of the planning process. But it is important to be clear about the role of the marketing department in planning. Planning means deciding what to do now in order to bring about a desirable situation in the future. It calls for the following steps:

1 Assessing what the true present position is.
2 Deciding what the most desirable future situation is.
3 Assessing alternative ways of getting there.
4 Selecting the most attractive of these alternatives.
5 Making detailed arrangements for pursuing the chosen course.

In terms of marketing plans, items (2) and (4) are clearly matters for top management decisions, and management will wish to be deeply concerned in (3). The remaining items may well be the direct responsibility of the marketing department (consulting as necessary with other specialists inside and outside the company).

Thus an important part of the task of most marketing departments is the detailed continuous monitoring of the present situation, and the preparation from time to time of detailed plans showing how top management's objectives (expressed in terms of profit levels, sales targets or market shares) can be achieved. On the basis of these proposals top management will make its decisions about future action.

9.4 The Marketing Department in its Functional Role

As well as co-ordinating the work of its own and other specialists, and preparing plans for top management, the marketing department will normally have its own specialized functions to carry out. Some of these, such as market research, will be necessary in order for it to perform its planning, monitoring and co-ordinating function. Others, such as sales and advertising, will play their part in implementing the plans when the top management decision has been taken. Those specialist functions that are grouped under the marketing department heading will vary from company to company, depending on the individuals employed, the kind of business the company is in, and the extent to which it has embraced the marketing concept.

9.41 *Core and Peripheral Functions*

Broadly speaking, there are two groups of functions that can be part of the marketing department – the core functions, at the centre of the marketing activity, and peripheral ones, which can often be performed quite adequately in some other part of the company, even though they have a close connection with the 'customer end' of the business.

The core functions are the following:

1 *Marketing Research*. Seeking, recording and processing all necessary data about the economy, the market, competitors, the effectiveness of sales and advertising programmes.
2 *Product Planning*. Determining the product mix and ensuring that the company's products are in line with customers' requirements, including packaging and pricing.
3 *Sales*. Field selling; selection of distribution channels; forecasting, budgeting and analysis of sales; sales office administration.
4 *Advertising and Promotion*. Advertising, trade and consumer promotions, point-of-sale and merchandising material, editorial publicity, sales literature.

The peripheral functions might extend to the following:

5 Product development.
6 Physical distribution.
7 Credit control.
8 Stock control.
9 Recruiting and training sales and other marketing staff.

Clearly, of these, (5), (6) and (8) could be controlled by production; (7) by finance; and (9) by personnel. In many companies they are. There is no 'right' organization – it depends on the company, the people and the circumstances and it will constantly be changing as these change. This is why the organization chart approach has its critics – they see organization as a fluid and constantly changing pattern, not as a fixed base structure that can be pinned up on a board for all time.

9.5 Organizing the Marketing Department

As well as being part of the total organization of the company, the marketing department must within itself be organized so as to operate as efficiently as possible. Organization of the field sales force is a subject in its own right, and is dealt with in Chapter 14. Here we look mainly at the remainder of the marketing department functions, although of course they cannot be divorced from each other in this way in reality.

The need for a clear-cut organization emerges as the size of the marketing department increases and the number of people and specialist functions proliferate. The number of people and tasks that can be effectively supervised (the 'span of control') is limited, although there are different views on whether a wide or narrow span of control (one man supervising a larger or smaller number of people) is better.

The wide span of control eases the co-ordination problem (since one manager is in charge of a wide variety of specialist functions), and the danger of dilution of objectives is less. The manager, however, may be forced to control more than he can effectively have personal knowledge of.

A narrow span of control makes it possible to have a manager with intimate knowledge of the work of his section. On the other hand, the proliferation of control centres adds to the co-ordination task, introducing the risk of each section developing its own goals and objectives and to some extent losing sight of (or being in conflict with) the general objectives.

There are four basic ways in which the work of the department can be sub-divided: (a) by function, (b) by region, (c) by market, and (d) by product.

9.51 *Organization by Function*

Here the marketing director will have a series of managers for each main function, as shown in Figure 9.4. As the number of functions increases and the span of control becomes too wide for comfort, a further sub-division might be introduced (Figure 9.5). This type of organization tends to be found where the product range is fairly narrow and where the markets are concentrated and clear-cut – especially in industrial or business-to-business markets.

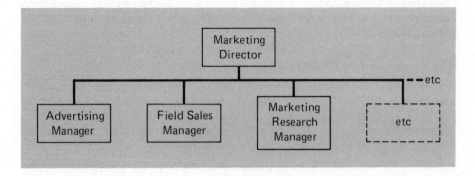

Figure 9.4 Marketing department organized by function

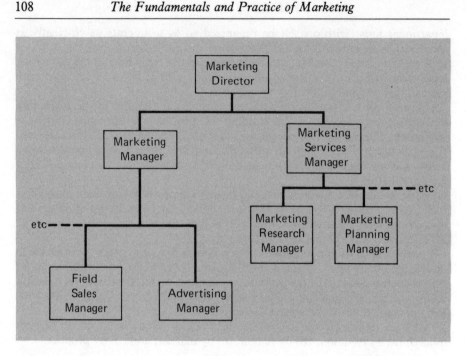

Figure 9.5 Alternative functional organization of marketing department

9.52 *Organization by Region*

Here the breakdown would be by geographical region, countries, continents, counties or arbitrary areas being the units. The marketing director has a territorial manager for each region. Each manager might have his own functional organization as above, or have responsibility within his area only for some functions, the rest remaining centralized and responsible to the marketing director. This is clearly the likely organizational approach for multi-national companies or those with a very large field sales force backed by many supporting functions over a very large area – especially where local variations are an important feature.

9.53 *Organization by Product*

A proliferation of products, perhaps all selling to the same or similar markets, introduces a different situation. Here the need is not so much for specialists in regions as specialists in products.

Each major product or group of products has its own marketing organization. This can be set up in one of two main ways, as follows:

1 *Product Divisions.* Each main group of products has a separate marketing division, each with its own sales force and marketing specialists. Thus a large electronics company might have divisions handling,

(a) telecommunications products,
(b) radio and TV products,
(c) aircraft control systems,
(d) radar systems.

Meanwhile the other functions within the company are split differently so that one factory, for example, might be manufacturing items to be marketed by all four of the marketing divisions, another for (a) and (c) only, and a third for (b) and (c). The position of the marketing division is then somewhat analogous to that of an independent marketing organization 'buying-in' products from the various factories.

2 *Product Managers* (also called Brand Managers). Alternatively, there can be a single sales force, with a product manager for each product or group of products. The product manager's task varies somewhat from company to company but normally includes the co-ordination of all advertising, promotion, packaging and product improvements for his personal products or brand. To a greater or lesser extent he will help in preparing the marketing plans and setting sales and profit targets for his brands. This pattern is very common in companies in fields such as confectionery, cigarettes, detergents, where there is a proliferation of brands. The main purpose is to ensure that each product or group of products is the responsibility of a person whose attention and enthusiasm is not diluted by his concern for other products at the same time. The sales manager may have fifty brands to worry about, but the brand manager has only two or three. This helps to ensure that no product wilts or dies from neglect and that all possible market opportunities are exploited.

9.54 *Organization by Markets*

Some products are sold to many different markets, and the marketing organization needs to have a clear knowledge and understanding of its customers' problems. We looked in the previous section at the example of an electronics company selling products in the fields of telecommunications, radio and TV, aircraft control, and radar. Let us now look at an electronics component manufacturer selling to many different companies making some or all of these four kinds of product, and adding computers to the list. To design and market such components successfully, the sales force must be able to talk technicalities with the designers and production engineers of their customers. But it is virtually impossible for one man to be thoroughly conversant with all five of these areas – each a technology in its own right – so that the marketing organization may be sub-divided by markets, as in Figure 9.6.

9.6 Buying in Specialized Services

It must not be assumed that all the functions referred to in this chapter are necessarily staffed wholly by people on the company's payroll. Advertising, as an example, can be carried out wholly within the company or wholly outside. Typically it is a mixture of the two. Similarly, market research, public relations, or new product development may be wholly or partly bought in from specialist

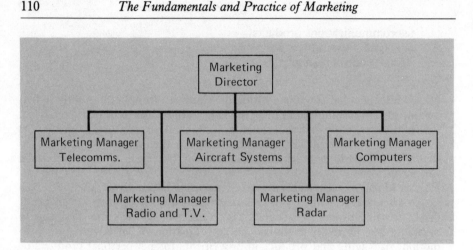

Figure 9.6 Marketing department organized by markets

organizations. It is not even essential for a company to employ its own sales force. In some cases suitable middlemen can take care of all necessary personal contact with customers; or the in-company sales force can be supplemented as necessary, e.g., by hiring a 'Commando Sales Force' to help with the launch of a new product or to 'sell in' a special promotion to retailers.

9.7 Summary

1 The marketing department may have responsibilities for (a) co-ordination, (b) planning, and (c) specific functions.
2 The main marketing functions are (a) marketing research, (b) product planning, (c) sales, and (d) advertising and promotion; but others may be added in particular circumstances.
3 Organization within the marketing department may be by (a) function, (b) region, (c) market, or (d) product.

Further Reading

Coventry, William F. *Management Made Simple* (W. H. Allen, 1970). A good basic introduction to the principles of management and organization.
Kotler, P. *Marketing Management* (Prentice-Hall, 1967), Chapter 6, 'Business Goals and Marketing Organization'.
Rodger, Leslie W. *Marketing in a Competitive Economy* (Hutchinson, 1965), Chapter 2, 'The Marketing Perspective'.
Smallbone, Douglas W. *The Practice of Marketing* (Staples Press, 1965), Chapter 2, 'The Nature of Marketing'.
Townsend, Robert. *Up the Organisation* (Michael Joseph, 1970).
Winkler, John. *Winkler on Marketing Planning* (Cassell/Associated Business Programmes, 1972), Chapter 5, 'Marketing Organisation Structures'.

Questions for Discussion

1 (CAM, June 1982) What is the thinking behind the appointment of a Brand or Product Manager? In what circumstances would you expect to appoint a Brand Manager and what would be his areas of responsibility? What are the disadvantages?
2 Many companies providing intangible products – insurance companies, for example – have no one with a 'marketing' or a 'sales' title. Does this mean they have no marketing problems? What other explanation might there be?
3 What would you suggest as the proper organizational relations between the research and development department of a company producing products for industrial use (e.g., machine tools) and its marketing department?
4 Some companies do not have any executives or departments with the word 'marketing' in their titles. How would you attempt to assess whether or not such a company was successful in marketing terms?
5 Outline a suitable marketing department organization for
  (a) a company providing a truck hire service for industry on a regional basis,
  (b) a firm selling ice-cream and yoghourts to supermarkets and also to hotels and restaurants, and
  (c) a company marketing throughout the E.E.C. a wide range of American-manufactured sports goods, garden tools and small electrical kitchen appliances (such as knife-sharpeners, can-openers, frying pans).

10. *The Changing Climate of Marketing*

'Indeed, the tendency to drift into set patterns or formulas, avoiding the painful necessity for original thought, has betrayed what should be a fundamental element in the marketing attitude – the flexibility to adjust rapidly to changes in a constantly monitored environment.'

Colin McIver. 'Back to Marketing'

10.1 The Complex Life of the Consumer

In Chapter 1 we saw how the object of marketing is to satisfy consumer needs, and that those needs consist not merely of purely physiological urges (to eat, sleep and be warm) but such other needs as to be loved and respected, to feel secure and unthreatened, and to develop one's personality to the fullest extent possible. We took the existence of these needs for granted and went on to discuss the means by which they are satisfied.

We shall now examine briefly some of the factors that shape these needs and give emphasis to one desire or another. Only by understanding these mechanisms can marketing ultimately be more than a mixture of carefully measured trial and error ('If we sold the goods they must have been what the customers wanted').

At present the mechanisms are not wholly understood. The newly developing science of social studies (also called behavioural studies) carries out many research programmes, and the results of these investigations are gradually becoming available. They are still fragmentary, not always easy to relate to the marketing situation and too complex to do more than touch on here. But students of marketing should be aware of a pattern of knowledge that is beginning to take shape.

Figure 10.1 shows some of the many influences that go to shape a person's needs and responses.

There are a number of 'models' of the way buyer behaviour operates. The simplest in the 'economic model', related to the perfect competition theory outlined in Chapter 1. It takes the view that man acts in a purely rational way to optimize the satisfactions gained from his expenditure, bearing in mind cost on the one hand and value on the other. This is probably true to some extent of industrial purchases (although how far it is true even there is disputed). But it is largely discounted by most marketing experts in the consumer field, especially for low-cost everyday purchases.

Much more favoured is the 'social-psychological model', which takes the view that man is a social animal much influenced by the groups to which he belongs –

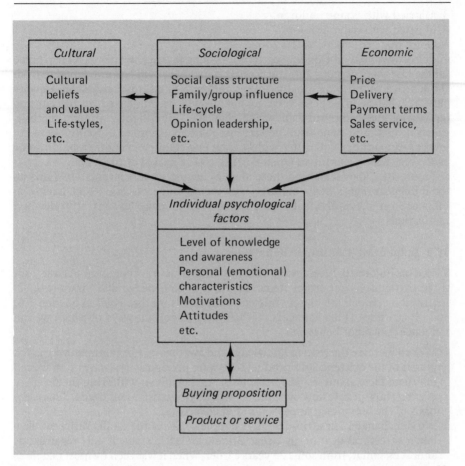

Figure 10.1 The complex pattern of buying influences (Source: adapted from Chisnall, Peter M. *Marketing – a Behavioural Analysis* (McGraw-Hill, 1975))

his family, workmates, his 'social class'. Friends, neighbours and other acquaintances, particularly those he would like to emulate and to whose life-style he aspires, are his 'reference groups' and have considerable influence on his behaviour ('Keeping up with the Joneses' is one everyday expression of this approach).

It is known that some individuals set the pattern within their own circle of acquaintances. They are the 'opinion leaders', the trend-setters – the first to have a home sauna or a video camera.

Several researchers have drawn attention to a difference in purchasing behaviour as people move through their life-cycle. This is defined variously but often by the following stages:

1 Unmarried.
2 Young marrieds, no children.

3 Married with young children.
4 Married with older children.
5 Older married, children left home.

Fairly obviously, the buying patterns of young married people setting up home for the first time (carpets, furniture, records, pictures) will be quite different from those with a young family (baby clothes, different foods, toys) and so on. Equally clearly, what people spend their money on will be influenced by the cultural outlook of the community in which they live – bullfights, Sunday football, carnival costumes, wine-drinking are just random examples of items where the level of expenditure will differ widely from one country to another and in some cases (e.g. wine-drinking in Great Britain) over a period of time.

Figure 10.1 above takes all these ideas as having some relevance. It shows all the influences mentioned – cultural, sociological and economic – each having an influence on the individual's own psychological make-up, his attitudes and motivations.

10.2 Influencing Consumer Behaviour

Listed on Figure 10.1, under the heading 'Individual Psychological Factors', are three particularly important items: (1) level of knowledge and awareness, (2) motivations (which are closely related to the needs we discussed in Section 1.6) and (3) attitudes. This list suggests three very important ways in which we can influence consumer behaviour:

1 We can increase the level of knowledge and awareness. For example, we can tell people of the existence of a product they were previously unaware of, or we can tell them facts about its performance or the benefits it will bring them.
2 We can show people how our product will help to satisfy their needs. This is the basis of the 'emotional appeals' used in advertising.
3 We can change their attitudes. An example of this is the totally different view taken of central-heating in Great Britain in 1983, when it was regarded as almost essential, from some 25 years earlier, when it was seen by most people as unnecessary or even a rather decadent extravagance.

10.21 *How Attitudes can be Changed*

To change attitudes can be a very desirable objective, sometimes in a positive, sometimes in a negative, way. Examples of changing attitudes in a negative way are the government campaigns against smoking and against 'drinking and driving'. Marketing will more often be concerned with positive change in order to win acceptance of a new idea or a new way of doing things.

Attitudes can be changed by the following means:

1 Reasoned argument leading the audience to judge the suggested conclusion as 'true' or 'false' (an example is the use of accident statistics to attempt to change people's attitude to the wearing of seat belts).
2 Positive emotional appeals, e.g. 'Stop smoking and you will feel fitter and food will taste better'.
3 Negative emotional appeals, e.g. 'Don't stop smoking and your lungs may end up looking like this'.

10.22 *The Importance of Brand Personalities*

Alan Hedges[1] emphasizes the importance of making it easy for people to identify with products. This means first that brands must have a clear identity which is a function of all forms of promotion as well as of the product itself, its name, packaging, etc. The identity of the product has three parts, suggests Hedges:

'– The prominence or salience of the brand (the extent to which it springs readily to mind)
– The clarity or distinctiveness of its identity (the extent to which it is seen to have clear and pronounced characteristics and properties)
– The nature of its identity (the *kinds* of feeling, thought and belief which people have about it)'.

All this means that what matters is not merely what people know about a product but how they feel about it and how they are able to relate it to their own personalities and life-styles. This is likely to be just as much a function of the right (creative/intuitive) side of the brain as of the left (rational/logical) side and often more so.

10.3 The Changing Social and Economic Climate

A failing of many marketing textbooks and a weakness in the make-up of many marketing practitioners is that they assume that things will go on in the same way. That is because society as a whole tends to take that view. But in recent years there has been a spate of books and articles talking about the rate of change and pointing out that marketing is dealing with a dynamic, not a static, situation.

Douglas W. Foster[2] is one of several first-rate marketing authors who draw attention to 'the increasing tempo of business' and 'the speed of technological change'. He and others like him rightly point out the increasing speed of change. But the assumption usually is that the 'direction' of change will be broadly the same. Authors like Alvin Toffler[3] and Herman Kahn[4] have highlighted the problems of moving ever more rapidly in the same direction. In fact, the very warnings they are uttering suggest the strong possibility of a change of direction. Indeed, *The Limits to Growth*, the summary of the famous Club of Rome study of the earth's resources, points out the absolute necessity of a change of direction, or at any rate a reduction in speed of change, if we are to continue in the same direction. Growing populations and diminishing resources make continuing at the same speed on the present course impossible to sustain, in their judgement.

Since the end of 1973 we have seen a series of 'discontinuities' – of changes in directions and severe setbacks to the rate of progress in the current direction. Until recently planners assumed an ever-increasing economic growth rate. We now are going through a time of decline in economic output or very slight growth from a low base.

Earlier prophecies drew attention to the widening gap between the wealthy industrialized countries and the under-developed 'Third World'. OPEC (the oil-producing countries' cartel) showed that the balance can be quickly changed. Two of the fastest-growing countries in the world in recent times, each with considerable natural resources, were Iran and Brazil – both classified as third world (under-developed) countries, at least until recently. Yet Brazil in 1975 was

Volkswagen's largest market outside Germany and said to be the only profitable one.

More recently many of these third world countries (the term is becoming less popular and the alternative term 'The South' as opposed to the rich countries of 'The North' in wide use) have run into severe financial difficulties because of their huge foreign debts. Throughout 1983 crisis threatened the international banking systems which had provided the money and could now not expect the anticipated rate of repayment.

At the same time 'The North' is experiencing huge unemployment due to economic cut-backs and structural change as industry and commerce uses more microcomputers and robots and high employment industries such as shipbuilding move to countries like South Korea, which not so long ago might have been regarded as part of the 'Third World'.

The 'island economies' of Hong Kong and Singapore are other examples of economic success among countries of 'the Third World' or 'The South' (although the future of Hong Kong is very uncertain until current negotiations between the U.K. and the Chinese People's Republic regarding the U.K.'s expiring lease of Hong Kong are complete).

Certainly, marketing is all about change. But change does not just mean more or less of the same, or even stops and starts heading in the same general direction. Some of the changes can be very surprising. Who can be sure what will be the main form of short-distance transportation twenty years from now?

We saw in the previous section that the prevailing culture and social climate have a big influence on people's needs and on their purchasing decisions. So does the economic situation. If there is social change, we must watch out for totally different marketing opportunities. (Just as, for a short period in 1974, we saw garages selling sugar and bread, owing to a breakdown in the normal channels of supply.)

In 1983 there is a proliferation in the U.K. of hand-crafted goods such as knitwear, toys, pottery as those made redundant or simply wishing to supplement their income take advantage of the affluence of others.

10.4 The Changing Attitude of Consumers

Another kind of change marketing has had to contend with is the growing awareness of 'consumers' rights' and increasing unwillingness by consumers to accept what they regard as a poor deal. The title of Robin Wight's book, *The Day the Pigs Refused To Be Driven to Market*, aptly expresses the situation. In the press, and on radio and TV, many articles and programmes give space and time to consumers' complaints and to attacks on poor goods and unsatisfactory marketing practices.

This seems strange when for many years the marketing concept has been accepted as an important principle by a large number of manufacturers and retailers in this country. Changing organization structures, in-company training and management education programmes witness a serious intent to carry the concept through into practice. Yet more than ever before there is this vociferous and growing consumer protest movement, usually referred to as consumerism.

If marketing was all that it claimed to be, why do we need consumerism now?

There is of course nothing new about movements and legislation to protect the interests of consumers. The first Weights & Measures Act in U.K. dates from 1878 and the Sales of Goods Act from 1893. Philip Kotler[5] recognizes in the U.S.A. three distinct consumer movements 'in this century' – the early 1900s, the mid-1930s and the mid-1960s – each leading to the strengthening of government controls over the buyer/seller relation.

As far as personalities are concerned, the consumer movement of the 1960s and 1970s is epitomized in Ralph Nader. His much-published clash with General Motors on safety standards[6] dates from 1965, but as early as 1962 President John F. Kennedy identified the four 'rights of the consumer':

1 The right to safety.
2 The right to be informed.
3 The right to choose.
4 The right to be heard.

Vance Packard[7] claimed to be writing 'About the way many of us are being influenced and manipulated . . . in the patterns of our daily lives', as far back as 1957.

The current wave of consumerism has thus been rising up for many years now. Earlier waves tended to be responses to particular limited situations and subsided when these were dealt with. The present one is much more widely based, shows no sign of abating and has largely triumphed with a whole flood of government legislation to its credit.

In all the EEC countries, in Scandinavia, Australia and many others there are strong consumer movements and legislation to protect the consumer. Derek Hollier writes: 'In Japan, women's organizations with memberships totalling several millions have produced price-shattering boycotts of colour TV sets and cosmetics.'[8] In many countries all round the world the consumer movement and the legislative reaction to it is well established. Derek Hollier also reports that even in the Soviet Union 'there are consumer clubs that try to improve the quality of production. The Minister of Consumer Services, Alesander N. Gandarin, spends much time appeasing consumers'.

In Great Britain there are the Government-sponsored Office of Fair Trading as well as many privately based groups that speak for the consumer. Each of the main local government areas offers consumer advice to its public free of charge.

The present consumer movement is thus stronger, more widespread and longer-lasting than similar previous manifestations. The reasons have been discussed by many authors, including Holloway and Hancock[9] and Kotler.[10] They include the following:

1 Rising incomes, standards of living and education, with a consequent greater concern for quality of life.
2 The increasing complexity of technology and marketing, putting the buyer more and more at a disadvantage in relation to the seller.
3 The stresses and strains developing in the economic/political system – the population explosion, inflation, pollution, loss of faith in political institutions.
4 The 'impersonality' arising from the increasing size of companies and institutions, coupled with automation and computerization.

5 The influence of writers such as Galbraith, Packard, and Rachel Carson, with political leaders ready to seize on the points raised.

10.5 Consumerism and the Marketing Response

For whatever reason, consumerism seems here to stay, and is a force that marketing people must reckon with. How does marketing respond to consumerist attitudes?

On the face of it, it should reinforce consumerism rather than conflict with it since the essence of the marketing concept is to generate customer satisfaction. However, the term 'customer satisfaction' is ambiguous. Kotler[11] suggests that 'most businessmen take it to mean that *consumer desires* should be the orienting focus of product and market planning. However, in efficiently serving customers' desires, it is possible to hurt their long-run interests.' He lists four examples of this situation, as follows:

1 Large expensive cars satisfy their owners' immediate desires, but pollution, congestion and parking problems reduce their long-term satisfaction.
2 The U.S. food industry produces new products with high taste appeal but low nutritional value.
3 Packaging provides short-run convenience but causes its users long-run problems of pollution and wasteful use of resources.
4 Cigarettes and alcohol 'are classic products which obviously satisfy consumers but which ultimately hurt them if consumed in any excessive amount'.

He goes on: 'While consumers buy as *consumers* they increasingly express their discontent as *voters*. They use the political system to correct the abuses that they cannot resist through the economic system . . . The problem is to somehow reconcile company profit, consumer desires and consumer long-run interests.'

The understandable automatic reaction of businessmen to the consumer movement is to condemn it. 'Consumerism has come as a shock to many businessmen because deep in their hearts they believe that they have been serving the consumer extraordinarily well.' But, as Kotler goes on to point out, 'perhaps (the marketing concept) is more honoured in the breach than the observance. Although top management professes the concept, the line executives, who are rewarded for ringing up sales, may not practise it faithfully'.

Holloway and Hancock[12] express the same basic attitude of businessmen under attack in this way: 'Consumerism looks like a threat to many businessmen. Many consumer demands create additional costs, impinge upon the freedom of business operations and push business in the direction of uniform standards and sameness.'

If this was the typical American reaction, British businessmen felt much the same. The average business sees itself as satisfying its customers' needs in the best way it can at reasonable cost. The criticism by *Which?* and the Automobile Association of car-servicing standards is a case in point. The reaction of many members of the trade was that they were being subjected to a quite unfair attack. Similarly, the beverage companies who pack in non-returnable glass bottles were rather hurt when heaps of them were dumped on their doorstep as a consumer protest.

Now that consumerism has largely made its point, industry finds itself under attack from many other 'lobbies' – the Greenpeace movement wanting to ban the use of whale-derived ingredients from the many products in which they have traditionally been used; the third world protaganists who want to outlaw goods from regimes, such as South Africa, which they see as treating workers shamefully; conservationists who object to mining and quarrying in areas of beautiful country.

There is still the danger that industry's response will be entirely negative. Yet all of the new threats also present new opportunities (just as the resistance to 'unhealthy' processed foods has given rise to a whole series of new markets for high-fibre and low fat dietary foods). Any signals from customers as to what they do and do not want must be eagerly listened to by marketing people.

Esther Peterson, the first special assistant for consumer affairs at the White House, went on in 1970 to set up a consumer relations programme for Giant Food Inc. Reporting in 1973 on its success, she observes: 'What seemed to some people to be a highly suspect and risky alliance has turned out to be a breakthrough for consumers as well as a great competitive asset for the company.'[13]

In the U.K. Lever Brothers provide an example of a manufacturer taking considerable pains to maintain continuing dialogue with representative consumer organizations and political spokesmen on sensitive issues such as unit pricing. Any communications from individual customers or from consumer organizations gain immediate attention, and are systematically analysed to determine what response is necessary, not merely as a defence mechanism but as a means of anticipating and reacting to changing attitudes in the marketplace.

Marks & Spencer's stress that putting the customer first in this wholehearted way cannot just be grafted on. It must be a reflection of top-management attitudes, and requires patient explanation and quiet insistence to gain acceptance as a policy right down the line. Esther Peterson makes the same point: 'Top management must be totally committed to the principles of open dialogue with consumers, maximization of quality, service and value . . . A programme designed solely to gain favourable publicity and win public support will fail. It must have substance.'[14]

10.6 Social Responsibility and Business Ethics

For many centuries legal judgements between buyer and seller were largely made on the basis of the dictum *Caveat emptor* – 'let the buyer beware'. The consumerist movement and the resulting legislation have changed this to the point where many businessmen ruefully feel it is now a question of 'let the seller beware'. However, the matter goes much farther than the question of buying and selling.

Businesses are now increasingly expected to exercise 'social responsibility' in all their actions. Thus a number of British companies have been under fire for employing black workers in their South African subsidiaries at wage rates regarded as unacceptable. Rio Tinto Zinc ran into stormy weather a few years ago over a proposal to carry out mining operations in Snowdonia. Quite apart from any legal requirements, it is no longer acceptable for a business to be carried on in a way that pollutes the atmosphere, the seas or rivers, or to cause excessive noise – things that a few years ago would have been regarded as 'necessary evils'.

This all means that far-sighted companies are themselves attempting to assess the social implications of any contemplated action well in advance of decisions being taken. Since marketing men are likely to be drawn into such decisions, they too are bound to be drawn into social responsibility discussions.

Along with the growing consumerism pressures and the blossoming of social responsibility, there is also an increasing interest in codes of practice and ethics. It is more and more realized that to be recognized as responsible professionals, managers must subscribe to and adhere to clear-cut standards.

Thus the Institute of Marketing has prepared a code of practice for managers, as have the British Institute of Management, the Market Research Society and the Institute of Public Relations. While the majority of people accept that most of these codes are at present too broad and unspecific in terms to be wholly satisfactory, they are a beginning and a public statement that the principle is accepted.

The Institute of Marketing Code of Practice follows:

Marketing's Professional Responsibility

I The professional marketing executive has responsibilities to his employer, to customers – both ultimate and intermediate – to his colleagues and to the public. The Institute requires its members, as a condition of membership, to recognise these responsibilities in the conduct of their business, and to adhere to the following Code of Practice. All members shall be answerable to the Council of the Institute for any conduct which in the opinion of the Council is in breach of this Code and the Council may take disciplinary action against any member found to be in breach thereof.

Professional Conduct

II *General* A member shall at all times conduct himself as a person of integrity and shall observe the principles of this Code in such a way that his reputation, that of the Institute and that of marketing shall be enhanced.

III *Instruction of Others* A member who knowingly causes or permits another person or organisation to act in a manner inconsistent with this Code or is party to such action shall himself be deemed to be in breach of it.

IV *Injury to Other Members* A member shall not knowingly, recklessly or maliciously injure the professional reputation or practice of another member.

V *Honesty* A member shall at all times act honestly and in such manner that customers – both ultimate and intermediate – are not caused to be misled. Nor shall he in the course of his professional activities knowingly or recklessly disseminate false or misleading information. It is also his responsibility to ensure that his subordinates conform with these requirements.

VI *Professional Competence* It is expected that, in the exercise of a member's profession as a marketing executive, he shall seek at all times to ensure that he attains and retains the appropriate levels of competence necessary for the efficient conduct of such tasks as are entrusted to him by his employers. He shall seek to ensure that all who work with him or for him have the appropriate levels of competence for the effective discharge of the marketing tasks entrusted to them and where any shortcomings might exist he will seek to ensure that they are made good as speedily as possible.

VII *Conflict of Interest*
(a) A member shall use his utmost endeavour to ensure that the provisions of this Code and

the interests of his customers are adequately and fairly reported to his Company in any circumstances where a conflict of interests may arise.

(b) A member holding an influential personal interest in any business which is in competition with his own employer, shall disclose that interest to his employer.

(c) A member having an influential personal interest in the purchase or sale of goods or services as between his own company and another organisation shall give his company prior information as to that interest.

VIII *Confidentiality of Information*
(a) A member shall not disclose, or permit the disclosure to any other person, firm or company, any confidential information concerning a customer's business without the written consent of the customer except where required by statute.

(b) A member shall not disclose, or permit the disclosure to any other person, firm or company or use to his own advantage, any confidential information concerning his employer's business without the written consent of his employer except where required by statute.

IX *Securing and Developing Business* No member may seek to obtain or obtain business in a manner which, in the opinion of the Council of the Institute, is unprofessional. In determining whether or not any behaviour is unprofessional, the Council will be guided, inter alia, by this Code and by any professional Codes of Practice in effect at the time the behaviour occurs. The Council of the Institute will always, unless it has determined to the contrary and so informed members, accept such other Codes of Practice as a minimum level to be expected of members of the Institute.

X *Other Relevant Codes of Practice* Members should be aware of other relevant Codes of Practice. The most important amongst these are:
(a) *Advertising* British Code of Advertising Practice (Advertising Standards Authority); International Code of Advertising Practice (International Chamber of Commerce)
(b) *Sales Promotion* International Code of Sales Promotion Practice (International Chamber of Commerce)
(c) *Market Research* Code of Conduct (Market Research Society/Industrial Marketing Research Association)
(d) *Public Relations* Code of Professional Conduct (Institute of Public Relations).
The Council of the Institute also issues from time to time **Schedules for the Guidance of Members** on facets of marketing process to supplement such Codes of Practice. These **Schedules for the Guidance of Members** are statements of minimal expected practice and do not preclude the Council from concluding that behaviour not covered in such schedules is, in fact, unprofessional.

Enforcement of the Code

XI *Role of the Individual Member* It is the duty of all members to assist the Institute in implementing this Code and the Institute will support any member so doing.

XII *Misuse of the Code* Unfair, reckless or malicious use of this Code by members or others to damage the reputation and/or professional practice of a member and/or his organization shall be deemed a breach of this Code.

XIII *Procedures for Handling Complaints* The Council of the Institute may nominate, at its discretion, a person or persons whose task will be to decide if there is a prima facie case to answer. If there is such a case, the Council shall initiate the necessary procedure for its investigation.

XIV *Sanctions for Breach of this Code* If the Council of the Institute, having duly and properly examined an alleged breach of this Code by a member, finds that member in breach of the Code, it shall be empowered to take such disciplinary action as it shall deem appropriate. If the Council decides to expel a member from the Institute, it shall act in strict accordance with the provisions of the Articles of Association of the Institute, of which Article 19 is set out below:

'Any member of any class who shall fail in observance of any of the regulations or by-laws of the Institute or whom the Council in their absolute discretion deem an unfit or unsuitable person to be a member of the Institute may be expelled from the Institute by the Council. Such members shall have seven clear days notice sent to him of the meeting of the Council at which the proposal for his expulsion is to be considered and he may attend and speak at the meeting, but shall not be present at the voting upon such proposal nor (except as afore-said) take part in the proceedings otherwise and as the Council allows. A member so expelled shall forfeit all claims to the monies paid by him to the Institute, whether upon admission or for fees or subscriptons or otherwise and shall cease to be a member of the Institute.'

10.7 Summary

1 Buying behaviour is the outcome of a number of complex factors – economic, cultural, sociological, and psychological.
2 The most valuable study from a marketing point of view is that of the social-psychological area.
3 To influence consumer behaviour, one may have to (a) increase customers' knowledge, (b) show how needs can be met, and (c) change customers' attitudes.
4 Attitudes can be changed by (a) reasoned argument, and (b) positive or negative emotional appeals.
5 The social and economic climate is liable to change, not merely in speed but in a discontinuous way and marketing people must be alive to the opportunities this presents.
6 A particular kind of change is represented by the following:

(a)   The growing strength of consumerism.
(b)   Insistence on the need for social responsibility in business.
(c)   The establishment by professions and quasi-professions of their own ethical standards and codes of practice.

7 The pressures of consumerism are giving rise to codes of practice.

References

1 In *Testing to Destruction* (I.P.A., 1974).
2 In *Planning for Products and Markets* (Longman, 1972).
3 In *Future Shock* (Bodley Head, 1970).
4 In *The Year 2000* (Macmillan, 1967).
5 In a paper in *Harvard Business Review* (May-June 1972).
6 In *Unsafe at Any Speed* (Bantam Books, 1973).
7 In *The Hidden Persuaders* (Penguin, 1960).
8 In 'Does a Consumerism Crunch Threaten Business?', *Business Administration* (January 1973).
9 In *Marketing in a Changing Environment* (John Wiley, 1973).

10 In a paper in *Harvard Business Review*, op. cit. See ref. 5.
11 As refs. 5 and 10.
12 In *Marketing in a Changing Environment*, op. cit.
13 In *Harvard Business Review* (May-June 1974).
14 ibid.

Further Reading

The Limits to Growth (Pan, 1974). No one book covers the subject matter of this chapter adequately, but any of those mentioned in the References are good on particular aspects. Perhaps *The Limits to Growth* is the one all students should have some familiarity with, in view of its challenge to the belief that things must necessarily go on the way they are.

McIver, Colin. 'Back to Marketing', *Management Today* (January 1976).

Quarterly Review of Marketing (Winter 1975). The section on consumerism is based on a paper presented by the author at a Marketing Education Group Conference at Lancaster University in July 1974 and reprinted in the above. Its bibiography contains many useful references.

Toffler, Alvin. *The Third Wave* (Pan, 1981). Gives a stimulating glimpse of many important social and other changes

Questions for Discussion

1 Identify two current advertisements which seem to you to contain inadequate or misleading information. Say why you think this and what changes you would want to see made.

2 (IM, June 1983) To what extent does the marketing concept take into account the potential conflict between consumer wants, consumer interests, and long-run societal welfare?

3 (CAM, June 1981) During the past decade there has been a number of changes in the pattern of distribution of goods and services to the consumer. Identify two major changes that have taken place and state what you consider to have been the causes.

4 (IM, June 1982) Discuss some of the main factors which give rise to changes in consumer needs.

11. *What Marketing Research Can Do*

'One no longer seeks to make decisions solely on the basis of hunch or flair. One now seeks first the facts upon which the hunch, or flair, can nourish itself.'

Market Research in Action – A Guide for Company Management

11.1 The Purposes of Marketing Research

11.11 *The Continuing Need for Facts*

The publication quoted above[1] has on its cover the caption 'Facts & Ideas . . . Decisions'. This highlights two important truths about market research:

1 Facts alone achieve nothing; they have to be processed. They need to be used imaginatively and creatively to produce good management decisions, which must then be well implemented.
2 But it is also true that decisions based purely on ideas (or hunch or flair), without the support of facts, can go sadly astray.

Managers need facts on which to base their decisions and their judgements – just as a judge in court would do, just as a scientist would do in testing a hypothesis, just as a general needs intelligence about the enemy's strength, position and movements before planning his own campaign. But there is a dimension in which business decisions differ from those of the judge or the scientist, although not those of the general. Generally judges and scientists make a once-for-all judgement. But, as we saw in Chapter 10, the business manager is dealing with a continuing situation. He cannot stop events at a particular point while he considers all the relevant facts and makes his decision. Even while the decision-making process is going on, the facts will be changing – a new competitor enters the market, an existing one changes his prices or introduces a new product, the pattern of distribution alters, or a new advertising medium becomes available. In one part of the company's global market the economic situation may change, for the better or for the worse; even the manager's own decisions change the situations in which he is operating.

This means that market research ideally needs to be built into the total activity of the business as a continuing operation, providing a steady flow of facts. There are, of course, many different kinds of fact. Adler[2] distinguishes between 'objective' and 'subjective' facts, listing the following types:

1 *Objective Facts*
   (a) Actions (buying habits).

124

   (b) Demographic facts (age, sex, marital status).
2 *Subjective Facts*
   (a) Knowledge (of a certain brand).
   (b) Perception (of an advertising message).
   (c) Notions (image of a brand or company).
   (d) Opinions (views, fashions, anticipations).
   (e) Intentions (to buy certain types of goods, say).
   (f) Wishes (to possess).
   (g) Motives (mainly subconscious).

In varying degrees, and depending very much on the particular situation, all firms need facts of all these kinds to assist in making sound decisions. Gathering such facts in order to improve the decision is what marketing research is all about.

Clearly, the ease of gathering facts and their reliability when gathered varies considerably. Facts about the numbers and ages of the population are readily available and highly reliable. Those concerning what people intend to do or why they behave as they do (motives) will almost certainly have to be specially collected; the cost may be high, the reliability low and the difficulty of correct interpretation very considerable.

11.12 *Marketing Research for Predicting the Future*

It must be stressed that marketing research can never be an infallible crystal ball. Facts about what is happening are relatively easy to obtain, but facts about what has happened are more difficult to come by (people find it difficult to remember and what they do remember may become confused). Facts about what will happen are even more of a problem, for people often have not thought about the situation in question and may well find it difficult to project themselves mentally into it. They may have intentions which, when the time comes, are not carried out (because other influences come to bear, because the situation changes, or simply because, like the ordinary human beings they are, they change their minds).

What will happen in given circumstances is, of course, what managers most wish to know. All that marketing research can offer (a not inconsiderable offering) is a firm basis for a clear appreciation of the present situation and perhaps a clearly delineated trend over time supported by some indication of what might happen in the future – a far better basis for decision than no real knowledge at all.

11.2 Ad Hoc and Continuous Research

A great deal of marketing research is carried out on a continuous basis. Many government statistics are gathered quarterly, annually, or at some other regular interval. Many commercial studies are carried out on a 'panel' or 'audit' basis. The great value of this is that we can plot trends and see whether a particular factor is increasing or decreasing, whether any of the elements being plotted are departing from what the trends were indicating, and so on. Any departures from the 'expected' trends may point to new factors of importance in the marketplace.

On the other hand, this is costly, and not every aspect of every market justifies the expense. Many marketing investigations, therefore, are carried out on an irregular, infrequent or even a once-for-all basis. The term usually applied to these cases is *ad hoc* research.

11.3 Panels and Audits

Panels consist of permanent samples of the universe concerned (see Chapter 12 for a full discussion of sampling). Members of these panels agree to give regular interviews and/or regularly record information in special 'diaries'. They are usually paid a small fee. This has obvious advantages in that sampling is itself costly, and using the same sample over and over represents a saving. But the main reasons for the use of panels are the following:

1 Comparison is easier and more reliable, since we are comparing over time the behaviour and/or attitudes not just of similar people but of the same people. It is even possible, if desired, to study individual behaviour over a period of time.
2 Because they are specially recruited and instructed, panel members are usually more 'forthcoming' than people interviewed 'out of the blue', and can be asked to carry out more complicated and extensive procedures.

Disadvantages of panels are that members may become self-conscious and no longer truly representative. Indeed, it may be that willingness to participate is in itself a non-characteristic response. Another problem is matching the succession when, for one reason or another, people leave the panel.

However, panels are used to gain regular information on such matters as the following:

1 Household purchasing patterns.
2 TV and radio viewing and listening habits.
3 Current stock patterns – an example of this is the 'pantry check', where a regular call is made by interviewers on a panel of households to check what products they are using (providing valuable information on such matters as changing preferences for pack size, quantities bought at a time, etc.).

11.31 *Retail Audits*

Panels are not confined to individual members of the public or to households. The retail audit technique uses panels of shops to establish brand shares and volume of sales from retail outlets to customers (which, because of changing stock levels, may be quite different from the volume of deliveries from factory to retailers).

A. C. Nielsen & Co. Ltd., operating in twenty-one countries, are leaders in this kind of research. Starting with their *Food Index*, then moving on to a *Drug Index* (based on audits of grocery and chemist shops), they now regularly publish indexes for confectionery, home appliances, D.I.Y., liquor stores and cash-and-carry wholesalers. The following extract from a Nielsen publication describes how the system operates:

> After special training in Nielsen's Head Office 'shop', auditors are assigned to a territory to work under the supervision of an area manager.
> They visit each sample shop in their territory at frequent intervals, usually every 2 months.
> At each visit they count the stock of all the product classes requested by Nielsen

clients, keeping a separate note of what they find in the selling area and stockroom. They don't just count a product class in total. They build up the total picture by making a separate check of the different sizes and types of brands.

They take the past stocks (which were recorded on the previous visit), add purchases made since then by the shopkeeper, then take away the present stock – and they have what has been sold. Purchases are recorded from documents kept by the retailer, such as invoices and delivery notes. Because of the number of transactions, this is a massive task in itself, requiring a tremendous eye for detail

PAST STOCKS + PURCHASES – PRESENT STOCKS = SALES FACTS

The Nielsen auditor now has not opinions or estimates, but the absolute sales facts. Nielsen knows down to the smallest pack size precisely what consumers have bought in that store. In addition to stocks and purchases, the Nielsen fieldman will also keep a record of selling prices, special offers, new products and display material. In fact, he keeps his eye open for any information which is likely to be of value to Nielsen clients.

On average an audit takes about 2½ man-days to complete. A large store such as a supermarket requires a team of auditors to carry out each check.

Page.01.   Total Great Britain

Food   Product class 2   Apr/May

Unit basis —packages in thousands—average and R.S.P.—packages

	Consumer sales £ at R.S.P.	Consumer sales	Retailer purchases	Stocks and months supply	Average stocks average monthly sales	Self service R.S.P. P	Distribution Shop sterling Max %	O.S. %	Purch %	Showing Shop sterling C %	A %	SS %	S %
Total all items	280,915 100.0%	2,909 100.0%	2,692 100.0%	1,456 1.0	29.3 29.3	9.7	45 71	2 4	32 60				
Brand A Small	41,665 14.8%	527 18.1%	486 18.1%	203 0.8	11.4 14.8	7.9	16 37	3 9	11 30				
Large	78,951 28.1%	691 23.8%	663 24.6%	387 1.1	12.3 11.0	11.4	28 51	3 7	19 39				
Cons.	120,616 42.9%	1,218 41.9%	1,149 42.7%	590 1.0	15.9 16.4	9.9	33 60	3 7	24 50	1 1 1 1		* *	* *
Brand B Small	22,473 8.0%	265 9.1%	202 7.5%	126 1.0	13.1 13.8	8.5	9 25	2 5	5 18				
Large	52,868 18.9%	440 15.1%	406 15.1%	342 1.6	15.0	12.0	21 42	3 3	11 31		* *	* *	
Cons.	75,341 26.9%	705	608	1.1	25.7 23.1	10.1	39 63	3 3	54		* *	*	
	9,352 3.3%	3.6%	99 3.7%	29 0.6	18.4 33.0	9.0	1 11	* 2	1 9	* * * *	* *	* *	
All others	69,144 24.6%	807 27.7%	772 28.7%	314 0.8	21.0 27.0	8.6	13 32	1 5	7 24				

Figure 11.1 Extract from a Nielsen retail audit report

By careful statistical analysis and selection (using 'weighting' techniques), a relatively small panel of stores gives accurate brand-by-brand information on a large number of brands on a regular basis. Figure 11.1 shows an example of the kind of information that can be obtained in this way.

A wide variety of consumer and retail panels is available and the companies offering them (along with other kinds of marketing research facilities) are listed in the *Market Research Society Year Book*. The Retail Audits Ltd entry, for example, includes: 'RAL operates 10 national audit panels and has national distribution checking services, covering such outlet types as chemists, grocers, garages, hardware, fertilizers, CTNs, licensed premises, electrical, toys and stationery.'

11.4 Syndicated Research

The results of retail audits, consumer panels and many other types of research are available to anyone who wishes to buy them. This cost-sharing approach, known as syndicated research, enables very extensive research to be carried out in a way that would be uneconomic if each client had to commission it separately.

An example of a quite different kind of syndicated survey is 'Monitor', carried out annually by Taylor Nelson & Associates Ltd. The survey is based on a random sample of 2,500 persons aged 15–65, and gives a wealth of information on twenty-eight social trends under the following headings: Consumerism, Psychology of Affluence, Anti-functionalism, Weakening of the Protestant Ethic, and Isolationism.

The TNA descriptive document says:

We call the reflections of trends 'manifestations'. These are behavioural or attitudinal responses to the social trends as well as manifestations in terms of product purchasing. Here are some manifestations of social trends:

> Interest in bulk purchasing of groceries
> Growth in wine-making and home-brewing
> Men showing more interest in new colours and styles of clothes
> Desiring warmer homes
> Having more adventurous holidays
> Developing new hobbies
> Interest in health foods
> The popularity of building society investment
> The appeal of the styles and art of the 1920s
> Women becoming financial decision-makers.

We show the relationship between trends and manifestations and also between trends, manifestations and exposure to certain media. The analysis of the data enables each report to stand on its own two feet. While the comparison over time is its prime objective, Monitor shows in individual reports:

– the description of those people who are strongly displaying each social trend
– the relationship between each manifestation (e.g. brewing beer at home) and demographics and trends
– the relationship between trends e.g. the overlap between Physical Fitness and interest in Technical Things
– the relationship between manifestations e.g. owning hi-fi and inviting friends round for drinks in the evening, antipathy to, for instance, the chemical industry and desire for

more government legislation restricting the action of manufacturing companies.

Some research companies operate a regular survey (often using a panel of interviewers) where a small number of questions can be bought by a series of different subscribers. Thus, the same survey might cover car servicing, shaving habits and a variety of other topics. These are often referred to as 'omnibus' surveys.

11.5 Qualitative Research

Marketing research is not only based on statistical analysis of the responses of large numbers of people (quantitative research), sometimes disparagingly referred to as 'head-counting'. Often it is valuable (and frequently more cost-effective) to have information which, although having little or no statistical validity, does give important insights.

We referred in Chapter 2 to motivational research and to group discussions – these are two of the techniques used in qualitative research. Here the aim is to explore in some depth the reactions, opinions or behaviour of a few people. While these people are chosen so as to be reflective of the universe, they are not numerous enough for the information obtained to be totally acceptable as being representative of the universe. However, information and insights obtained in this way are often used as a starting point for drafting questionnaires. The latter are used in surveys that do give a statistically accurate view of the whole. Even where this is not the case, however, qualitative research can often have great value in helping to understand why people behave as they do, instead of merely telling one what they do – which is largely what is obtained from such research as retail audits.

11.6 Advertising Research

Marketing research carried out as an aid to advertising decisions has become so extensive as to be a subject, and an industry, in its own right. Two main areas of research are important, as follows:

1 *Advertisement Research.* This includes testing proposed advertisements to determine whether they are likely to have the desired effect (advertisement pre-testing), and also research to assess what the effect actually was (advertisement post-testing)
2 *Media Research.* This consists primarily of identifying the size and nature of the audiences for the various media, but also tries to determine such matters as the effect of varying size and position of advertisements.

11.61 *Advertisement Research*

Many of the standard techniques of marketing research – questionnaires and group discussions, for example – can be used to yield information about the ways in which people have reacted to advertising or how they will be likely to react. Interviewees can, for example, be shown a publication and then asked questions about which advertisements they can recall. This, of course, is a 'post-testing' technique, but a similar 'pre-test' can be obtained by making up a folder or dummy magazine containing one or more projected advertisements – perhaps alongside existing ones – to obtain reactions to them before incurring the cost of placing them in publications.

Television commercials similarly can be tested before or after showing over the air. In one method members of the public are invited to a private film show. Following a brief feature or cartoon film, a number of commercials are screened, including the one being tested. There are then a number of techniques enabling the audience to record their reactions, one of the simplest being the question-naire, perhaps supplemented by group discussion. Sometimes a 'brand-aware-ness' questionnaire is completed before and after the showing, giving a measurement of change in awareness brought about by seeing the commercial or commercials under test.

At the more complicated extreme a whole battery of physiological tests have been used, measuring such things as sweat response (with a 'psychogalvano-meter'), or pupil dilation (by means of a special camera). These had a great vogue among some researchers at one time but now are very little used. Many of these 'ironmongery' techniques are far too expensive for other than experimental use and, in any case, few of them are universally regarded as totally reliable. Increasingly, group discussions are used whenever possible as they provide a great deal of information at low cost.

The brand-measurement check referred to above is frequently used to test an entire advertising campaign. 'Brand-awareness' (i.e. how readily a particualr brand comes to mind, how it is regarded in relation to other brands etc.) is measured before the campaign 'breaks' and at suitable intervals thereafter in a suitable sample of people. Awareness of a company and its 'image' can also be checked regularly by standard research techniques, and this is frequently done in the case of 'corporate image' campaigns.

It should be noted that post-testing can in some situations be carried out much more simply, particularly where the purpose of the advertising is simple and clear-cut. Thus, the number of coupons returned, articles bought (in the case of mail order advertising) or leaflets requested can be a direct measure of advertising effectiveness. Only in relatively few cases is the matter so simple, however, and even then pre-testing may still be desirable.

11.62 *Media Research*

In the U.K., a number of joint bodies supported by the advertising industry are responsible for basic readership/audience research for the main media. The *National Readership Survey* is organised by JICNARS (the Joint Industry Committee for National Readership Surveys). The figures are based on annual interviews with 30,000 adults and covers over 100 publications – national daily and Sunday newspapers and some magazines.

Subscribers to the NRS receive detailed breakdowns of readership sub-divided in a number of ways, including:

- by sex, age, six social grades, survey regions and ITV Regions;
- by weight of ITV viewing and radio listening;

– readership among special groups, such as housewives with children, possessors of certain consumer durables, etc.

Television audience research is carried out by the Broadcaster's Audience Research Board (BARB). The main method used is to attach electronic meters to receivers in a representative sample of over 2,500 homes throughout the U.K. The meters record, on a minute by minute basis, whether the set is switched on and if so to which channel it is tuned. In addition all members of the households whose sets are metered complete on a quarter-hour basis a 'diary' record of what they viewed. This information is analysed weekly to provide subscribers with a detailed minute-by-minute statement of the composition of the audience for all BBC and ITV television transmissions.

The Joint Industry Committe for Radio Advertising Research (JICRAR) under the guidance of the IBA initiates additional research into radio listening.

At one stage the Joint Industry Committee for Poster Audience Surveys (JICPAS) operated but seems to have been inactive in recent years.

In addition, there are many other surveys carried out for special purposes, for example, in the field of specialist publications Table 11.1.

Table 11.1
Extract from a readership survey published by Management Today.

	Director		Manager		Neither	
Unweighted sample	415		690		1,186	
Est. population (000's)	138		243		418	
	000	%	000	%	000	%
The Daily Telegraph	51	37	89	37	152	36
Financial Times	51	37	58	24	69	16
The Times	26	19	32	13	64	15
The Guardian	11	8	18	7	57	14
The Sunday Times	74	54	97	40	160	38
The Observer	29	21	37	15	86	21
Sunday Telegraph	27	20	38	16	69	16
Punch	17	12	28	12	44	10
The Economist	14	10	24	10	40	9
Country Life	14	10	20	8	32	8
New Scientist	3	2	14	6	41	10
Investors' Chronicle	13	9	16	6	17	4
Management Today	30	22	69	28	69	16
Illustrated London News	18	13	35	15	57	14
Director	40	29	29	12	23	5
Business Administration	15	11	24	10	23	6

11.7 Product and Package Testing

So far we have considered marketing research in connection with products already 'in the marketplace', but an important use of research is in screening

Table 11.2

Extract from a BARB report on television audiences

Reproduced by kind permission of The Broadcaster's Audience Research Board Ltd.

LONDON   TUESDAY

QTR HR BY QTR HR			ITV PROGRAMMES	CH 4 PROGRAMMES	Minute-By-Minute TVR	BBC1 PROGRAMMES	BBC2 PROGRAMMES

(Table of audience figures for London, Tuesday 8 Feb 83. Columns: ITV, CH 4, BBC1, TVR/TOT; ITV Programmes title, start time and duration (mins), Homes 000's, % Share, TVR; CH 4 Programmes title, start time and duration (mins), Homes 000's, % Share, TVR; Minute-By-Minute TVR graph 0–60, TVR = 4,206,000 HOMES; BBC1 Programmes title, start time and duration (mins), TVR; BBC2 Programmes title, start time and duration (mins), TVR.)

ITV programmes listed include: DAYBREAK 0600 60; GOOD MORNING BRITAIN 0700 135; SCHOOLS 0930 149; COCKLESHELL BAY 1200 11; ONCE UPON A TIME 1211 16; THE SULLIVANS 1230 26; NEWS 1300 23; THAMES NEWS 1323 5; CROWN COURT 1330 27; A PLUS 1400 29; SECOND CHANCE 1434 53; ONE OF THE BOYS 1530 27; COCKLESHELL BAY 1600 11; THE MONKEYS 1615 26; STIG OF THE DUMP 1621 15; FIVE MAGIC MINUTES 1640; CH TV CHANNEL; EMMERDALE FARM 1714 26; NEWS 1730 27; THAMES NEWS 1800 26; HELP 1825 5; CROSSROADS 1834 22; REPORTING LONDON 1900 30; SHE CRIED MURDER 1936 78; FOR WHAT IT'S WORTH 2034 26; THE HARD WORD 2100 46; THE HARDER THEY COME 2104 109; NEWS AT TEN 2200 29; THAMES NEWS HEADLINES 2232 2; TITANIC/DUSTIN HMGR 2234 56; CITY PRIEST 2335; LIVE AT CHILLIONAIRE 0002; LAST PROGRAMME.

CH 4 programmes include: YEARS AHEAD 1644; WAYNE AND SHUSTER 1730 27; MINI POPS 1800 28; COMMON INTEREST 1832 25; CHANNEL FOUR NEWS 1900 55; BROOKSIDE 2000 28; FOR WHAT IT'S WORTH 2034 26; THE HARDER THEY COME 2104 109; EASTERN EYE 2258 52; CLOSEDOWN.

BBC1 programmes include: BREAKFAST TIME 0630 149; SCHOOLS PROGRAMME 0905 135; SCHOOLS PROGRAMME 1140 47; NEWS AFTER NOON 1230 35; PEBBLE MILL AT ONE 1301; FINGERBOBS 1347; YOU AND ME 1401; SCHOOLS PROGRAMME 1415; SIR WALTER SCOTT/HERE 1434; SONGS OF PRAISE 1515 34; PLAY SCHOOL 1550 24; YOGI BEAR 1617 7; JACKANORY 1628 14; ANIMAL MAGIC 1642; JOHN CRAVEN'S NEWSROUND 1707 10; GRANGE HILL 1717 21; NEWS AND WEATHER 1740 19; NATIONWIDE LONDON 1759 26; NATIONWIDE 1825 24; DOCTOR WHO 1850 24; BEST OF THE WEST 1916 23; VOX POP 1940 30; BRITSH ROCK/POP AWARDS 2011 48; 9 O'CLOCK NEWS/WTHR 2100 27; NCYS/FROM/BLACKSTUFF 2120 68; CUP SOCCER SPECIAL; PEOPLE AND POWER 2307; NEWS HEADLINES 2347; TOP BILLING 2348; WEATHER; CLOSEDOWN 0021.

BBC2 programmes include: PLAY SCHOOL 1100 24; WORLD BOWLS 1500 161; ROBINSON CRUSOE 1740 18; CHARLES BROWN 1759 24; THE WALTONS 1824 46; NEWS AND WEATHER 1910 6; WHEN WORLDS COLLIDE 1915 74; RUSSELL HARTY 2036 27; DOCTORS' DILEMMAS 2103 43; ARENA 2144 55; NEWSNIGHT 2243 41; WORLD BOWLS 2334 40; CLOSEDOWN 0014.

products so that only those likely to be acceptable to customers reach the market. Not only the product as such but its packaging and everything about it can be subjected to testing before the product launch.

Some of this is by completely straightforward questioning of carefully selected samples of people. Often, however, subjective reactions are provoked, and rather more subtle techniques need to be used. For example, groups of housewives can be asked to choose between a number of alternative products with (unbeknown to the group) only minor differences, such as colour or design of pack. This 'blind' approach can give more reliable results than open questions such as 'Which of these three packs do you prefer?'

Products can be tested by getting a suitable sample to taste them and give their views. Two commonly used ways of doing this are the following:

1 Invite people in from a busy shopping street to a rented room (e.g. in a church hall), give them a cup of tea and a snack, and then ask their reactions to the taste of the snack. This approach is known as a 'hall test'.
2 Give people a sample to try in their homes and call back a few days later to collect their views ('placement test'). This is a more expensive method but has the advantages that the whole family's reactions can be gathered, and that it is carried out under more natural conditions than the 'hall test'.

11.8 Test Marketing

In a sense, the reason for all marketing research is to reduce the level of costly failures. The best possible way to know whether your marketing mix is correct is to try it on the customers and see whether they buy (and go on buying) it in sufficient numbers. But a failure at this stage can be very costly indeed. Yet research can only attempt to measure whether some of the ingredients in the marketing mix are likely to be successful; as we said earlier, no research can predict what will actually happen.

The compromise between a full-scale, potentially very risky, national launch of the product, and research that, at best, can only give useful pointers is a test-marketing operation. That is to say, one part of the total market is chosen for a launching of the new product. If this is successful, we can then go on to the complete national launch or step-by-step, area-by-area (a 'rolling launch'), build-up to the national marketing stage. If the test is unsuccessful, then less money and effort have been wasted than would have been the case with an immediate national launch.

Test marketing is of value not only with new product launches. Successful marketing necessitates correctly adjusting a large number of variables – weight and kind of advertising, price levels, distribution patterns and so on. Changes in any one of these may improve or worsen the competitive position. Thus, before making changes of this kind right throughout a market, it may be valuable to test the proposed changes in one section of the market first.

There are some key points to consider when selecting a test market area, in particular the following:

1 It must be as representative as possible of the market as a whole, in terms of age, class, sex, size of households; in terms of proportion of large and small shops,

independents and multiples: in terms of relative weight of one's own sales organization; and in terms of behaviour patterns. For example, are people in the area typical of the whole in their purchases and usage of the type of product concerned? One area may have higher car-ownership or keep fewer pets than another.

2 As far as possible, it should be self-contained. A town with a big shopping centre, serving a wide 'hinterland' area, for example, presents problems when it comes to analysing the significance of sales patterns generated during a test.

3 The area should offer advertising media that can be duplicated when sales become national. For this reason (and for reasons connected with 2) a television coverage area is often chosen. Even so, there are problems of overlap (people in some areas have the choice of two or three TV transmitters). Other problems are that the local press does not have exactly the same characteristics as the national newspapers, but the latter offer few regional test facilities (although a number of colour magazines do now offer, at a price, the facility of including an advertisement only in those copies delivered in a particular area.

4 Size – the larger the area the better (but more expensive) the test. Small areas are not only more likely to be atypical but also tend to present greater problems of overlap and non-availability (without colossal wastage) of national media.

It should be noted that test marketing is not a precise instrument. The conditions listed above are difficult to achieve in any completeness; there are usually many variables, and attributing success or failure to particular variables is almost impossible. There are also other problems: for example, an extensive test gives competitors an opportunity to beat you by launching their products virtually before your tests are completed. It is not even unknown for competitors to devise ways of 'spoiling' a test.

For all these reasons, test marketing is no longer thought to be the panacea and the near-necessity it was once considered. In many situations (especially where the price of failure is not very high) it may be more cost-effective to go straight into a national launch, particularly with products (e.g., in the fashion world) which have a short life-cycle.

Test marketing must be accompanied by a well considered and probably substantial programme of research if it is to be of great value. Thus, it is of little use to find that sales of a new snack food are too low to be profitable if we do not know why. Research may tell us that customers do not like the taste sufficiently, that they regard the price as too high, that too few retailers are prepared to stock or display it, or that the advertising was noticed by too few people. With an array of facts such as these we are in a much better position to make further changes or to develop the next new product more successfully.

11.9 The Full Scope of Marketing Research

The above are some of the more important types of marketing research, but there are many others. The full scope of marketing research is summarized in Figure 11.2.

11.10 The Positive Use of Marketing Research

There is a tendency to view the use of marketing research in a negative or a passive

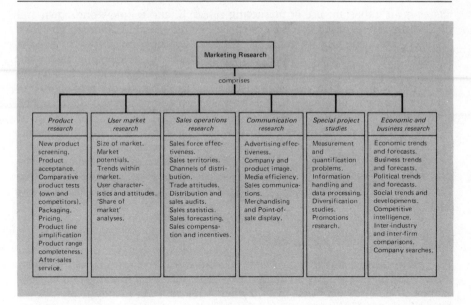

Figure 11.2 The scope of marketing research

way. Thus, it is used to help solve problems, such as why our brand share is falling, why customers prefer an alternative product, and what the best advertising medium for the desired audience is; merely to monitor progress – what our brand share is now, or what the overall market trend is.

But research can also be used positively, as follows, in order to expose marketing opportunities, which can then be exploited:

1 What are the ways in which our product is used? (Johnson's were able to open up a whole new market when they discovered that adults were using their baby talcum powder.)
2 What customer needs are not at present well met by our products or our competitors'? (See gap analysis in Section 5.61.)
3 What might be the customer reaction to an advertising approach no one is currently using?

Using research to expose gaps in the marketplace can reveal opportunities potentially far more profitable than can simply plugging away with existing products to known customers in the traditional way.

11.11 Cost-effective Marketing Research Decisions

In Section 2.9 it was pointed out that the two main limitations of marketing research are time and cost. It is particularly important not to become over-enthused by the undoubted value of research to the point of ignoring its cost implications. For example, we have said several times that knowledge of brand shares is an important use of marketing research, and to know one's own and one's competitors' brand shares an important matter. But it is not important for a company holding a tiny share of the market. To know precisely whether the market share is 2 per cent or 3 per cent will hardly be worth spending money on, since the knowledge will be unlikely to affect management decisions on marketing strategy. At anything up to 5 per cent brand share, one is likely to be a minnow in a pond full of big fish, being totally ignored by them and unaffected by their actions.

Similarly, if a marketing decision will lead to only a small potential profit, research costs may wipe out or severely reduce the profit gained from taking a better-based decision. Marketing research expenditure must be related to the potential benefit it can bring, just like any other business expenditure. Marketing research is not in the business of producing knowledge for its own sake or at any cost.

11.12 A Test Marketing Case History

An example of the way in which vigorous and exhaustive test-marketing over a long period of time can pay off handsomely is the success of Aquafresh toothpaste in the U.S.A. The story began in 1974 when Aquafresh was already an established brand in the U.K. The owners of the brand were the Beecham group whose Macleans brand had for around 20 years had a modest share of the $650m. a year U.S. market – dominated by Procter and Gamble and Colgate Palmolive.

In 1974 several thousand unmarked tubes of Aquafresh were distributed to housewives in different areas of the U.S.A. and after two weeks the households were surveyed. Most said they liked the taste but were unconvinced of the toothpaste's ability to prevent cavities.

After minor reformulation a further test was carried out a year later. This time half the adults preferred it to competitive brands but children showed a marked liking for the new product.

At the same time consumer reaction was sought to the U.K. commercial (dubbed for the American market). American housewives to whom – in groups of 15 – the commercial was shown, felt that the commercial was strong on creating an exhilarating feeling but weak on telling the benefits of the toothpaste (the commercial was based on a schooner ploughing through Caribbean waters).

A more practical down-to-earth approach was produced and the two commercials tested against each other in Dallas, St. Louis, Denver and Indianapolis (each commercial used in two of the cities). Finally, the toothpaste colour was changed from blue to green, the name amended to read Aqua-fresh (i.e. hyphenated) in response to customer reactions and further test-marketed.

Ultimately a product now believed to be formulated and promoted completely in line with American tastes was given a full-scale launch with a massive sampling (a 1.4 ounce free sample posted to 2 in 3 households). The cost for postage alone was almost $4m. and a $30m. advertising campaign, using the 'down-to-earth' commercial was mounted.

Result; Beecham captured 40 per cent of the US market, with Colgate in second place with 19 per cent (reported in *The Times* 30th November 1980).

11.13 Summary

1 The purpose of marketing research is to deliver facts that can be used to make better management decisions.
2 Marketing research is no crystal ball – it cannot predict the future, but only reduce the amount of hunch and intuition that has to be used.
3 Both continuous and *ad hoc* research have a part to play.
4 Continuous research (such as consumer panels, retail audits, TV audience research) is based on a panel of respondents, selected on the sampling principles outlined in Chapter 12.
5 Much research is syndicated, i.e. the cost is borne by a number of subscribers rather than by one company.
6 Qualitative research has its own special value and may sometimes be more cost-effective than quantitative research.
7 Advertising research deals both with the effectiveness of advertisements and with who reads, watches and listens to the various media.
8 Pre-testing of products and packaging – using 'hall test' or 'placement test' techniques, among others – can give valuable advance notice of the likely reactions of potential customers.
9 Test marketing is simulating on a large or a smaller scale what is likely to happen in the marketplace as a whole. It can be used as an insurance against expensive mistakes but is often in itself very costly.
10 Marketing research can be used not only to monitor a position or explore problems, but also, more creatively, to identify profitable opportunities.
11 Because market research can be expensive, it must be used with judgement to ensure that any information gained is really worth the cost of getting it.

Reference

1 Mechanical Engineering E.D.C. *Market Research in Action – a Guide for Company Management* (H.M.S.O., 1971).
2 In *Lectures in Market Research* (Crosby Lockwood, 1969).

Further Reading

Willsmer, Ray L. *Directing the Marketing Effort* (Pan, 1975). This has an extremely vivid chapter on Test Marketing, which gives the 'feel' of how it is used, with many practical examples from the author's experiences with J. Lyons & Co., and an exploration of the theoretical aspects.

Questions for Discussion

1 Consider the relative value of the methods of continuous research that are used by manufacturers of fast turnover consumer goods.
2 Give three examples of situations where qualitative research would be of great value in decision-making, stating in each case which factors you would recommend investigating and the methods you would suggest using.
3 There will always be more marketing information that could be useful than funds available to collect it. How would you go about ranking possible

marketing research projects in order of priority?
4 What possible disadvantages can you see in the use of syndicated research from the point of view of a company buying it?
5 (CAM, June 1982) You are the Advertising Manager of a major Bank. You have received a number of complaints from branch managers who do not like your trendy new TV commercial.
Write an article for your house magazine fully explaining the research steps taken to ensure that your money is being well spent.

12. *How Marketing Research Works*

'It is not always understood that research can be carried out with varying degrees of precision according to the type of information wanted and the type of research done.'

D. Thomas. *'Riddles of Market Research'*

12.1 The Importance of Sampling

Sampling is a very important aspect of most market research. Why is it necessary and how does it work?

First, let us be clear that marketing research without sampling is perfectly possible. If, for example, we need to obtain certain information about all housewives in the U.K., we can, in theory at any rate, question every single one of them. Indeed, information about the U.K. population is regularly obtained on this basis, by surveying every single household in the country. This we call a census.

In some industrial markets the number of users of a particular product may be so small that it is perfectly feasible to interview them all. Indeed, it could be dangerous not to do so, since any one of them may be a sufficiently large user to have a significant effect on the total picture (computer-manufacturers, for example).

However, normally a census is not the preferred method of obtaining information, (a) because of the cost, and (b) because of the time it would take. For most products, to interview all households would cost far more than the potential profit over many years. Because of the time it takes to carry out a full census, even government population statistics are now regularly gathered in the U.K. on a sampling basis – with a full census only occasionally. Using the figures from a full census means inevitably working with out-of-date information, and it will often be preferable to have up-to-date information, even if it is slightly less accurate.

12.2 The Basis of Sampling

The use of sampling is based on the concept that, if a small number of items or parts (the sample) are selected at random from a larger number of parts of a whole (the universe), then the sample will tend to have the same characteristics in approximately the same proportion as the universe. The 'universe' is sometimes called the 'population'.

'Random' has a special meaning in this context. It does not mean, as in everyday usage, aimless or haphazard. A random sample is one selected in such a way that every single individual unit in the universe from which it was chosen had

139

a full and equal chance of being included in the sample. Its implications are perhaps best understood by looking at examples of sample selection that are not random:

1 A sample of housewives obtained by selecting numbers from the telephone directory cannot be random, since housewives not on the telephone have no chance of being selected and so are not representative of the universe.
2 A sample of marketing men selected from the membership list of the Institute of Marketing cannot be random, since it excludes those who are not members.
3 Questionnaires inserted in a motoring magazine for completion and return by readers cannot provide a random sample of all car owners because

 (a) it excludes non-readers,
 (b) it excludes readers who did not see that particular issue,
 (c) it excludes those who are too busy or disinclined to fill in the questionnaire and return it.

We said in the definition at the beginning of this section that the sample tends to have the same characteristics as the universe. However, it may well not precisely match the characteristics of the universe – how closely it matches will depend largely on the size of the sample.

We can see in principle why this will be so by considering the simple case of tossing a coin. The proportion of 'heads' to 'tails' must be 50 : 50 if we toss the coin enough times. But we know from experience that, purely due to chance, there are 'runs', so that, in a small number of tosses, we may get a higher number of heads than tails or vice versa. The more times we toss, the more likely we are to reach the 50 : 50 balance. Similarly, with a sample, the nearer it approximates in size to the total universe, the less likely we are to get chance deviations from the total pattern.

Fortunately, as the sample size increases, we fairly rapidly reach the point when there is a high degree of 'match' with the total universe, and further increases in sample size give only relatively small increases in accuracy. Provided we have a good idea of the total size of the universe, we can, using statistical formulae, calculate the size of sample needed to give the desired degree of accuracy. Since these calculations would normally be carried out by specialists within the marketing research team, we do not need to concern ourselves with precisely how they operate.[1]

The main point to grasp here is that the use of sampling techniques enables us to trade off an acceptable loss in accuracy for a substantial reduction in cost and in time taken to provide the information. Since it is rare that 100 per cent accuracy is necessary in any case, and since percentages in the 90s are fairly readily obtainable with relatively small samples, this is a good bargain.

12.21 *Size of Sample*

As to what all the above actually leads to in terms of sample size, the following quotation, from Adler[2] gives a good general idea:

Surveys with more than 15,000 (0.05 per cent of the adult population of the United Kingdom) are very exceptional. A nation-wide sample often contains no more than

2,000 cases and is rarely greater than 5,000 cases. Samples of only a few hundred cases are often regarded as sufficient for the purposes of a particular survey.

The aim is to include the optimum, not the maximum, number of cases. The optimum size depends upon:

I Deriving the greatest amount of relevant information, per £1 spent on the survey.

II The size of sampling error which can be tolerated without seriously impairing the results. A very high degree of precision is often unnecessary for particular studies, depending on the purpose of the survey results.

III The size of the smallest sub-group relevant to the aim of the study. There should be a sufficient number of cases in it to make the results meaningful.

IV The homogeneity of the universe. The more homogeneous it is, the smaller the sample can be.

V The length of time allowed for the survey. Larger samples require longer spans for data collection and tabulation than do smaller samples.

VI The type of sample used.

We have been talking in terms of sampling individuals. Samples are of course drawn not only from groups of people but from other 'populations' or 'universes', such as shops, farms, posters, or sites. People can be sampled in such groups as customers, readers of publications, shoppers etc.

12.3 Types of Sample

So far we have been talking of sampling in terms of random sampling of the entire universe. But we have also referred to the need for marketing research to operate within cost limitations. This latter point means that in practice other approaches to sampling are frequently used. The main division is between the following:

1 *Random Sampling*, where each unit in the universe has the same chance of being included in the sample. Units are selected by precise means and the interviewer is given detailed instructions on who or what to include.

2 *Quota Sampling*, where the interviewer selects the individuals to be interviewed, but is given detailed instructions on the characteristics (age, sex, class, occupation etc.) of the people to be interviewed, numbers of each category to be interviewed, conditions of interview (at home, at work, etc.)

Random sampling needs a 'sampling frame', i.e. a complete and up-to-date list of all members of the universe, such as that provided by the electoral roll, for example (although it, like any sampling frame, is never totally accurate). The units to be included in the sample are then selected along the lines of the following example.

On any given section of the electoral roll randomly select (by means of a more sophisticated version of the 'drawing lots' principle) a starting point, such as the 10th household. The interviewer is instructed to interview the head of that 10th household, then the 25th, 40th, 55th and so on, or the 30th, 50th, 70th and so on – the interval depending on the total sample size required. The interviewer must interview the person specified and must, if necessary, call back repeatedly until he or she finds the interviewee at home. Strict rules are laid down to cover such contingencies as death or permanent absence, and the interviewer can only include someone else in the sample instead if he is so instructed.

In the case of a quota sample, the interviewer selects the people to be interviewed, although strict criteria are laid down to ensure as far as possible that the final sample, when all the individuals interviewed by the different interviewers are put together, does represent the universe.

The following is an extract from the instructions given by Pegasus Research Ltd to their interviewers.

'Work in a systematic fashion. Never wander about aimlessly wondering where to begin and do not be put off by shabby houses or dirty curtains. On the other hand, don't feel you must stay in the *same* area for the whole of your assignment – if contacting rate is slow, change areas within the sampling area named.

It is easy to find shift workers and housewives in during the day, but the views of working housewives and men who always work during the day are equally important and must be sought out. In the same way, people in the street should not be avoided simply because they appear to be in a hurry or you do not like the look of them. First appearances are often misleading. Clearly, when you have a quota to fill you must select people by assessing their age and class but other personal opinions should not be allowed to intervene.

An interviewer must use her commonsense and not let any one group be over-represented, therefore avoid interviewing more than one or two people on an army estate or in a block of police flats. (See Page 18 for interviewing in places of work.)

Towards the end of your quota establish both the age and occupational group of the respondent at the *beginning* of the interview, otherwise you will interview people who do not qualify and we cannot accept interviews outside the quota.

Interviewers have individual methods but a suggested introduction might be:

'For the purpose of our survey we are interested in interviewing a cross section of the population. Please tell me, what was your age last birthday?'

Pause here for the reply; if the age is in the group you require, then:

'Also, what is the occupation of the head of the household?'

If the person is not in the required age or occupational group she may be able to suggest someone who lives nearby who might be able to help you.'

The main advantage of a quota sample is that the cost per interview is much lower than with a random sample, as particular individuals do not have to be found and interviewers can conduct more interviews in a day. The disadvantage is that, unless they are very well trained and reliable interviewers, personal bias in selecting people for an interview may affect the sample adversely. For example, there is a natural tendency for interviewers to select people they know or suspect will readily respond, and to choose locations near their home or easy to travel to.

12.31 *Stratified Sampling*

Sometimes it is specified that there are to be proportionately more sampling units from some levels or strata of the universe than from others. Thus, in order to be able to make the necessary sub-divisions, it might be necessary to sample a higher proportion of rural households than urban ones (which are a much bigger stratum).

In industrial market research it is often possible to stratify companies according to number of employees or by turnover. A number of different strata can be fixed – e.g. up to 500 employees, 501–2,000, 2001–5,000, and over 5,000 – and a different percentage taken from each category according to its size and importance.

One important factor that may lead to the use of stratified sampling arises when one or more strata are so small a proportion of the universe that they would yield only a very low number of interviews. Suppose that, in a total sample of 1,000, one stratum is expected to yield only fifty interviews, when the sub-division required in the analysis of results may call for at least 200 in the smallest group. It is then necessary either to increase the total sample to 4,000, and thus considerably increase the cost, or to add 150 interviews within the particular stratum, at much lower cost. In tabulations of results proportionality can be restored by 'weighting' the various strata according to the size of sample taken from each.

12.32 *Multi-stage Sampling*

If the universe is a big one, such as a whole country, selecting a relatively small number of units over the whole universe will mean that widely scattered (and therefore costly) interviews have to be carried out. A way of reducing this problem is to divide the universe into sections (such as administrative areas), sample the sections on a random selection basis, and then take a random sample within each section. Clearly, there can be a number of stages – for example, counties, then towns within selected counties, electoral areas within towns and, finally, individuals within selected areas – the selection of each stage being established on a random basis.

Cluster sampling is a form of multi-stage sampling in which sales areas, residential blocks or similar groupings are chosen randomly and then either all units within the 'cluster' interviewed or else a further random selection made within each cluster. Area sampling is a similar process, in which a geographical area of some kind is selected randomly.

12.4 Questionnaires and the Problem of Bias

Although sampling can be a complex process, it is in some ways easy to handle (by experts, that is) because it is susceptible to precise statistical analysis. The limitations arise not so much from inadequate techniques as from the difficulty of obtaining suitable sampling frames.

Some other aspects of marketing research are much more a matter of judgement, and questionnaire design is one of them. There are some simple rules, which are briefly listed below, but experience, care, good judgement and careful cross-checking are necessary if bias is to be avoided.

12.41 *The Problem of Bias*

In all marketing research there must be a constant fight to prevent bias creeping into the results, i.e. to avoid the situation where the results are not in fact representative of the universe. Richard D. Crisp defines bias as 'any force, tendency or procedural error in the collection, analysis or interpretation of data which produces distortion'.[3] Among the sources of bias are the following:

1 *Faulty sample selection.* The various sections of a universe may not be represented in the sample in the correct proportions. An extreme case might be

using the telephone directory to select a sample that should include the same proportion of poor people as in the population as a whole, when the poor have fewer telephones than the rest.

2 *Prejudiced interviewing.* Crisp[4] quotes a 'classic case' of an ardent prohibitionist who interviewed down-and-outers. They blamed liquor for their situation to a much greater extent than did similar people questioned by less prejudiced interviewers. Generally speaking, it is desirable for interviewers not to be too different from respondents in age, education and socio-economic status.

3 *Leading questions.* Bias here springs from questions that suggest the answer required. There is a strong tendency for people to give the 'accommodating answer' – the one they believe the interviewer wants. If the sponsor of the research is known, the respondent's attitude to the organization may well affect the answers given. Questions that have strong connotations of social acceptability (such as 'How frequently do you bath?') are likely to lead to respondents giving the answer they believe they ought to give. Other sources of bias are questions that are ambiguous or not clearly understood.

It is partly because of these problems that it is customary to include a pilot survey as part of most market research projects. This enables questionnaires to be tested and many potential difficulties overcome.

12.42 *The Content of Questionnaires*

In most surveys the interviewer is provided with a questionnaire (but see Section 12.5). The purpose is the following:

1 To list the questions the interviewer is to ask, in the precise words to be used and in the right sequence.
2 To provide space for recording the answers, usually in such a way that they can be readily analysed. Frequently a 'magnetic' pencil is used, so that an electronic device can read off the marks and transfer them directly to punched tape ready for computer analysis.
3 To record details of the respondent – age, sex, occupation etc., and sometimes such other factors as whether he is a car-owner or not, or a householder or not, depending on the needs of the particular survey.

12.43 *Types of Question*

Questions asked in interviewing are of three main types, as follows:

1 *Dichotomous*, i.e., answered by a simple yes or no (usually with a 'don't know' column as well).
2 *Multiple-choice*, where a number of possible answers are listed and the interviewer indicates which are selected (sometimes more than one).
3 *Open-ended*, where no particular kind of answer is presupposed and the interviewer has to write in the respondent's answer.

Open-ended questions have the disadvantage of being slow, difficult to analyse, and yielding answers which are perhaps irrelevant or incoherent. On the other hand, they allow the possibility of much fuller answers, with shades of meaning, they reduce the possibility of bias from answers suggested by the researchers, and they may overcome the reluctance of some respondents to answer direct questions. The selection of types of question will depend on the kind of information being sought and the depth required, the type of respondent, and the cost limitations imposed on the research.

12.44 *Some Rules for Framing Questions*

In order to reduce bias, care has to be taken in working out the sequence and wording of questions. Some of the 'rules' are as follows (but judgement and experience play a large part):

1 Questions on matters of a private or emotional nature should come at the end of an interview, as should complicated questions and those requiring thought, so that these are not asked until the respondent's interest is engaged.
2 Conversely, easy questions and those most likely to capture a respondent's interest are placed at the beginning.
3 Questions should be short, easy to understand, and phrased in colloquial language.
4 There should be no ambiguity and, 'double-barrelled' questions should be avoided ('Did you drink coffee with lunch and dinner yesterday?' comprises two questions).
5 Leading questions (i.e. where it appears obvious what answer is expected) must be avoided.
6 Questions that rely heavily on the respondent's memory (Which magazines have you read during the past six months?) must be avoided.
7 Questions must be as precise as possible. For example, in the previous point what do we mean by 'reading' a magazine? From cover to cover? A quick glance? Editorial or advertisements, or both?
8 There are severe limits to the length of questionnaire that will hold a respondent's interest. To go beyond them increases the risk of ill considered or flippant answers.

12.5 Structured and Unstructured Interviews

So far we have considered interviews in which the interviewer asks specific questions listed on a questionnaire (or, for example, in postal surveys, in which the respondent is asked to read and answer the questions). These are known as 'structured interviews'. Often, especially in industrial marketing research, it is not possible, or not the best technique, to do this, and an 'unstructured interview' is used. In these the interviewer has a general idea of the ground to be covered (and may be given a list of questions for his/her guidance), but extracts the information through a guided conversation with the respondent instead of through specific questions. The respondent is encouraged to talk about the area of interest in his own way. The interviewer makes notes or (with the respondent's permission) uses a tape-recorder.

12.6 The Socio-economic Classification

Although the idea of 'class' is becoming increasingly suspect, at any rate in this context, it is often convenient to be able to break down the population into groups. Since there is often a degree of correlation between occupation and life-style (the latter in turn having some influence on buying habits etc.), the classification now commonly used is based on occupation of 'head of household'. This is described in great detail in a document published by the National Readership Survey, for which it was originally developed. In outline the classification runs as follows:

		% of UK Population
A	(Higher managerial administrative or professional)	3.2
B	(Intermediate managerial administrative or professional)	13.4
C1	(Supervisory, clerical, junior administrative or professional)	32.2
C2	(Skilled manual workers)	31.7
D	(Semi-skilled and unskilled manual workers)	20.9
E	(State pensioners, widows, casual and lowest grade earners).	8.6

By using this classification (usually simplified into AB, C1, C2, DE), data produced in different surveys can achieve a higher degree of comparability than would be the case if a different classification were used. It is for this reason that the system continues in use, although many people have reservations about it.

12.7 Using Secondary Data

Because it avoids the cost of sampling and interviewing, the use of secondary data (See Section 2.5) has obvious advantages. Naturally there are snags, too, for the sources are not always obvious or easy to locate, and the information is not always available in a form that makes it easy to use for the purpose in hand. There is also the question whether the cost of re-analysing data will be so high that gathering fresh primary data will in the long run be cheaper.

Sources are an easier matter to deal with. There are a number of 'sources of sources', i.e. books of reference that indicate where various kinds of information may be found. Most government statistical offices issue a guide to what is available in their own files, as do organizations such as O.E.C.D., UNO, GATT and the E.E.C. Commission.

Good reference libraries contain many books, of which one example is Gordon Wills's *Sources of U.K. Marketing Information*. A cheap ready-to-hand source list is *Principal Sources of Marketing Information*.[5]

12.8 Analysis and Interpretation

The results of the fact-gathering part of a marketing research operation will be a large pile of completed questionnaires in the case of a survey, or masses of figures gathered as secondary data from various sources. The way this material is analysed and presented is a crucial factor in how valuable the research will be.

Questionnaires must frequently be edited as a first stage in processing: that is, they must be carefully scrutinized by an experienced person who will reject obviously unreliable questionnaires, and correct or complete any answers not clearly written in by the interviewer (but where it is obvious what is meant). In appropriate cases the editor will check that the various answers in the questionnaire are consistent with each other, that the answers are not merely frivolous and so on.

The questionnaires screened in this way will then be processed to extract the data in tabular form. This is almost invariably carried out by computer as even small surveys can be processed using standard soft-ware.

Once the information is available in the form of tables of figures, their significance must be examined and interpreted. This interpretation will emerge finally as a report, which will draw attention to the similarities, discrepancies, changes and other important features the analysis has uncovered. This stage must also be carried out when secondary data is being used, although most of the actual processing of figures may already have been done.

Opinions vary on how far marketing researchers should go in pointing out what can be inferred or deduced from the figures they present. Normally the report will be read by people unfamiliar with figures of this kind, so they will need some guidance as to what the figures mean. How much help depends on the individual situation. However, the key point is one made in Chapter 2. Marketing research is only of value when it enables better decisions to be made. So taking a management decision will normally be the final stage in the process.

12.9 Summary

1 Most market research uses statistical sampling methods to obtain a close approximation of the views or behaviour of an entire universe by interviewing a relatively small representative selection from it.
2 Sample size is determined by:

   (a) the degree of accuracy required,
   (b) the cost that is acceptable,
   (c) the size of the smallest sub-unit of those interviewed that has to be analysed.

   In practice (c) is most often the decisive factor.

3 The two main sampling methods are the following:

   (a) Random sampling, in which each unit in the universe has an equal opportunity of being included and interviewers are instructed who to interview.
   (b) Quota sampling, in which the interviewer selects people to be interviewed, but according to instructions designed to ensure that each group within the universe is proportionately represented.

4 Stratified sampling and multi-stage sampling are ways of arriving at a representative sample without incurring the cost of a widely scattered sample of the entire universe.
5 Bias – the tendency for distortion to creep in for various reasons – must be guarded against in all marketing research. Common sources of bias are:

   (a) sampling errors,
   (b) prejudiced interviewing,
   (c) faulty questionnaire design.

6 Interviews may be structured (based on specific questions the interviewer must ask) or unstructured (consisting of 'guided conversation').
7 Questionnaires must be carefully framed and worded so as to encourage response and avoid ambiguity and bias.
8 The socio-economic classification is commonly used in order to stratify members of the public in terms of occupation and income.
9 Secondary data can often provide the necessary information at lower cost.
10 Analysis and interpretation of the results is a key stage, which should lead to management decisions.

References

1 For those who wish to have some idea, Smallbone, Douglas W. *The Practice of Marketing* (Staples Press, 1965) gives an outline of the basic statistical approach, and any introductory textbook on statistics will do the same.
2 In *Lectures in Market Research* (Crosby Lockwood, 1969). Adler's book is outstanding in its clarity and still the best source of a quick general understanding.
3 In *Marketing Research* (McGraw-Hill, 1957). Crisp's book is an excellent 'bible', in which to delve deeper into particular aspects.
4 ibid.
5 Published by the Information and Marketing Intelligence Unit of The Times Newspapers Ltd.

Further Reading

Davies, Anthony H. *The Practice of Marketing Research* (Heinemann, in association with CAM, 1976).
Thomas, D. 'Riddles of Market Research', *Management Today* (March 1968); included in *Modern Marketing Management* (Penguin, 1971), p. 121.

Questions for Discussion

1 (IM June 1983) Random sampling is regarded by theorists as giving much more reliable results in survey research than quota sampling, but the latter is much more frequently employed in market research surveys. How would you account for the fact that practice is so willing to accept a theoretically inferior method?
2 Why is a pilot survey frequently an important stage in carrying out a marketing research survey?
3 (CAM Nov. 1982) What are the advantages and disadvantages of the following survey techniques: personal interviewing, telephone interviewing, post questionnaires?
4 What likely sources of useful secondary data can you suggest for the following?

   (a) A civil engineering company seeking opportunities to tender for road building contracts on new housing estates.
   (b) A car radio manufacturer wishing to establish what his approximate market share is.

5 (IM Nov. 1982) Outline the main rules of questionnaire design for *either* a telephone *or* a mail research survey. Use these rules to show how you would distinguish between a well designed and a poorly designed questionnaire.

13. *How Personal Selling Works*

'When all the theorists and planners have had their moment and the production, finance and labour problems have been solved . . . then someone, somewhere has to go out and knock on someone's door and sell.'

L. A. Rogers, *Sales Management*

13.1 The Importance of Personal Selling

We saw in Section 8.4 that, although advertising and related forms of promotion can often communicate with customers far more cheaply, personal selling still normally has a more important role. This is mainly for two reasons, as follows:

1 Personal selling can deal with the whole of the selling process from making initial contact with a customer to closing the deal and taking the money. Other forms of promotion rarely can.
2 The person-to-person situation is far more flexible than other forms of promotion. An advertisement can only deliver a standard message to the average customer, but a trained salesman can establish each customer's individual needs and frequently can help to shape the product to fit these needs. At worst he can highlight those attributes of an existing product that fit in with the customer's requirements particularly and thus score heavily over alternative, impersonal methods of persuasive contact.

We also saw in Section 8.4 that the terms 'selling' and 'salesman' embrace a very wide range of different situations – from the dairy or bakery roundsman, whose task is primarily to deliver the goods and take the money, to the highly qualified salesman of technical products, who may help to establish the precise need and then join with designers or technicians in developing the product. There will sometimes be a need for 'creative' selling, in order to capture the imagination of the customer and show how his needs can be better met in ways he had not previously considered (for example, by a numerically controlled machine tool or a new materials handling system that will substantially cut production costs).

In Section 13.2 we consider the qualities called for in selling of this professional and creative kind. But remember that there is the wide range of selling jobs touched on in Section 8.4 and listed more fully in Section 13.4.

13.11 *Who Needs Salesmen?*

It can be argued that, if the marketing job has been done properly, there is no need for the selling function. If customers' needs have been properly established through marketing research, if technical research and development have produced a product that meets those needs, and if a sound distribution system has

150

been established to make the product readily available to customers, who needs a salesman?

A supermarket, for example, appears to present a picture from which the salesman is totally missing. The customers select their own purchases from the shelves without advice or persuasion from anyone except the advertiser. However, the salesman is still of enormous importance. Salesmen will have worked very hard to ensure that their companies' products are bought in large quantities by the buying departments of the supermarket chains, since many alternative sources of similar products are usually available. Other salesmen (perhaps with a different name, such as 'merchandisers') will have worked with each store manager to get the best position and the most eye-catching display possible for their companies' products. The salesmen are there – even though unseen to the casual observer.

13.12 *The Role of the Salesman*

There are, in fact, a number of jobs that have to be done, and frequently only the salesman can do them, even when the marketing task has been thoroughly and carefully carried through and a product that does match the need has been developed. One important reason for this is that very few purchases are made on purely objective criteria. Certainly a product will need to do the task expected of it satisfactorily, but with most consumer products and very many industrial products that is virtually taken for granted. The customer is then choosing from a whole range of products, any one of which will do the job. Other factors then come into the picture.

Thus, visual design, colour and 'appearance' generally have great importance, even with industrial products. Concepts such as reliability are partly a matter of objective assessment, but include such subjective factors as 'Can I trust this company to put it right if anything goes wrong?'

The role of the salesman, therefore, includes the following:

1 To understand the customer's subjective (psychological) needs and to demonstrate how his products will satisfy them. In some cases (such as life insurance) the customer may initially have only the vaguest idea what his requirement is, and the salesman will have to work it out for him.
2 To negotiate. Very often there is a gap between the price being asked for a product and what the customer is willing to pay. The easy way to close the gap is to cut the price, but profit is then sacrificed. The salesman can solve the problem in another way, which is to enhance the value of the product by demonstrating its particular benefits to the customer and showing how paying a higher price will bring additional value. In some cases (such as cars and certain industrial equipment) the negotiation will frequently necessitate agreeing a 'trade in' price for the customer's present model.
3 Two-way communication. The company needs to communicate information to its customers. Often the salesman is the most effective channel (letters, leaflets and other written communications may never be read, partly because they are likely to be couched in general terms rather than speaking directly to the customer's particular situation). The company also needs feedback from its customers – what pleases them and what annoys them about the service being

provided. What are their future plans and what opportunities for profitable sales will these offer?

13.2 The Selling Process

We saw in Section 10.1 that the mechanisms of the buying process are not yet
clearly understood, although the section went on to summarize some of the
complex factors known to be present. Similarly, the selling process is not totally
understood. Communication is part of it (Sections 8.5 and 16.61), as is persuasion
directed to the changing of attitudes (Section 10.2).

Richard R. S. Hill and Edward W. Cundiff[1] stress that most theories on the
selling process are 'experiential', i.e. they are based on experience of what is
known to work, rather than any understanding of why and how it works.

One of the 'experiential' theories most commonly used is the AIDAS one,
outlined in 16.61, which can help to describe the personal selling process as well
as the advertising one. However, AIDAS does not explain in any depth how the
process works. Another is the 'Buying Formula' theory, which puts the emphasis
on the buyer, who is seen as having a clear understanding of a problem he is trying
to solve. The salesman's role is then to help the buyer towards a satisfactory
solution, as follows:

$$\text{Need (problem)} \rightarrow \text{Solution} \rightarrow \text{Purchase} \rightarrow \text{Satisfaction}$$

However, all approaches of this kind, while they help one to appreciate the
steps in the buying/selling process, give little insight into the psychology of
buying and selling, and a much more complex model (such as that suggested in
Section 10.1) is necessary to demonstrate all the factors that may play a part.
Simplistic approaches such as AIDAS have their main value in sales training.
They help the salesman to organize his actions better without expecting him to
grasp the full complexity of why people react the way they do.

A fuller understanding is likely to come eventually through the behavioural
sciences and the following two examples of this kind of approach will give an
indication of what may eventually emerge.

13.21 *The Theory of Cognitive Dissonance*

This theory has been the subject of a number of experiments, but mainly in
respect of advertising. Dissonance (disharmony, frustration) is a state of
psychological tension, which may result from purchasing a product, especially if
it is an expensive one. People try to keep their 'cognitions' (their set of beliefs
about people, products etc) in a state of harmony. When a choice has been made
between several products, the buyer may experience 'cognitive dissonance'
through anxiety and doubt as to whether the product will perform as he expected
and whether his expenditure was wise. An important part of the salesman's task is
to reassure the buyer that his decision was sound and to re-emphasize the benefits
the purchase will bring. Car salesmen generally do this instinctively or through
experience when, as their customer takes delivery, they make remarks such as
'This car will give you hundreds of miles of happy motoring, Sir; you and your
wife are really going to enjoy travelling in it'.

13.22 *The Buyer-Seller Dyad*

Here, the salesman and his customer are viewed as a 'dyad', that is a social situation for two persons, and the essence of the selling process is the interaction between the two. An important finding of these studies is that the more alike the salesman and his prospect are, the greater likelihood of a sale (this is true not only for physical characteristics such as age and height but also for such factors as education, politics, smoker or non-smoker). Particularly interesting is the fact that people who have bought from a salesman tend to see him as more like themselves than is in fact the case. 'Selling as a dyadic relationship – a new approach', writes F. B. Evans.[2]

13.3 What Makes a Salesman?

In the light of what we have said so far, is it possible to list the attributes of a good salesman? Only to some extent, mainly because the attributes required will vary enormously, depending on the kind of selling situation. For example, in many industrial selling jobs a high degree of technical competence will be necessary; and special qualities will be needed for a man who is expected to seek out his own 'prospects', as against one who has merely to call regularly on established buyers of his company's products.

After seven years of study, David Meyer and Herbert M. Greenberg[3] came up with just two vital qualities:

1 *Empathy*. The ability to feel as the customer does.
2 *Ego Drive*. A strong personal need to make the sale (not simply for monetary reward).

In many situations the ability to communicate effectively will be important, and in others some strong *creative* qualities will be necessary, in order to identify ways in which potential customers can benefit from the products available. Occasionally the tough-skinned, 'foot-in-the-door', rather brash type of selling may be called for (perhaps still what comes to many minds as 'typical' salesmanship). But this is increasingly rare, as the general level of sophistication of both products and customers rises.

13.4 The Kinds of Selling Situation

We have already touched on the fact that there are many different kinds of selling situation. One excellent breakdown of these is that given by Robert N. McMurray,[4] who lists the following 'positions':

> *Positions where the salesman's job is predominantly to deliver the product, e.g., milk, bread, fuel oil* – His selling responsibilities are secondary. Obviously good service and a pleasant manner will enhance customer acceptance and hence lead to more sales. However, few originate many sales.
> *Positions where the salesman is predominantly an inside order-taker, e.g., the haberdashery salesman standing behind the counter* – Most of his customers have already made up their minds to buy. All he does is serve them. He may use suggestive selling and upgrade the merchandise they buy, but his opportunities to do more than that are few.
> *Positions where the salesman is also predominantly an order-taker but works in the field, as*

the packing house, soap, or spice salesman does – In his contacts with chain store personnel, he may even actually be discouraged from applying the hard sell. As with the delivery salesman, good service and a pleasant personality may enhance his personal acceptance, but he too does little creative selling.

Positions where the salesman is not expected or permitted to take an order but is called on only to build good will or to educate the actual or potential user – Examples here are the distiller's 'missionary man' or the medical 'detailer' representing an ethical pharmaceutical house.

Positions where the major emphasis is placed on technical knowledge, e.g., the engineering salesman who is primarily a consultant to the 'client' companies.

Positions which demand the creative sale of tangible products like vacuum cleaners, refrigerators, encyclopaedias – Here the salesman often has a double task: first he must make the prospect dissatisfied with his or her present appliance or situation, then begin to sell his product.

Positions requiring the creative sale of intangibles, such as insurance, advertising services, or education – This type of sales is ordinarily more difficult than selling tangibles, of course, because the product is less readily demonstrated and dramatized. (Intangibles are often more difficult for the prospect to comprehend.)

13.5 What a Salesman Does

It will be clear from what has gone before that a salesman's job may include many different tasks and call for many different skills. He will normally have to drive a car and organize his journeys, write reports and keep accurate records. He may need to analyse his territory and pinpoint good prospective customers. He may deliver goods, set up in-store displays, expedite deliveries from the factory and deal with customers' complaints. Certainly, in most instances, he will be responsible for ensuring a continuing happy relation with customers rather than just conducting a once-for-all sale.

Even apart from all these peripheral duties, the selling process is a complex one, which may include some or all of the following stages:

1 Creating effective contact, at all levels. In industrial selling particularly, the purchase will be influenced by a number of different people (a decision-making unit – D.M.U.). Design engineer, works manager, buyer and finance director, make up one typical D.M.U. (See Section 13.5). The salesman will need to identify and communicate with them all. In other cases only individuals need be contacted, but they must be found from a wide population. Locating a householder who is currently in the market for a washing machine or a car is not easy. Where do you start?

2 Establishing effective communication, with all the relevant people and in both directions.

3 Establishing the customer's needs, which may include identifying problems the customer himself is not clearly aware of.

4 Demonstrating how the company's product can satisfy those needs, which may necessitate the full range of informative and persuasive techniques.

5 Getting a profitable order, which may mean detailed negotiations, arranging credit and bringing carefully calculated pressure to bear on the customer to 'close the sale.'

6 Ensuring customer satisfaction, by making certain that the right product is

delivered on schedule and performs well, that installation is correctly carried out, and pre- and post-sales service is given (including perhaps such things as training customers or their staff to operate and maintain equipment).

7 Creating goodwill and a situation in which future business will develop.

In addition to all this, the salesman must be able to plan his own time and activities so that they are as productive as possible.

13.51 *Decision-making units*

Identifying who are the members of a decision-making unit, what their precise role is and how they can be influenced is a most important aspect of the sales force task. Although this is especially true in industrial markets, it may well apply in other situations. For example, insurance and double-glazing salesmen know that it pays to talk to both husband and wife as both play a part in the decision to buy (even in everyday purchases like breakfast cereals, various members of the household – especially children in that example – have a strong influence and this fact is recognized in the way such products are advertised).

Decision-making units may contain people in some (or even all) of the following categories:

1 *Users*. Those who will actually operate the word-processor or drive the truck; they may well be consulted by those authorizing the purchase and certainly can have a vital effect on post-purchase satisfaction and hence future sales.
2 *Buyers*. The professional purchasing people; their influence tends to be very strong with routine purchases (such as raw materials, standard components, etc.) but other voices become more important if a high technical input is necessary or if heavy capital investment is involved.
3 *Influencers*. People not obviously involved in the buying process may yet influence it strongly (e.g. doctors are unlikely to prescribe a drug not approved of by specialists and consultants).
4 *Deciders*. Decisions may be taken 'down the line' for low-cost or routine purchases but are usually at top level for those where big money is involved; however there can be surprising departures from this norm.
5 *Gatekeepers*. Those who 'get in the way' (buyers who resist the desire of a salesman to talk to design engineers, secretaries who 'protect the boss', etc.); advertising, exhibitions and so on can be a way of by-passing them.
6 *Specifiers*. Architects specify building materials, design engineers specify components and it is very difficult to have the specifications altered later, sometimes making selling impossible if one's own product does not 'meet the spec.'; such situations have to be recognized and the specifier convinced early on that a specification embracing our product will satisfy his requirement.

13.6 Recruiting and Training Salesmen

13.61 *The Importance of Good Salesmen*

With this complexity of tasks and with the characteristics of a good salesman, including such subjective matters as empathy and enthusiasm, it is clear that finding good people for the job will not be easy. Yet it is extremely important. The difference in performance between the best salesmen and the worst can be very marked. A salesman costs his company a great deal of money, too, £10,000 p.a. on average according to a survey summarized in *Marketing*, December 1976 (by 1983 the figure had doubled). The following key questions will decide whether this money is being well spent:

1 Was the right man selected in the first place?
2 Has he been trained to bring out his full potential?
3 Is he motivated to give of his best?
4 Is he being properly managed and given sound direction?

The last point is the subject of Chapter 14. Clearly the sales force is a vital (and expensive) part of a company's resources. Its effective management is a matter of extreme importance.

Motivation is dealt with in Section 13.7. We go on here to discuss selection and training.

13.62 *Good Salesmen – Born or Made?*

This is an old question with no final answer. Clearly some qualities, such as empathy, are to some extent inborn and cannot easily be acquired by those who do not possess them. But often they exist in a latent form and can be 'brought out'. Other qualities, such as technical know-how, are acquired by training and experience.

This raises another hoary question. Is it better when seeking a technical salesman to start with a salesman and give him the technical knowledge, or should you start with a technical man and attempt to teach him how to sell? Again there is no final answer. Much will depend on the selling situation. If, in essence, it calls for a highly technical discussion, then a high degree of technical knowledge on the part of the salesman will be essential, because the matching of customer need with technological solution is the essence of the sales task. Some understanding of how the sales process works will be an additional advantage, and can easily be provided by suitable training. In many other situations a good salesman can quickly be given sufficient technical knowledge – a car salesman does not have to be able to design cars or even discuss their technicalities in great detail; and a washing-machine salesman needs to know what his product will do, but requires no knowledge of hydraulics or turbulence effects, or of the design of electric pumps.

In general, then, while it will be helpful to seek out individuals with the 'right' personal characteristics, some degree of training can be and usually must be given. But in many cases specific experience (e.g. in some technical field) will be sought.

13.63 *Recruiting Salesmen*

In a sense recruiting salesmen is no different from recruiting other staff. The problems will be the same and failures and inadequacies will result from the same causes. The essentials are the following:

1 Be quite clear what is the job to be done. A job specification should be drawn

up, setting out in some detail what the job comprises. All too often this is not done, or is inadequately done, and the recruiter has no clear knowledge of what he is looking for.

2 Be clear what qualities the job calls for: e.g. if the sales job is for a technical product, some technical knowledge may be necessary. How much and in what areas? If the salesman has to find his own 'leads', he may need to be a much more 'aggressive' type than if he is simply calling on existing customers.

3 Be clear how the job will be organized and controlled. Are we looking for someone who will work under close supervision or on his own? Is meticulous record-keeping called for or not? Will he be given training or is previous experience of this kind of selling essential?

There are three main sources of recruits: (a) from within the company, (b) from another sales force (maybe a competitor or maybe from a different field), and (c) from some other kind of job entirely. Choices (a) and (b) each have their merits: someone already in the company will need less training in the ways and background of the company, and perhaps will already have a high level of product knowledge; and someone who has done a precisely similar job with another company has obvious advantages, but may find it difficult to adapt to different ways and to switch his loyalties quickly. Alternative (c) may pose a heavy training burden if the job demands a high level of product knowledge, especially if the man has little sales experience.

13.64 *The Selection Process*

Selecting salesmen is basically no different from selecting any other type of employee, except that it may be marginally more difficult to spot a potentially good salesman because of the importance of the personal qualities of empathy and drive referred to above. Many companies, therefore, now use psychological tests in an attempt to select on the basis of these characteristics. Otherwise, the following normal 'screening' procedure is used:

1 Preliminary selection of 'possibles' on the basis of letters or telephone calls giving brief details of the applicant.

2 Pinpointing of 'probables' by scrutiny of application forms sent to those selected at stage 1.

3 Final selection on the basis of one or more interviews with each 'short-listed' candidate. An important principle here is that normally the final decision should be open to very strong influences by the person (area sales manager or whatever) who will directly supervise the new recruit. Since he will carry the praise or blame for the success or failure of the team, he must take part in choosing its members.

A most important aspect of interviewing is that the interviewers will be asking themselves 'How will this man appear to our customers?' It is the customer who must ultimately find him satisfactory.

13.65 *Training Salesmen*

As with recruiting, the vital need in training salesmen (or anyone else) is to be clear about what purposes they are being trained for, and precisely what they need to know. While too little knowledge can be dangerous, to attempt to make people acquire more knowledge than they need is very expensive, and may provoke resistance through boredom or frustration ('Why don't they stop wasting my time and let me get on with the job I was hired for?').

Training generally will fall into the following categories:

1 *Knowledge of the company*. Since the salesman represents his company, he will need some knowledge of its size, structure and achievements to pass it on to his customers and others. A salesman who is ignorant of his own company is unlikely to command respect or generate confidence.

2 *Knowledge of his product(s)*. He will need to have detailed knowledge of his product(s), especially of what they will do for the customer (how they are made is usually of much less importance).

3 *Technical knowledge*. Some salesmen will need to have considerable technical knowledge of how the customer will use the product, in order to carry out, for example, discussions in the buyer's own language and in order to establish clearly what the buyer's needs are.

4 *Procedural knowledge*. All salesmen need to understand clearly how orders are processed, how delivery and servicing are carried out, what credit can be permitted and so on, (a) so as not to misinform their customers, and (b) to ensure smooth processing of orders. Similarly, they must be clear what records they are required to keep, what expenses they can claim, how their car is to be maintained and serviced and similar 'good housekeeping' details.

5 *'Professional' knowledge*. A salesman needs regular training and up-dating in the job of selling. Even the best needs to be helped to improve his techniques from time to time. What the training consists of will depend on the situation and the men, but might include, for example, cold canvassing (how to locate new customers), effective demonstrations, overcoming typical buyers' 'objections', and closing the sale (ways of bringing the customer to the point of buying or signing an order).

Training can be given by training organizations outside the company or on an 'in-company' basis, the latter either (a) on the job, or (b) in-house, i.e. at the company's own training centre or in premises hired for the purpose, where the company's own staff or specialists brought in from outside (often a mixture of both) act as trainers.

Much of the training will need to be given as part of a planned induction process. However, there is normally also a need for continuous training, for the following reasons:

1 The amount of training required may be too much for the total process to be completed in one session.

2 Further training after practice 'in the field' is often a good way of reinforcing acquired skills.

3 The urgency of getting the man or woman into action may make a 'crash programme' necessary, with the gaps filled in later.

4 Products change, policies change, market conditions change, and such changes need to be communicated to all staff on a planned basis.

5 Skilfully used, a series of training sessions can help to keep salesmen fully

motivated – it is very easy for people operating on their own to become apathetic and no longer fully aware of the total team effort supporting them.
6 As the members of the sales team gain experience, they may need training specific to their personal situation, so that they can develop their own full potential and also bring maximum benefit to their customers and their company.

Ideally, each member of the team should be kept under regular scrutiny, and talked with at intervals to establish in what ways he needs help. Appropriate training should then be made available. In this way people can constantly progress and improve their (and the company's) performance. Regular and well conducted training contributes to a good level of morale.

13.66 *Methods of Training*

Continuous training does not necessarily mean pulling people away from their normal area of operation to the company training centre or some similar location. Much training can be done 'on the job' by the immediate supervisor. Area sales meetings can similarly be used for training purposes by the area manager, perhaps supported on occasions by specialist (e.g. technical staff or sales trainers from head office). The company's sales manual will cover most of the headings set out in Section 13.65 (*see* also Section 14.7).

Some companies' need for sales training is so large and so continuous that they maintain a full-time staff of trainers to carry it out. In others the sales director or marketing director and members of his staff will carry it out personally. This can be supplemented by people from specialist sales training companies. They will, if required, survey training needs, make recommendations and supply the staff to carry them out.

All this is the 'in-company' approach to training. An alternative is to send sales staff on courses and seminars (along the lines of those run by the College of Marketing, for example) offered by specialist organizations on an 'allcomers' basis. These have the merit that delegates can share experiences and benefit from insights gained in situations other than their own. Furthermore a small number of people (even individuals) can be trained in this way without the company having to bear the cost of mounting a special training exercise. But such courses are inevitably less precisely focussed on the training needs of a particular company.

13.7 Motivating Salesmen

Motivation has been described as the difference between 'Can he?' and 'Will he?' A man or woman may have all the necessary personal attributes and all the necessary knowledge, but without being activated these are valueless.

Those factors that motivate a person to purposeful activity are commonly called incentives, and those which deter him from it disincentives. To motivate a salesman, we need to provide the maximum weight of incentives, counter-balanced by as few disincentives as possible.

The word 'incentives' has become associated with direct or indirect financial reward, but this is only one factor in motivating a salesman. Good support from his company, a structure that enables him to feel he has command of the situation, and timely praise and encouragement are all important, as is the good performance of his colleagues. Disincentives include frustration through lack of support from his 'boss', poor product performance and deliveries etc. (and consequent complaints from customers), and lack of reward or commendation for 'a job well done'. Since selling is frequently a lonely job and very dependent on the individual's own efforts, motivation is a very important ingredient in success.

It is usually found that salesmen more than most (although it is true of everyone to some extent) need constantly remotivating. This is probably due to the following reasons:

1 The job is a lonely and isolated one, and frequently the salesman feels 'rejected' because he cannot make a sale on most of his calls.
2 Like everyone else, he has personal and family troubles. Because the job takes him away from home and is in other ways demanding, he may have more than the usual difficulty in handling them.
3 Most people in any case operate below their true capacity unless there is some special gain to be had in terms of money, personal satisfaction or social recognition.

Management's response to this can come in three areas:

1 Creating a generally congenial climate within the company, with good working conditions, opportunities for advancement etc.
2 Personal interest by the salesman's immediate 'boss', with whatever help and support is possible through any personal difficulties.
3 Direct incentives – these we discuss under the next heading.

13.71 *Methods of Remuneration*

Salesmen either earn a salary or are paid a commission on sales. Important decisions have to be taken as to (a) whether one or the other or both of these methods is to be employed, and (b) if commission is paid, on what basis it is to be calculated.

Many people feel that there should be at least some element of commission in order to provide a very necessary incentive; otherwise, they argue, the last call of the day may not be made, the extra effort may not be summoned to convince a potential customer to buy. With a commission system the good hard-working salesman will be rewarded, the less good and the idle will be penalized.

Unfortunately there are complications. For example, what do you do about the 'lucky' salesman who happens to have a territory with many large potential buyers and rather weak competition (while his colleague a few miles away has fierce competition in an area of much lower total potential)? Many sales, especially in the capital goods field, may take many months to negotiate. Is the salesman to have no income meanwhile? And what about the person who closes the deal someone else has been negotiating for many weeks? Who gets the commission?

Even from the company's point of view, all is not simple. Fixed salaries have the advantage of being known in advance and therefore easy to budget. On the other hand, although salesmen operating on commission means that the company only pays out when it has sales to generate the money, larger sums than anticipated can be payable when sales increase sharply and there will be a problem

of drastic cuts in income when sales fall off for any reason.
Some advantages of salary only are the following:

1 The salesman can be expected, if necessary, to carry out duties, such as merchandising, which are not directly geared to his sales.
2 There will be less temptation to sell only those lines most likely to yield a quick return.

The main advantages of commission only are the following:

1 It may be the only way for an inadequately financed firm to survive until sales start coming in.
2 It may be the only way of paying a part-time agent.

Normally, in large, well established companies at any rate, we are likely to find a basic salary structure probably augmented by some form of commission on sales, bonus schemes (another way of achieving the same result) or an incentive scheme based less directly on simple sales figures (but taking into account, e.g. call rates, new customers obtained or other factors judged to be important).
Commission can, of course, be calculated in a number of ways, as follows:

1 Commission on all orders from the salesman's territory.
2 Commission on sales over and above a basic quota.
3 A differential commission system designed to boost sales of selected products.
4 Annual bonus based on total sales turnover by the team of which the salesman is a member. Payment on the group's, rather than the individual's, results does help to equalize distribution of commission as between different territories, duties and types of customer.

Each of these, and there are other variations, has attractions and disadvantages, and a choice needs to be made according to the demands of the situation.
Often instead of commission as such, success is rewarded in other ways, e.g. prizes (holidays, luxury goods) for salesmen who achieve specified targets.

13.8 Summary

1 Personal selling is a most important form of promotion because (a) it can deal with the complete selling process, and (b) it can react flexibly to meet individual customers' needs.
2 Salesmen form a vital link in the chain of communication for most companies. Their role may include all or some of the following: (a) understanding customers' needs, (b) negotiating, and (c) two-way communication.
3 The selling process is a complex and not completely understood relation between buyer and seller.
4 The qualities required of a good salesman will vary according to the selling situation, but empathy and drive are usually vital ingredients.
5 A good salesman will proceed in the following way:

   (a) create contact,
   (b) establish effective communication,
   (c) establish the customers' needs,
   (d) demonstrate how the company's product can meet those needs,

(e)   get a profitable order,
(f)   ensure customer satisfaction,
(g)   create goodwill leading to future business.

6 Recruiting salesmen entails a clear assessment of the job to be done and the qualities needed.
7 Training should be a continuous process of upgrading the salesman's performance.
8 Motivation is a very important factor in ensuring that performance matches ability; its positive achievement may go far beyond material incentives, such as financial rewards.

References

1 In *Sales Management* (Prentice-Hall, 1969), one of the most authoritative works on the subject.
2 In *The American Behavioral Scientist* (May 1963).
3 In 'What Makes a Good Salesman', *Harvard Business Review* (July–August 1964).
4 In 'The Mystique of Super-Salesmanship', *Harvard Business Review* (March–April 1961).

Further Reading

Chisnall, Peter. *Marketing – a Behavioural Analysis* (McGraw-Hill, 1975). Very clear on the selling process, especially Chapter 12, 'Models of Buying Behaviour'.
Lidstone, John. *Training Salesmen on the Job* (Gower Press, 1975).
Rogers, L. A. (ed.). *Sales Management* (Pitman Paperbacks, 1970).
Smallbone, Douglas W. *Control of the Field Sales Force* (Staples Press, 1966). Gives a detailed study of recruitment and training of salesmen, as does Lidstone above.
Tack, Alfred. *Sell Your Way to Success* (Panther, 1967). Unfortunately for the present purpose most books on selling are of the experiential kind – 'This is how I did it and see how successful you will be if you follow my example'. Tack's is a very good example.

Questions for Discussion

1 Would you expect the information aspect or the persuasion aspect to be more important in selling each of the following products? Say why in each case.

(a)   A brand of cigarettes with low-tar rating.
(b)   A computer controlled machine tool.
(c)   A long-range supersonic aircraft.
(d)   A multigrade engine oil.

2 (IM, June 1983) Sales managers frequently complain that 20 per cent of their salesforce make 80 per cent of the sales. How would you account for this phenomenon and what recommendations would you make to a sales manager

with this problem?

3 Who might be members of the decision-making unit considering the purchase of the following?

(a) A fork-lift truck for stacking reels at a paper mill.
(b) Sheet steel for manufacturing domestic appliances.
(c) Continuous stationery for the computer department of a large nationalized industry.
(d) Car parts for the stores department of the maintenance unit of a large brewery's road tanker fleet.

4 What special qualities might be required in a salesman for

(a) management consultancy,
(b) aircraft,
(c) books,
(d) life insurance,
(e) breakfast cereals?

5 (IM, Nov. 1982) Why is it that although for many companies advertising can communicate with actual or potential customers far more cost effectively than personal selling, in many circumstances there still remains an important role for selling?

6 Would you expect to find more emphasis on salary or on commission in the pay structure for salesmen in the following situations?

(a) Area salesman for a major oil company, calling on independent and company-owned sites.
(b) South American representative of a large civil engineering company.
(c) Junior salesman for a small local printer.
(d) Door-to-door salesman for a company selling plastic bowls and similar household equipment.

14. *How Selling is Managed*

'A sales organization, like any organization, is a group of individuals striving jointly to reach certain common goals . . .'

Richard R. Still and Edward W. Cundiff. *Sales Management*

14.1 The Task of the Sales Force

The kind of sales force a company needs and the way it organizes it, will depend on its marketing objectives. These in turn will be influenced by the kind of markets it is operating in, and its position in those markets.

The sales approach will be very much affected by the company's present position. If it is in control of the majority of the business in an area or in its particular field, it will concentrate on regular service calls to retain existing business. At the other extreme, where competitors dominate the scene, the emphasis will be on pioneering – developing a sales approach appropriate to each major potential customer and backing it with senior management staff (appropriate to the decision-making level within the customer's company) and a full technical team if necessary. The typical situation may call for a mixture of these two approaches. Clearly, however, the type of people needed and the organization and back-up required to support them could vary considerably.

Other factors will similarly influence the type and size of sales organization employed. A company aiming at rapid growth will want a large sales force geared to winning new accounts. A marketing strategy designed to 'pull' products through retail outlets by massive advertising aimed at consumers will lead to a quite different sales organization from the one which emphasizes the 'push' techniques of offering retailers big cash and other incentives to carry stock and then encouraging them to display and sell the goods to consumers.

A company very concerned with creating a long-term build-up of strong customer relations will have a different sales force from one aiming principally at quick short-term profits. A company whose marketing strategy is to sell direct to end-users will need a different sales force from one dealing through a multi-layer distribution chain.

Sections 8.4 and 13.4 outlined the many different types of selling, and which of these the company is concerned with is strongly relevant. The concentration of customers in many markets into a small number of very large customers calls for special sales treatment (see Section 14.12).

14.12 *Key Accounts*

Increasingly a high proportion of a company's revenue may come from a small number of large companies. These 'key accounts' need special treatment partly because of the mere fact of the importance of their business, partly because the way they place contracts may be quite different from the way a small company buys.

Special cases are the large national organizations such as banks, supermarkets, etc. where local managers have some autonomy but where head office exerts a greater or lesser degree of control over buying policy and may want to place large national contracts on favourable terms.

Sometimes the local manager can only place orders for products which are 'listed' by head office. It is then a major sales task to achieve this listing – normally the job of the 'National Accounts' (another term for Key Accounts) sales force. Only when they have succeeded can the rest of the sales force achieve success.

14.2 The Organization of the Sales Force

The company's situation will determine the kind of job a sales force needs to do and the kind of people best fitted to do it. Other factors come into play when we start to consider how many salesmen we shall need. For example, how many points need to be called on, and how frequently? How many effective calls can be made in the average working day?

In Section 9.5 we saw how the marketing department could be organized in various ways, including possible sub-division by region, product, and market. Clearly, the sales force organization would fit into this same pattern.

The Concise Oxford Dictionary's definition of the word 'organize' includes 'make into living being . . . form into an organic whole . . . give orderly structure to,

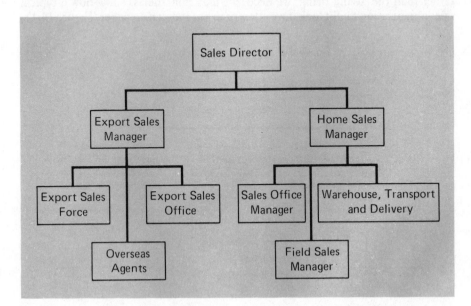

Figure 14.1 Typical sales organization

frame and put into working order'. But by its nature the selling task tends to be fragmented and unorganized. Salesmen are apt to be individuals, whose work takes place away from direct supervision; necessarily, they operate very largely 'under their own steam'. Hence there is a very strong need for an overriding framework that will 'give orderly structure' to the work. But, because the salesman's own personal contribution is so vital, the organization must not be a dead set of boxes and lines on a piece of paper; it must 'make into living being' the various people and facilities that it brings together and whose activities it exists to guide and direct.

This organization will include not only the salesmen calling on customers but many other people as well. In most cases a considerable clerical staff or well-designed computer-based information system is needed to process orders fed in by salesmen. Orders must be recorded and a 'follow-up' system operated to see that they are delivered when due, instructions must be passed to production and/or despatch departments, and sometimes quotations must be prepared or special delivery arrangements made. Thus, behind the salesmen in the field, there will usually be a considerable number of supporting staff, as well as the sales manager and his immediate aides, whose duties include supervising and directing the field sales force.

At the end of the day, the whole of the sales organization, like every other part of the company, must be concerned with producing maximum profit at minimum cost. Anything that contributes to this goes into the organization, and anything that does not comes out.

Having warned of the danger of organization charts becoming dead things rather than the 'living being' we need, we may nonetheless show how a typical sales organization might look if we attempt to put it down on paper (Figure 14.1).

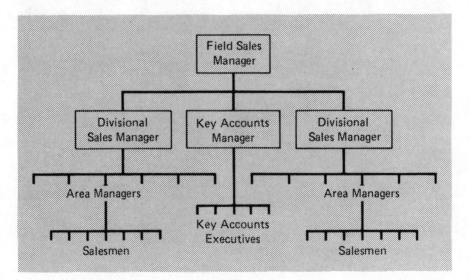

Figure 14.2 Field sales force organization

Depending on the size and nature of the operation, the field sales organization itself might become quite complex, along the lines of Figure 14.2. The 'divisions' of course could follow any of the patterns suggested in Section 9.5.

In management theory terms, most of the people in the various levels in these organizations have a 'line' relation to each other. The commanding officer of an army regiment is able to exercise authority down through the organization, so that his orders eventually result in actions being taken by the privates at section level. At each level the officers and N.C.O.s have 'command' over those beneath them in the organization. This is known as a 'line' relation. By contrast, staff officers, intelligence units and the like have the task of providing information and giving advice, so that theirs is a 'staff relation'. Marketing research is one of the marketing functions of the 'staff' rather than 'line' category.

The sales director and everyone in his organization is very much concerned with causing things to happen, not merely planning and advising. That is therefore a line relation.

An important aspect of the importance of a good organization is the avoidance of conflict. Every member of the team must be clearly aware of what his job is and have a fair idea what he can expect from others. If this is not the case, there will be situations where two people are trying to carry out the same task, leading to wasted effort and needless irritation. Conversely, there is a danger of 'gaps' in the organization, where important tasks (seeing that a customer's order is properly processed, up-dating the salesman's stock of literature) do not get done because it is not clearly a particular person's task to see that it is done.

14.3 The Function of the Sales Office

A valuable outline of the task and importance of a sales office is given by L. A. Rogers:

> There is no standardization of duties in sales offices but undoubtedly the majority of work performed is in servicing salesmen and customers. Such activities will include customer correspondence, telephone enquiries, salesmen's correspondence, order preparation, progressing of order with the works, customer record cards, stock records, statistical records and returns, credit control and possibly market research, advertising, sales training and sales promotion. From this list, one would need to distinguish strictly routine, day-to-day matters from specialist functions. In a consumer goods company which is highly oriented to the consumer market, advertising may form a major part of its sales activities and, as such, would not be classified as a routine daily operation. In a company manufacturing, say, packings and packaging for industry, advertising may be a very minute part of its sales operations and relegated to a routine consideration. The activities which can be regarded as routine or as specialist will depend on the type and size of the company.[1]

14.31 *Export Sales Office*

Exporting comprises a whole series of additional office functions, which can be very burdensome. They include arranging the following as necessary:

1 Shipping and despatch.
2 Customs and currency exchange clearance.

3 Insurance of goods and perhaps of credit (possibly through the government sponsored Export Credits Guarantee Department).
4 Initiating and progressing all necessary documentation.
5 Routine contact with overseas customers and agents.
6 Calculating quotations and prices (which may entail detailed awareness of exchange rates etc.).

Quotations can be made on a variety of bases, but the two most commonly used are f.o.b. (free on board), i.e. delivered to the vessel or other point of departure from the country; and c.i.f. (cost, insurance, freight), i.e. delivered to the port of entry in the country buying the goods.

14.32 *Inside Sales Staff*

We have perhaps so far given the impression that the real selling task is done face-to-face with customers out 'in the field', and that the tasks of people in the sales office are supporting ones. But this is often not the case. Many companies (printers and art studios, for example) have 'inside sales staff', who carry out a great deal of the day-to-day liaison with customers, leaving the 'outside' people free to seek out new business or spend more time with especially important customers.

Where the sales task is of the 'order-taking' type, especially when this is repetitive, virtually the whole selling job can be done on the telephone. A number of companies supplying retailers with a standard consumer item (for example, canned or frozen food, or confectionery) make a regular telephone call to ask the retailer for his re-stocking requirements. The field salesman can then concentrate on opening new outlets, introducing new products, and merchandising.

In the media field the television companies do a great deal of their selling of 'spots' on the telephone, and, in classified advertising particularly, newspapers are well aware of the cost-effectiveness of this approach (many owe a high proportion of their revenue to their highly trained Tele-Ad staff).

Where these inside selling functions are taking place, they will still further complicate the organizational structure. A constant task of sales management is to review the methods being used in the light of their costs and the profit they generate. Since relative costs are constantly changing (1975, for example, saw an enormous increase in telephone and postal charges in the U.K.) and market situations are very fluid, so the sales organization in all its aspects must respond to the changes.

14.4 The Management of the Sales Team

Management has been defined as 'getting things done through other people'. Except in the most unusual circumstances, or when the scale of operation is very small indeed, no one man can carry out by himself the sales task for his company. The sales manager is therefore faced with having to achieve certain aims with the help of many other people. It is his function to direct their efforts so that those aims are achieved. His job will include the following responsibilities:

1 Defining the tasks to be done.

2 Selecting the best people to do them.
3 Setting them individual tasks and objectives.
4 Guiding, instructing and training these people as necessary in the performance of their tasks.
5 Making them accountable, i.e. setting up ways of ensuring that the appointed tasks are carried out or that any shortcomings are noted and corrected.
6 Devising the best form of organization within which all the members of the team can work.

Some of these responsibilities we have already dealt with, but (3) and (5) are given further consideration in Sections 14.5 and 14.6.

14.5 Allocating Sales Territories

We have just indicated that an important aspect of sales management is to define the individual tasks each member of the team is to carry out, and make sure that each of them is accountable. So far as the field sales force is concerned, an important aspect of this is the allocation of sales territories. The starting point, as ever, is the company's marketing objective. If a particular market is to be tackled, how can it be best done? With a typical consumer product, are sales to be direct or through distribution channels, and which distribution channels? If certain types of retail outlets are required, how many are there, how are they spread geographically, and how often will they need to be visited?

With a sophisticated industrial product, such as telecommunications equipment, the market may well be the whole world. But which countries represent the main potential? How do they buy? Is it better to negotiate directly or through agents? Either way, how many salesmen, with what characteristics, will be required, and how many buying points in how many countries can each handle?

From these kinds of question we can begin to develop an idea of the kinds of task each person has to perform and over what area. The amount of support he can be given will further influence the answers – for example, by follow-up phone calls from head office, by merchandising teams or by technical demonstration teams. (Some companies have a 'travelling circus', often in a caravan or even a boat or train, to demonstrate their products and answer technical queries.)

Once the load, in terms of number of customers and their size and complexity, which each man can carry has been arrived at, we can start splitting the total market into 'territories' or 'areas'. Depending on the nature of the market and the product, an area could be a continent (in the case of a technical product with few potential users) or a small part of, say, London or Frankfurt (in the case of a consumer product needing widespread retailer stocking).

A basic dilemma in the allocation of sales territories is whether to divide the total market into areas of equal sales potential or areas of equal work-load. The difficulty arises from the fact that a compact territory with a small number of large users is much easier to work than a much larger territory with smaller users scattered about in it. Many factors go to determine the effective length of a salesman's working day, including driving time, waiting time, administration time (writing reports etc), non-selling activities (e.g. investigating complaints), breaks and selling time. The vital selling time will be influenced by the compactness or diffuseness of the territory. Thus, a salesman's performance will be much affected by the nature of his territory.

The shape of a territory may also have a bearing on the efficiency with which it can be covered. A salesman who is based at one end of his territory will spend more travelling time than one sited in the middle. A territory designed around the transport system can be more efficient than one that ignores it.

14.6 Evaluating Sales Performance

Because of the point made at the end of the previous section, it is not possible to judge a salesman's performance purely by the total volume of turnover he is able to achieve. Turnover will depend very much on the factors just referred to, as well as on the salesman's own efforts and capability.

Yet an important part of sales management is to ensure that people perform as well as they can. This in turn means setting targets that can be achieved. A further important part of the sales manager's task, therefore, is to devise effective ways of evaluating performance. This can become a very complex affair, especially as a salesman's job is rarely simply to increase total sales in the short term, but is likely to include such other matters as the following:

1 Gaining new customers.
2 Keeping numbers of lost customers at a low level.
3 Introducing new products effectively.
4 Carrying out or monitoring merchandising plans.

Thus, any comprehensive evaluation scheme must take account of these and other relevant factors. Actual sales performance will probably be evaluated against a quota, based on what the salesman is judged to be capable of achieving in the light of the particular circumstances of his territory, the tasks he has to perform etc.

Total evaluation will then be under a series of headings, such as (a) performance against quota, (b) new customers gained, and (c) customers lost. A short-term assessment of performance could be made on the basis of (a) number of calls made, (b) ratio of orders to calls, (c) average size of order etc.

14.7 Sales Force Communications

It is obvious from the previous section that a well organized system of communication is an important aspect of sales management. Most salesmen are required to compile regular reports, usually on a daily and/or weekly basis. This reporting provides the sales manager (or the regional sales manager acting on his behalf) with the vital control information he needs to assess whether things are going according to plan. The need for information and its value when received must, of course, be balanced against the loss of effective selling time it may represent (although salesmen are often required to complete their records 'out of hours').

Regular communication is a two-way necessity. The salesman needs a reaction to his reports, both for guidance on how to use his efforts most effectively and also as a boost for his morale (nothing is more soul-destroying than spending hours completing detailed reports that no one seems to read). He also needs a regular supply of information from head office: information about the state of the market, competitors' activities, his own company's forward plans, advertising activities, guidance on how best to present his products and overcome objections, and (depending on circumstances) a whole host of other aspects. Increasingly of course this rapid two-way information system is best provided by equipping salesmen with portable terminals so that they can key straight into a sales office computer.

The sales conference is another important method of imparting information and, at the same time, developing a sense of team spirit and company loyalty, which is otherwise made difficult by the 'lone operator' nature of the salesman's job. Cost pressures may sometimes operate against the large 'set piece' sales conference, and smaller regular conferences with less 'ballyhoo' may take their place. In any case, small regional conferences can be held on a more regular basis.

Newsletters are another important method of keeping salesmen up-dated. There is a danger, however, that they may either usurp or duplicate the vital regular person-to-person communication (face-to-face, by phone or by letter) from the immediate superior – area manager, district manager and so on. In other words, effective public relations is essential (see Section 15.21).

Wherever possible, the salesman should be provided with a full range of sales aids. These can perform the dual function of reinforcing the salesman's own words and ensuring that the company's message reaches the customer exactly as it left head office. Sales literature, sales manuals, visual aids, all have a part to play.

14.8 Summary

1 The nature of the sales task will derive from the company's marketing objectives.
2 Because of the nature of the selling task, effective organization is vital.
3 Organization must be viewed in a flexible way, with changes being readily made in reaction to the fluid situation in the marketplace.
4 The field sales force must be complemented and supported by a suitable sales office team. In some cases a large part, or even the whole, of the selling task will be carried out by 'inside' staff, rather than by a 'field' sales force.
5 In some situations telephone selling assumes special importance.
6 In export selling documentation and administration put additional burdens on the sales organization.
7 The management of the sales organization entails the vital job of translating general objectives into individual tasks and targets.
8 The allocation of sales territories, setting up targets, quotas and the evaluation of performance in relation to them are further crucial aspects of the management task.
9 Effective management is dependent on a good system of two-way communications.

Reference

1 In *Sales Management*, 5th ed. (Pitman, 1970), p. 121.

Further Reading

Kennedy, Gwain. *Everything is Negotiable* (Business Books, 1982).

Kotler, P. *Marketing Management* (Prentice-Hall, 1967), Chapter 19, 'Sales Force Decisions'. Gives clear insight into the key decision areas.

Willsmer, Ray L. *Directing the Marketing Effort* (Pan, 1975), Chapter 15, 'Selling'. Puts the practical point of view, and is consequently a good counter to some of the more theoretical approaches. The books referred to at the end of Chapter 13 all have relevant chapters.

Winkler, John. *Bargaining for Results* (Heinemann, 1982). This and Kennedy's book deal in a stimulating fashion with the increasingly important topic of negotiating business with key accounts.

Questions for Discussion

1 What characteristics would you look for in a regional sales manager:

    (a) in charge of the Midlands region of the U.K. for a grocery products company,

    (b) responsible for Central and South America for a telecommunications manufacturer?

2 Suggest three different situations in which telephone selling could be a suitable sales method?

3 What are the key factors to be taken into account when allocating sales territories?

4 (IM, June 1982) Describe the main elements involved in the management of a salesman by his sales manager and show how these are discharged.

5 What sales aids would you recommend for a sales force selling a range of agricultural machinery?

6 (IM, Nov. 1981) Different sales forces have different roles. What are the main factors that determine the role of a sales force?

15. *What Advertising and Sales Promotion Can Do*

'Each time the decision is made to spend money on advertising it is only because the manufacturer does not know of a more efficient, more economical way to help the sale of his product.'

Simon Broadbent. *Spending Advertising Money*

15.1 What Advertising Is

It is important when discussing advertising to be fully aware of what it is we are talking about. Especially in critical comment, the view taken of advertising is often very narrow, whereas in fact advertising consists of a wide variety of types of message transmitted through many different media.

Generally, when people talk of advertising, they think mainly of advertising on television for household goods such as detergents, for drinks and food, for clothing and confectionery. In fact, the breakdown of advertising expenditure in the U.K. in 1982 (Advertising Association figures) shows a different picture (Table 15.1).

Table 15.1

	£ million	Per cent
Press	1986	63·5
TV	928	29·7
Poster and transport	124	4·0
Cinema	18	0·6
Radio	70	2·2
	3,126	100·00

The next surprise is that, of the £1,986 million spent in the press in 1982 only £515 million (16.4 per cent of total advertising expenditure) was spent in the national newspapers (*Daily Express*, *The Times*, *The Sun*, etc.). A considerably larger amount £737 million (23.5 per cent of total advertising expenditure) – went into the regional newspapers (the local weekly, daily and evening papers).

The breakdown of press expenditure is shown in Table 15.2.

So advertising is not just the beer, soap and cigar commercials on TV. It is also the shop in the High Street advertising its sale in the 'local rag'; the housewife

173

Table 15.2

	Per cent
National press	16·5
Regional press	23·6
Magazines and periodicals	6·7
Trade and technical publications	7·9
Directories (incl. Yellow Pages)	4·0
Press production costs	4·9

63·5 of total advertising
—— expenditure

wanting to sell her old bedroom suite or her husband his sailing dinghy through the 'small ads'; job announcements and company reports; the Government urging us to stop smoking, wear our seatbelts and save fuel; the engineering company announcing a new machine or the mail order company offering its new catalogue; the poster telling us what is on at the local cinema or the Festival Hall; the card in the Underground offering to find us a job or clear our blocked drains; and the back of a bus telling us where we can buy our next car.

Advertising is often the conspicuous part of marketing, the visible 'tip of the iceberg'. Most people know nothing of the complexities of the distribution process, of pricing policies or of product development. But they cannot help being aware of advertising, especially if they are television addicts (and the average person in the U.K. watches TV for some 20 hours a week).[1]

15.2 What Sales Promotion Is

Here we have yet another term that is used by different people to mean different things. The distinction made by a number of authors and one we shall follow here is that 'advertising' describes messages carried in media owned and controlled primarily by people other than the advertiser, and 'sales promotion' messages are carried by media controlled by the company itself.

This puts direct mail in the sales promotion camp, which not everyone would accept, and leaves trade exhibitions a little uncertain. For convenience, we shall deal with them under the sales promotion heading. The terms advertising and sales promotion, then, closely correspond with the 'above and below the line' distinction that is commonly used, in advertising agencies especially. The distinction developed there because 'above the line' media – press, TV, radio – pay advertising agencies a commission, and 'below the line' come direct mail, exhibitions, point-of-sale displays and sales literature, not carrying a commission. The agency's work on them, therefore, must either be 'all part of the service', paid for by the above the line commissions or be the subject of separate charges. The latter is becoming more and more common, as agency profit margins are squeezed harder and harder.

Most frequently the term 'sales promotion' is used to describe a special campaign, usually fairly short in duration, to boost sales of a particular brand or product. Typical techniques are temporary price reductions, gifts, competitions and special displays or events (such as Dutch Dairy Products girls dressed in Dutch costume touring a neighbourhood).

15.21 *The Place of Public Relations*

Still left out on a limb by the above definition is public relations. This is not totally 'controlled' by the company itself, but, although it includes messages carried in media owned and controlled primarily by people other than the advertiser, it differs sharply from advertising. In particular, the content of an advertisement is decided by the advertiser, although the media owner may impose some limitations. With a public relations message, however, the company initiating it has no control at all over the way it finally appears in the medium. Advertising is clearly identified with the company sponsoring it; public relations frequently is not. In any case, messages in the media (press relations) form only one part of what public relations is concerned with. Public relations is a vast subject needing an entire book and only partly is it directly concerned with marketing (see Section 17.8).

15.3 The Role of Advertising

The relative importance of advertising as part of the promotional mix is determined by the following.

1 *The Circumstances*. Advertising is more likely to be used in the following circumstances:

  (a) There are many customers, widely scattered, for a low-cost product (direct personal selling is then usually not economic and retailers do not really 'sell' the product).
  (b) Many people need informing very quickly (e.g. about a new product, an improvement, a price change).
  (c) The distribution chain is long and complex (ultimate customers are remote from the manufacturer).
  (d) The opinions of many people are required in the buying decision (often the case with capital goods).
  (e) The potential customers are not easy to identify and advertising can be used to 'flush them out'.

2 *The Task*. Advertising is particularly good at effecting some stages in the selling process (for example, arousing initial interest, creating brand-awareness, giving post-purchase reassurance). It is less good at others (e.g. making a specific proposal, closing a sale). Whether advertising is the best means of communicating depends on what is being communicated and to whom.

3 *The Product*. Some products can be simply and easily explained in the short time available on radio or TV, or in the limited space of a press advertisement. Others need discussion or specially designing to fit them to the customers' requirements.

4 *Economics*. It is all a matter in the end of cost-effectiveness. Advertising should be used if it enables more people to be given the right message more effectively than in any other way.

15.31 *Some Typical Advertising Tasks*

Because of its strengths, advertising is commonly used to carry out certain marketing tasks.

1 *Announcing New Products and Product Changes.* A new product is introduced, an existing one changed, a new pack or a different price is brought in, the distribution is increased to include new retailers, a special offer is available for a short period – customers and potential customers must be made aware of these changes, and quickly. Short of writing or telephoning to them all, advertising is the only way to do it, especially as in most cases customers cannot be listed by name and address. Even if they could, the cost would be astronomic, and it would still be difficult to achieve overnight. Some industrial markets in which there are a very small number of well known customers are at first sight different. In this case they can best be informed by the sales force or by direct mail. Even here, though, we often have the problem of the decision-making unit (see Section 13.5), not all of whose members will be easy to identify. Advertising may still have a job to do in that case.

2 *Aiding the Salesman.* In industrial marketing, particularly, the reputation of suppliers is a very important factor in purchasing decisions. No one will be eager to buy an expensive and vital piece of equipment from a company he has never heard of. Buyers will be very reluctant to spend time with a salesman from an unknown company.

A similar situation applies in the consumer products field when salesmen call on retailers and other middlemen. He will find it easier to sell to them if (a) they know his company, and (b) they have been informed in advance of the product he wants them to buy. Another factor in this field is that many retailers are reluctant to take in stocks of products unless they will be advertised to the ultimate consumers. Thus, one of the objectives of consumer advertising on T.V. or in the press may be to back up salesmen in their efforts to persuade dealers to stock the product during the crucial 'launch' period.

A subsidiary effect of advertising can often be that it boosts the morale of the sales force.

3 *Entering New Markets and Expanding Old Ones.* As we have already seen, customers have to be both informed and persuaded to try out new products. Except in markets where the cost per unit is high and the number of customers is low (typical of industrial products), advertising is again the only economical way of reaching them.

Retailers are generally not good at selling products, especially new and untried ones, and normally act only as dealers, regarding it as the manu-facturer's task to persuade customers to buy. Very rarely is it sufficient to put products on the shelves and wait for customers to come in – and, as we have already seen, retailers will be reluctant to do even this unless they can be sure of advertising support.

Advertising probably has a job to do when (a) a product has been a success in one area and is now to be introduced to another, and (b) many buyers already exist but more must be found in the same area(s) (e.g. by attracting customers from other socio-economic groups).

4 *Keeping Existing Customers 'Sold'.* It is a mistake to think that, once a product is established in the market, it can simply be left to carry on. This is not so, for three reasons.

First, customers who have bought a product need reassuring that it was a 'wise buy' in the light of all the alternative purchases they could have made. Section 1.6 spoke of 'post-purchase feelings' (see also Section 13.21 on Cognitive Dissonance). These are determined partly by the customer's actual experience of the product in use (does it do what he hoped it would do?), and partly they are psychological. A well known phenomenon is 'buyer remorse' – having made a purchase, it is quite common for people to be worried as to whether they have done 'the right thing'. Reading advertisements for the product they have just bought is one way they obtain the necessary reassurance (it has been established that a high proportion of the readers of car advertisements are people who have just bought the model being advertised).

Second, competitive or alternative products are constantly being offered; 'our' customers are constantly exposed to advertising, displays in shops and other invitations to buy them. The advantages of 'our' product need constant reiteration.

Third, established customers grow old and eventually die, and the new generation has to be told about the product afresh. Products such as Guinness, Bovril, and others, which have been flourishing for 50 years and more, owe their longevity largely to persistent advertising.

5 *Inviting Enquiries.* Many businesses depend very largely on inviting enquiries. Such companies are as diverse as hoteliers, mail order traders and seedsmen advertising their catalogues. They include insurance, unit trust and similar organizations offering details of their services; and manufacturers of industrial products offering to send a salesman to discuss a would-be customer's requirements or to provide a free quotation (e.g. for an office installation or car-leasing agreement). Generally advertisements of this type carry a coupon for the enquirer's name and address – it has been found that this considerably increases the enquiry rate and can also be used to add to the advertisers' list of addresses of potential customers.

This technique is used when a constant stream of new customers have to be found, in contrast to the typical 'packaged household goods' product, where an objective of advertising will probably be to encourage repeat business – part of what Section 17.4 is all about. Most classified advertising falls into this category or the next (houses, used cars and other personal effects are advertised in the 'small ads' columns to attract enquiries from would-be buyers).

6 *Selling Direct.* Some display advertising and much classified advertising aims to complete most of the selling process. Not only many unit trust advertisements but also many for household goods ask for the money and an order to be sent often referred to as 'selling off the page' (see Section 7.31). Many classified advertisements expect to attract enquiries leading to sales that can be 'clinched' over the telephone (e.g. local advertisers of fencing, turf and other garden products). But this is the exception. Most advertising is expected to achieve only part of the total selling process.

7 *Creating a Brand or Company 'Image'.* In Section 8.31, we spoke of the importance of 'branding' in some situations. The way a product is viewed by customers and those who might become customers can be a very important influence on the level of sales. People need to be able to 'relate' to a product, to be able to feel 'this one is for me'. So the way a product is presented, its

personality, must all be expressed in its 'brand-image'. Advertising lends itself well to this task, especially cinema and television advertising, where a wide range of aural and visual ('audio' and 'video' in the jargon of the trade) effects can be used to project the desired 'image'. The product can be made to look staid and reliable or young and 'with it', exciting and new or well-tried and trusty, expensive and exclusive or economical for everyday use – just as the same actor can appear young or old, boring or dashing. Clearly the product when sampled must fit the image created, but this is rarely a problem. The same car, for example, may be both fast and safe, economical on fuel and comfortable to sit in, dashing in appearance and also reliable. It may appear cheap to some and expensive to others. How we talk about it depends on who we believe to be our target market. If it consists of middle-aged civil servants, we may wish to stress the economy, comfort and reliability; if it is young business executives, we may emphasize the dashing appearance and the speed. The car is the same, but with a choice of two quite different brand-images.

Similarly, a company may need to present an 'image' of itself. Business buyers, in particular, have a liking to 'know with whom they are dealing'. Advertisements can present facts about the company – its resources, its financial status, its present customers, its product range and research facilities – which will create a picture or 'image' for its potential customers of what kind of company it is. Clearly, again, the desired image can, to some extent, be selected. The company can stress its financial standing and its long record in the business, its capacity for innovation and quick action, and its reputation for reliability and quality. Advertising can establish this image fast and with a wide audience – a task that might take years to achieve through salesmen or by customers talking to each other 'on the grapevine'.

15.4 The Role of Sales Promotion

In Section 15.2 we drew a distinction between advertising and sales promotion in terms of the media used. We can also make other distinctions, as follows:

1 *Sales Promotion is Often Tactical.* To a large extent advertising is used strategically, i.e. it is part of the continuing 'attack' on the marketplace, often with long-term objectives in view. To create a brand-image, to generate a flow of enquiries, to influence a whole new market favourably towards a product, calls for carefully planned advertising (usually in conjunction with other forms of promotion) over a long period. Even when short-term results are expected, as in direct sales advertising, this response will usually need to be on a frequently repeated basis, so that the advertising must be continuous.

   Sales promotion, on the other hand, is more often tactical, i.e. designed to achieve a short-term and limited objective, possibly in a limited area or through certain outlets. For example, an introductory price cut or premium offer may be made, coupled with special discounts for dealers, in order to encourage dealers to stock and customers to sample a new product. The promotion would continue for a few weeks only. However this tactical aspect must be kept in perspective because continuing use of sales promotion does have long-term effects (see Section 17.2).

2 *Sales Promotion Is Normally Concentrated at Point of Sale.* In general, advertising speaks direct from the marketing company to the customer. Sales promotion usually takes place in close association with the dealers who stock the product. Very frequently, the whole thing takes place 'at the point of sale', i.e., at the place where the customer buys the product. You, the customer, get the free beer mugs from the garage when you pay for the petrol that has just been put in your tank, or the entry forms from the supermarket check-out desk for the holiday competition being run by the makers of the jam you have just bought. Some sales promotion activities ('personality promotions', for example) do take place in the street or (as with some forms of sampling) on a door-to-door basis, but even then there is usually a strong tie-in with local dealers.

15.41 *Some Typical Sales Promotion Tasks*

Sales promotion includes a very wide range of activities, which can be used in all kinds of situations, but some of the most common jobs it is used for are the following:

1 *Encouraging Dealers to Stock.* Most retail dealers feel they already have far too many different products, and every new one means dropping an old one or having more capital locked up in stock. So they need considerable persuasion to take in a new line. They must be convinced it will be profitable for them, which means they must be convinced that customers will buy it in reasonable volume. Sales promotion activities can be used both to help in this argument and provide direct cash incentive (e.g. by way of cash discounts or deals like the '13 bottles for the price of 12' used in the wines and spirits trade).
2 *Encouraging Customers to Sample.* With food products, confectionery etc., for example, it is often crucial that customers try the new product – they are almost certainly already buying an alternative they find reasonably satisfactory. They must be given an incentive to try something new. A special price offer, a 'two for one', or even an exciting display may tempt them sufficiently to make the test.
3 *Combating Competition.* A competitive situation, such as someone else introducing a new product, may call for an intensive short-term promotion of an existing product to ensure that not too many present customers are wooed away, and that, if possible, some new ones are gained to fill any gaps in the ranks.
4 *Improving Distribution.* A similar situation to (1). An existing product may have 'patchy' distribution, and sales promotion techniques can be used to fill in the gaps and gain extra dealers in the poorly represented areas.
5 *Adding Excitement.* A well-established product may suffer from pure familiarity. Since most people are well aware of it, it can become boring. Sales promotions liven it up again and revive interest in it.

15.5 The Social and Economic Justification of Advertising

Advertising (and sales promotion, since the two are not at all distinct in the mind of the general public) comes in for frequent criticism on grounds such as the following:

1 It is a waste of money that would be better spent in price reductions or product improvements.
2 It encourages people to spend money they can ill afford on things they would be better off without.
3 It frequently appeals to the less attractive emotions, such as envy, snobbishness, etc.
4 The sheer weight of advertising 'forces' people to buy things they would not otherwise buy.

Criticism along these lines led to the production of a British Labour Party Green Paper, which proposed in particular a tax on advertising and the setting up of a 'National Consumers' Authority' financed from the proceeds of the tax. The advertising industry in the U.K. has for long believed in voluntary controls by the industry itself (see Section 15.6), and produced a spirited reply to the Green Paper.

This document, *A Commentary on the Labour Party 'Green Paper' on Advertising of March 1972*, was published by the Advertising Association in October 1972, and contains the case in favour of advertising in reply to criticisms of the kind referred to above. Some of the points made are the following:

1 'The consumer not only has the power to choose but exercises it ruthlessly.'
2 'The consumer has spending power nowadays for many goods and services over and above the necessities of life. Industry responds by offering a wide variety of such products to suit as many tastes as possible. No one would want, or can afford, them all. People have to choose.'
3 'The consumer can pick and choose what advertisement he wants to consider. It is well known that his mind and eye shrug off instantly those of no interest to him.'
4 'The process of advertising . . . achieves no more than an interest to try the product and, if that product does not live up to expectations, it is not bought a second time.'
5 'In general economics, the contribution of an efficient low-cost communication system lies in the fast pay-off of investment cost; the avoidance of wasteful production hanging about in the warehouses, the maintenance of steady production and therefore of employment.'
6 'The special value of advertising is its cheapness and rapid spread of product information.'
7 'Consumer attitudes may not be as the writers of the paper would like them to be. They are, however, the product of the material betterment of the mass of the population over the last century. They are the consumers' own choice, and industry and advertising have merely responded to their needs and wishes with products, services and communications. The communications have not created the attitudes; and to restrict the communications will not change the attitudes.'

This book is not the place to try to resolve the argument, but most marketing people – at least in the U.K. – would take the view that our present economic system, in spite of difficulties and disruptions like inflation followed by severe depression throughout the early 1980s, is better than any other available to us. Certainly it is the one we have to work within at present. A key element in it is that consumers are offered a wide choice of products and services by competing organizations. Consumers' choices, in the end, contribute largely to the decisions as to which products and services will continue to be provided, since, without consumer support, companies cannot provide them at a profit. Most people are above the level of 'bare necessities', so that many of the purchases will be used to satisfy needs higher up the hierarchy of needs (see Section 1.6). There will be a wide discrepancy in what different groups of people believe they need. Advertising and sales promotion are among the ways in which competing companies signal to customers what is available to them. The customers then decide.

A survey carried out regularly on behalf of the Advertising Association reported in 1981 that:

> 'Advertising remains extremely low on people's list of concerns. Few people talk about it, fewer still hold strong opinions on the subject, and a tiny minority (2%) feels that a major change is needed in this area. This contrasts with 34% demanding change in the Government, 23% change in education, 30% in trade unions and 11% in politicians.
>
> 77% of the sample approve of advertising and 16% disapprove (7% have no opinion). This follows the trend shown by attitude surveys since 1972, of a continuing increase in the proportion of the sample approving of advertising and a decline in the proportion disapproving. In 1972, 67% of the sample approved and 24% disapproved. It is also clear that young people are more strongly in favour of advertising than older ones; 89% of the 15–24 age group approved, as against 6% disapproving.'

15.6 The Ethics of Advertising and Sales Promotion

Even if the view is taken that advertising and sales promotion are in themselves a valuable part of the economic scene, it is still possible that individual advertisements or campaigns will use methods that are unethical. In the U.K. there is a unique system of voluntary controls, supported by all the major bodies concerned with advertising and representing advertisers, advertising agencies and media. In addition, radio and TV advertising must by law be vetted (the latter before transmission) by agencies of the Independent Broadcasting Authority.

The Advertising Standards Authority, financed by a levy on all advertising in the main media, will examine any advertisements or sales promotion activity complained of by a member of the public. The Authority has prepared a *Code of Advertising Practice* and a *Code of Sales Promotion Practice*, and ensures that activities offending against these *Codes* are amended or withdrawn.

In addition, there is much legislation, such as the Trade Descriptions Acts 1968 and 1972 and the Sale of Goods (Implied Terms) Act 1973, which limit what may be done or said in any selling situation. Other laws, such as the Hire Purchase Acts 1964 and 1965, lay down rules for advertising particular goods or services.

15.7 The Limitations of Advertising and Sales Promotion

It must not be thought that advertising and sales promotion are all-powerful activities. In spite of much loose talk, advertising is not 'brainwashing'; it cannot make people do what they firmly wish not to do. Its power of changing attitudes is real but certainly limited. Indeed, over-enthusiastic statements about a product will probably rebound, because those who try the product themselves will be disappointed with it.

A further limitation is cost. Advertising can be a very expensive activity. Only when it is accurately assessed and given its rightful place in the marketing mix, as part of a properly conceived plan, will it pay dividends. The 'accurate assessment' and 'properly conceived plan' will owe a great deal to sound knowledge of customers and their needs, and much hard work and good judgement in determining how best to meet those needs.

15.8 A Dramatic use of Advertising and P.R.

An important role of advertising is often to help establish or reinforce customers' relationship with a product. A particularly dramatic example hit the headlines in the U.K. during 1983 (see for example *Marketing*, 27 October, 1983).

In the mid–1970s the lawnmower market was dominated by the garden products division of Birmid Qualcast, the established brand leader and biggest advertiser (spending around £250,000) with its cylinder type mowers.

Flymo at this time was also well established with its petrol driven hover mowers, regarded as especially useful for rough grass, holding about 10 per cent of the mower market. But in 1977–8 it had begun to make inroads into the mass end of the market with a lightweight electrical model, backed by TV advertising (previously only explanatory press advertising had been used) and with improved distribution.

As a possible defensive measure Qualcast developed its own hover machine, the Airmo, but did not push it very hard. Trials suggested that the traditional cylinder design was still most appropriate for the average consumer, taking into account the 'finish' it gave to the grass, together with speed and ease of operation. However attitude research showed that two-thirds of the market preferred the hover type because they were perceived as modern and easy to use. When people actually tried both types however the percentages swung the other way.

Further research into consumers' reactions to proposed advertising themes (in story-board form) suggested that an underlying reason for consumers' preference for the hover was that people were a little lazy and saw the hover mower as easy and fast.

Eventually, the arguments for and against seemed to turn on the fact that hover mowers left the grass on the lawn and therefore entailed an extra operation to achieve the same clean result as the cylinder mower. Qualcast developed a strong TV and press advertising campaign (£650,000 expenditure in 1980) with the theme 'For a perfect lawn, the Qualcast Concorde: It's a lot less bovver than a hover'. The advertising also emphasized the Concorde's ability to cut banks and overgrown grass (one of the perceived advantages of the Flymo).

In 1983 Flymo introduced the hover mower with a grass bag. The new Qualcast commercial, based on independent tests, showed the new Flymo and said that it left as much as 40 per cent of the cuttings behind. The uproar created by this 'comparative advertising' (or more unkindly called, by some, 'knocking copy') approach was considerable and led to massive editorial comment in the press, well orchestrated by the Qualcast P.R. consultancy. The outcome appeared to be that Qualcast merely managed to halt the decline in their share of the market. But as the *Marketing* article commented 'Qualcast is clearly happy with its long running and controversial campaign. One is left, however, with a bovversome riddle. The company has gained in turnover and profitability since it began its advertising drive. But it has taken until this year to reverse the march of the hover, perhaps only temporarily. What will happen in 1984?'

15.9 Summary

1 Advertising is the term used to describe 'paid-for' messages of all kinds in media owned and controlled by people other than the advertiser.
2 Sales promotion activities, on the other hand, use tools and media controlled directly by the advertiser.
3 The place of advertising in the marketing mix is determined by (a) the circumstances, (b) the task, (c) the product, and (d) cost effectiveness.
4 The tasks advertising can be usefully employed in include the following:

    (a) Announcing new products and product changes.
    (b) Aiding salesmen.
    (c) Entering new markets and expanding old ones.
    (d) Keeping existing customers 'sold'.
    (e) Inviting enquiries
    (f) Selling direct.
    (g) Creating a brand or company image.

5 Sales promotion is normally tactical (whereas advertising is mainly strategic) and concentrated at point of sale.
6 Sales promotion can be used to

    (a) encourage dealers to stock,
    (b) encourage customers to try,
    (c) combat competition,
    (d) improve distribution,
    (e) add excitement.

7 Advertising and sales promotion are essential ingredients in the competition between companies, which is an important element in our economic system.
8 The unethical use of advertising and sales promotion is restricted both by legal restraints and by the voluntary control system.

Reference

1 During February 1975. See *Facts in Focus* (Penguin, 1975).

Further Reading

Broadbent, Simon. *Spending Advertising Money* (Business Books Ltd, 1975).
Wilmshurst, John. *The Fundamentals of Advertising* (Heinemann, 1985). A general study of the whole subject at a basic level and contains many up-to-date facts and figures.

Questions for Discussion

1 (CAM, Nov. 1982) An advertiser's budget is often said to be split into 'above the line' and 'below the line' activities. Explain the exact meaning of this classification and describe the activities which are most usually referred to as 'below the line'. Does the classification have any relevance to campaign planning?
2 How far is it true to say that the purpose of advertising is to create sales?
3 (IM, June 1981) In what ways can sales promotional activities be used to support or encourage the marketing efforts of distributors or dealers? Illustrate your answer with practical examples.
4 Suggest current advertising or sales promotion campaigns that seem to have as their objectives

   (a) announcing new products,
   (b) inviting enquiries,
   (c) improving company image,
   (d) stimulating immediate sales.

5 Are there any current advertising campaigns that seem to you unethical? If so, discuss why and what alterations you believe should be made.
6 Why do you think pet foods are so widely advertised on television? Why is insurance more frequently advertised in the press?

16. *How the Advertising Business Works*

'Advertising is more complicated than it might seem to the uninitiated. It is not possible to trace cause and effect in advertising, as under the controlled conditions of the physical sciences.'

Dunn and Barban. *Advertising – Its Role in Modern Marketing*

16.1 The Story So Far

In Chapter 3 we saw that 'promotion' is an important element in the marketing mix – the combination of product, price, place and promotion that provides the satisfactions the customer is seeking. The way the product is promoted (e.g. as a 'fun thing', as an exclusive article, as a reliable mechanism) is inseparable, in the customer's mind, from the product viewed purely 'as it comes from the drawing-board'.

In Section 8.5 we used the term 'marketing communications' as a convenient phrase to embrace the many methods by which companies may pass messages to their customers and prospective customers – messages that attempt to persuade as well as to inform (Section 8.3). The precise way in which the various methods of communication (including personal selling) are blended together in the appropriate proportions to fit a given marketing situation is called the 'promotional mix' (Section 8.2). In Chapter 15 we looked at some of the tasks advertising and sales promotion can perform.

16.2 Planning for Advertising

We go on in this chapter to examine the mechanisms by which advertising is actually carried out. But, first it is essential to remind ourselves that this will all be done as part of a carefully planned operation. We shall not start preparing an advertising campaign without first asking questions such as the following:

1 Who are our customers?
2 What are their needs?
3 What do we have (or what can we develop) that will meet those needs?
4 How important to the customers are the various elements in the marketing mix and how can we best handle each?
5 If promotion is an important element, what promotional mix do we need?
6 In particular, is advertising of value in this situation and, if so, what must it communicate (facts, atmosphere, customer benefits) and to whom (customers, dealers, salesmen)? How can we define our 'target audiences'?

In Chapter 19 we shall be looking more closely at the whole business of devising marketing plans. For the present, it is enough to say that advertising decisions must be a part of a whole complex of decisions that together form the total marketing plan.

16.21 *How Advertising Plans are Developed*

Like so much in marketing, developing a sound plan for advertising is largely a matter of asking the right questions. If, on answering the questions in the previous section, it seems that advertising has a part to play, then we go on to ask the following:

1 What is the objective of advertising in this particular situation? It could, for example, have any of the tasks set out in Section 15.31, and there are many others. There may be more than one task (e.g. to make customers more aware of the product *and* to secure wider retail distribution).
2 What is the audience we are communicating with? We must be very clear what our 'target audience' is. There may be more than one, in which case can we communicate with them all at once or do we have a number of quite separate communication tasks to do?
3 What is the message we have to convey? It may well be different for each audience: consumers may need to be told of the product's performance, whereas dealers will be more interested in the profit they can make; in an industrial context the factory manager will want to know that a machine will give him fewer breakdowns and higher output, and the financial director that it will reduce capital outlay and hence reduce overdraft charges.
4 What is the best medium? Is this a job for television, the press, posters or some kind of 'below the line' activity?
5 What is the best timing and frequency? Do we need to advertise now, in 3 months, in 6 months, over what period? Is it better to have a short sharp burst or would a larger campaign 'spread thin' be better?
6 How much should we be spending?
7 How can our message be expressed most effectively?

16.3 Deciding on Advertising Budgets

One of the questions just posed, 'How much should we be spending?', is a crucial one, for how much we have to spend will have a big influence on what kind of advertising we can do. It is not much use thinking of national television if the budget comes out at £1,000. Unfortunately, it is a particularly difficult question to answer.

Up to a point we can arrive at it by way of the break-even approach (Section 6.31). Since our promotional costs are probably an important element in our variable costs, we can plot them against anticipated sales and try to assess at what point further promotional expenditure should show diminishing returns. But, in the first place, there is likely to be a fair amount of guesswork in it (how else can we arrive at the level of 'anticipated sales'?) More important, however, is that we are still dealing in total promotional costs. These may well include the expense of a sales force, sales literature (sometimes very costly indeed in the case of high technology industrial products) and other forms of sales promotion. In a sense adding, say, £20,000 to the advertising budget means operating with one less salesman. What is the correct approach to this difficult question?

Some well tried approaches exist, the main ones being the following:

1 *Arbitrary Methods*. While, clearly, they cannot be recommended, many companies simply pick a figure 'off the ceiling' or on the basis of 'that's what we can afford'.

2 *Percentage of Sales*. An 'easy' and superficially attractive method is to allocate a proportion of sales revenue to advertising. But which sales revenue? Last year's, this year's, what we anticipate next year? All are used by various companies in various ways. The method has the advantage of making calculations easy – if anticipated turnover is £X,000, then the advertising budget is Y per cent of £X,000. But the underlying assumption is either that the level of sales is directly determined by the level of advertising expenditure or that advertising is a luxury you buy according to how much profit you are making. A variant of this approach, often used in a fairly predictable market, is to allocate an amount for advertising on a per unit basis, e.g. 5p per case or per dozen of anticipated sales.

3 *What Competitors Are Spending*. Clearly competitive expenditure cannot be ignored, since it may provide, especially for a company entering a new field, a good general guide to the kind of expenditure that may be necessary. But it can be very misleading:

   (a) because it assumes that competitors know what they are doing, when, in fact, their level of expenditure may be hopelessly uneconomic and based on sheer guesswork;

   (b) because companies in the same field have a quite different promotional mix, e.g. in the cosmetics field Avon concentrate on direct selling, Boots rely largely on 'captive' customers in their own retail outlets, and many others spend heavily on advertising.

4 *On a 'Task' Basis*. If it can be decided what task(s) advertising needs to perform in the particular circumstances, a suitable advertising programme can be worked out and costed to give the budget necessary to achieve the task(s). In principle this must be the correct approach, but unfortunately there are always many ways of achieving the desired result, often with wildly different costs. Nor is it easy to decide what concentration of advertising is necessary to achieve a particular effect.

Dr Simon Broadbent[1] suggests asking four questions (in fact, a combination of most of the above approaches), as follows:

1 What can the product afford?
2 What is the advertising task?
3 What are competitors spending?
4 What have we learned from previous years?

In an example he suggests that the approach might give answers such as the following:

1 £175,000 is all that is allocated in the preliminary budget.

2 £230,000 would achieve the advertising exposures regarded as desirable.
3 £200,000 will buy a share of advertising equal to the product's share of the market.
4 £200,000 was spent last year, but there are indications that brand share is responsive to the amount of advertising support.

Dr Broadbent goes on to say: 'You can imagine the discussions which take place around the range of £150,000 to £230,000. Ultimately, the decision will lie in the character of the firm. The conservative firm will settle at a low figure, the thrusting, expansionist firm will invest in its future.'

16.4 Advertising Agencies

The production of advertising material is a complex business. A number of different parties work on it, but principally the advertisers (companies marketing products, including manufacturers, retailers, importers, franchise holders etc.); advertising agencies (companies specializing in the development and production of advertising campaigns for a variety of 'clients'); and the media (newspaper and magazine publishers, TV and radio programme contractors, cinema owners, transport authorities, poster contractors and the like).

It is perfectly possible for the whole process of advertising to be carried out within the company. Selecting media, designing and writing advertisements, taking photographs, making printing plates and many other things are then all done within the advertising department. There is a particular tendency for this to happen when the company has a very large number of products, each with a high technical content. The promotional mix will contain a high element of sales literature, exhibition material and so on, all of which must be carefully worked out in close collaboration with technical experts. Even press advertisements may contain a fair amount of technical information, e.g. in fields such as tele-communications, plastics, and building materials.

This is the exception, however. More usually the technical content of advertising materials is small. To produce promotional material for coffee, underwear or furniture, it is rarely necessary to go into the technicalities of how they are produced. Even for products such as electrical appliances, the technical content of the main promotional material is very small (although there may well be some service manuals and other supporting material that are technical).

In general, then, the people who write and design advertising material do not need to be skilled in the technicalities of the products themselves. Rather, they need to be experts in the advertising business – in communicating. Such people are mainly (though by no means solely) found in advertising agencies, and it is in advertising agencies that most advertising material is produced, for three main reasons:

1 The obvious advantages of bringing together within one organization all the skills that go towards producing good advertising.
2 The fact that an agency can usually afford to employ a much wider range of skilled and experienced people than an individual advertiser.
3 Historically, in the U.K. (and in many countries, though not all), advertising agencies received a commission from the media owners (usually 15 per cent) for

all space or time bought on behalf of their clients. This means that they could afford to pay writers, designers, media experts and advertising planners to act on their clients' behalf. Clients could not obtain these commissions so that it cost them more to 'do it themselves'. Increasingly now 'fair trading' laws are abolishing the enforced commissions not payable to clients so this consideration becomes less relevant.

An advertising agency has various specialist departments, the main ones being the following.

16.41 *Account Management*

The clients of an advertising agency are referred to in advertising jargon as accounts. Agency people speak of 'the Volkswagen account', 'the Kleenex account', 'the I.C.I. account' and so on. Responsibility for providing appropriate service to clients is then the responsibility of the 'account management team'.

Each client of the agency will have one or more 'account executives' (depending on the size and complexity of the task and the level of expenditure). Other titles, such as 'account managers', are also sometimes used. They are the point of contact between client and agency. It is their job to understand the client's business and his advertising needs sufficiently to translate it into a 'briefing' to the other agency staff. Usually the account executive (or his senior, the 'account director') is largely responsible for all campaign planning within the agency on the client's behalf. Normally this will be done in close consultation with the client's own staff.

16.42 *Creative Department*

The creative department contains the 'ideas men', able to express in words and pictures the essence of the benefits that have to be communicated to customers. They work to a briefing from the account management staff. Copywriters produce the verbal, and visualizers the visual, elements of the story, usually working side by side, and the basic idea of the advertising coming from either or both of them.

16.43 *Media Department*

Other specialists have the function of analysing readership and viewing figures, comparing costs of space and time, and recommending which media should be used for a particular advertising task. They are the media executives. (Computer techniques are used for the complex data-handling which may be necessary.) Their job is twofold: media planning and media buying. Once the plan is agreed, the space and time must be bought (often some hard bargaining takes place), and 'media schedules' (Figure 16.1) drawn up for everyone to work to. These will show 'copy dates' – the dates, often weeks ahead of publication, by which the publishers need material.

16.44 *Production Department*

Designs for advertising campaigns will emerge from the creative department in

PRATT & COMPANY
Media Consultants
19, Holland Park
London W11 3TD
Tel. 01-221-6417

PRESS SCHEDULE

Advertiser... Sunshine Cereals Ltd. ......   Product... Morning Glory Flakes .... Approved by...................

Campaign Period... Jan-Mar 1984 ......   Target Market... Housewives with children ...... Date.................. 4.9.83

Publication Title	Circulation	Advertising Space	Advertising Space Costs				Publication Cover Date			Copy Date	Readership by Target Market		
			Rate-Card Cost £	Agreed Cost £	No.	Total Cost £	January	February	March		Coverage %	Readers 000's	CPT £
Woman's Own	1,317,246	Full page, facing editorial, full colour, bleed	18,040	16,500	5	82,500	7,21	4,18	10	23 Nov	23	1532	10.77
Woman	1,266,400	Full page, facing editorial, full colour, bleed	17,380	16,000	5	80,000	14,28	11,25	24	16 Nov	22	1465	10.92
TV Times	3,288,228	Full page, facing	21,560	20,000	3	60,000	22	9	15	16 Nov	24	1549	12.91
Family Circle	483,367	Double page spread first in issue, full colour, bleed	13,810	13,000	2	26,000	Feb	Mar		24 Oct	15	953	13.64
Living	422,084	Double page spread first in issue, full colour, bleed	8,830	8,500	2	17,000	Feb		Apr	10 Oct	9	610	13.93

Total Space Cost : 265,500   Total Campaign Coverage : 60%
Production Budget : 34,500   Frequency : 5.8 Opportunities
                    £300,000   To See (O.T.S.)

Notes : 1. Circulations are Jan-Jun 1983 ABC UK figures
          2. Rate-Card prices as at Spring 1984
          3. Coverage data based on Jul 82 - Jun 83 NRS

Figure 16.1 Typical media schedule for a familiar type of consumer product (provided by Pratt & Company, Media Consultants).

rough form – as 'copy and layout' (typescript and a drawing or photograph) for material to be printed, and as 'storyboard' (a series of 'stills', again with typescript) for television. Although these are spoken of as roughs (or visuals), they may look quite polished. Instead of storyboards, for example, TV campaigns may be presented as videotape. Whatever method is chosen, the aim is to let everyone concerned in the client's (advertiser's) company and in the agency see what the campaign will look like without incurring the full cost of photography, finished illustrations, typesetting, models and actors, and scenery and 'props'.

From these roughs the finished work must be developed. It will be the task of the creative department to supervise the development and ensure that the finished result is as intended.

However, there is a planning and logistics problem as well, and that becomes the job of the production department. They will order material, plan dates, 'chase up' suppliers and generally ensure that jobs are completed in time to meet copy dates. Sometimes there is also a 'traffic control' department to ensure the smooth passage of each campaign through all its stages in order to meet all the important copy dates, when films or blocks or artwork must reach the media.

16.45 *Other Specialist Departments*

Each agency will have a series of other departments (in addition to those, such as accounts and personnel, that will be found in any company) for special functions.

These vary from one agency to another, but may include marketing research, sales promotion, direct mail, exhibitions and display, and P.R. The exact 'mix' will depend on the agency's specialization and on the kind of clients it works for. As profits become harder to maintain, there is a growing tendency for the specialist departments to be 'hived off' as separate trading units, or even separate companies, and made to stand on their own feet commercially.

Advertising agencies, of course, use the services of many other people and organizations – film production companies and photographers, model agencies, art studios, individual freelance writers and artists, blockmakers, printers and so on. Advertisers, too, deal direct with these people for much of their promotional material, even when they use an agency for most of their work.

A recent tendency is for some of the traditional agency functions to be offered by companies specializing purely in, for example, the creative function (creative 'boutiques' or 'hot-shops') or the media function. These offer their services at lower rates, or set out to provide a more highly specialized service at normal rates, but the advertiser loses the advantage of co-ordinating and general planning other 'full service' agencies offer, and has the inconvenience of dealing with several sources instead of only one.

16.5 How Media Decisions are Made

Having arrived at a set of advertising objectives and established a budget, we are then faced with decisions on how to implement them. (It works the other way round, too, of course, for if the budget is set by the 'task' method, we must have some idea early on of how the objectives will be reached in order to work out the approximate cost.)

Nowhere is the choice of methods more varied than in the media aspect of the job. A wide variety of kinds of media are available, including the following:

Broadcasting (TV and radio).
The Press (Newspapers and magazines, both consumer and trade).
Outdoor (Posters – buses, trains).
Direct mail (sending out letters through the post).
Exhibitions

If we want to reach financial directors of large companies, for example, we can choose between newspapers (such as *The Times* and *Financial Times*), magazines (the accountancy journals, the *Economist* and so on), or direct mail.

Usually the selection must be made in four stages, as follows:

1 What kind of media (from a list including the above)?
2 Which particular medium (which newspaper, which radio stations or whatever)?
3 What size/type of space, how much time, how many posters of what size, what frequency of appearance over what length of time?
4 How much will our budget permit us to buy?

It is not possible here to go into all of these areas in depth,[2] but, as an example of the kind of approach, we can take a short look at the way in which one newspaper or magazine might be selected rather than another. This is done by progressively narrowing down the list of possible publications to find the one that will reach the maximum number of our target audience (though sometimes it may be better to concentrate on only a small section of the target audience, to gain maximum impact). Sometimes, of course 'maximum number' will conflict with 'lowest cost' and a compromise may have to be decided upon. This is normally a progressive process going through a number of stages as follows:

1 Select those publications that are likely to reach as many of the target audience as possible.
2 Establish the cost of reaching those readers (usually on a 'cost per thousand readers' basis).
3 Arrive at the best publication in terms of maximum number of readers within the target audience at lowest cost per thousand.
4 Consider whether any supporting publications are needed (for example, the 'best buy' publication may reach only 65 per cent of the target audience; to use a second would reach a further 25 per cent).

Sometimes other criteria have to be taken into account, e.g. a particular product may need illustrating in colour (fabrics, paint), whereas the 'best buy' may only carry black and white advertisements.

16.51 *The Importance of Concentration*

We have just suggested that it is important to select the 'best buy' rather than to advertise in all publications that reach the target audience. This is one example of an important general principle in advertising – that of concentration. It may be very tempting to try to cover all the options but this is never the most effective use of money. In general it is better to (a) use the one best publication rather than many, (b) publish a small number of large advertisements rather than many small ones, and (c) reach a small part of the total potential market strongly than all of it with a feeble message. The aim should always be dominance, if need be in a carefully chosen sector, rather than to be just 'one of the crowd' of advertisers.

16.6 How Creative Decisions are Made

16.61 *The Communication Process*

It is still not known precisely how advertising works, and almost certainly it works rather differently in different situations. There are, however, some 'models' of the process that have stood the test of time, one of them being expressed by the mnemonic AIDA, the initial letters of Attention, Interest, Desire, Action. (Some authors add Satisfaction, and use the letters AIDAS to summarize this approach.) (See Section 8.5 for a development of this model.)

The supposition here is that advertising helps take the customer through one or more of these stages ('action' may be purchase, or some other specific action such as asking for a test-drive or sending for a leaflet). Some people now feel, however, that this model attempts to assign too specific a role to advertising, and that the purpose of much advertising can be better expressed in terms of increasing 'awareness' of the product. It may encourage 'testing' of the product and it helps to provide 'reinforcement' of the purchasing habit.

This latter approach is perhaps a better description of much of the 'brand-awareness' advertising that appears on television. Rarely is it now expected that an advertisement on TV will convert a purchaser to a product for life. The most important contribution of all made by most advertising is the development or reinforcement of a favourable brand image (see Section 10.22).

16.62 *The Creative Task*

Section 16.2 listed the key questions that determine the outcome of the advertising planning process. The creative stage of producing advertising campaigns is concerned with two of them:

1 What is the message we have to convey?
2 How can our message be conveyed most effectively?

Advertising a new burst-proof tyre will call for different treatment from reminding customers of the existence of a brand of baked beans or canned soup. But, of course, these questions must be answered in the light of the answers to some of the other questions in Section 16.2, in particular:

1 What is the objective of advertising in this particular situation?
2 What is the audience we are communicating with?

Telling doctors about a new drug is clearly a different proposition from announcing a new pop record or persuading companies to consider leasing vehicles rather than buying them.

The advertising budget and the choice of media will also have a bearing.

16.63 *Devising Advertising Campaigns*

Note the word 'campaigns'. Very rarely should a single advertisement be developed (advertising jobs or specific offers such as sale bargains are clear exceptions). Advertising generally is a long-term strategic activity (see Figure 16.2).

The creative team, therefore, will be faced with the need to develop an advertising campaign bearing in mind the following:

1 The audience.
2 The task advertising is to perform.
3 The media being used.
4 The amount being spent (which may well influence, for example, the size of space, or whether colour can be used).
5 The length and frequency of the campaign (can we rely on a steady build-up or must the story be told all in one go?).

These are not necessarily the only factors (in some situations what competitors' advertising is saying will be very important, for example). Any ideas for the campaign must then be matched against these criteria. They should also have the following attributes:

1 Be able to command attention against all competing influences. People do not

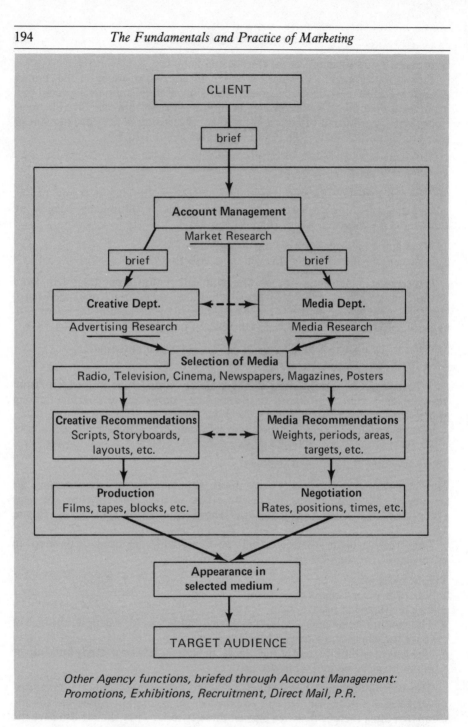

Figure 16.2 Sequence of activities involved in preparation of a campaign by an advertising agency. This chart was provided by Benton & Bowles, Ltd.

watch television and read newspapers primarily to see the advertisements.
2 Be able to sustain interest. Boring or dull advertising is unlikely to exert much influence.
3 Be memorable.

16.7 Summary

1 Advertising plans are developed on the basis of

    (a) objectives,
    (b) audience,
    (c) message,
    (d) medium,
    (e) budget.

2 Advertising budgets can be worked out by a number of methods, of which the task method is normally regarded as the most significant.
3 The business of advertising is done by (a) advertisers, (b) agencies (and companies supplying ancillary services), (c) media.
4 Advertising agencies are companies concentrating on the development and production of advertising campaigns on behalf of clients. The main departments are account management, creative, media, and production.
5 Media selection decisions are made on the basis of coverage (of the target audience), and cost (on, e.g., a cost per 1,000 readers or viewers basis).
6 Concentration of resources is an important principle of advertising.
7 Creative decisions are made on the basis of selecting a message that will (a) command attention, (b) sustain interest, and (c) be memorable; and also carry the desired message in a way which is appropriate to the target audience.

References

1 In *Spending Advertising Money* (Business Books Ltd, 1975). Broadbent's book deals in detail with media selection decisions, but Chapters 1–4 provide a succinct introduction to the principles of advertising.
2 ibid. The book does it admirably.

Further Reading

Hedges, Alan. *Testing to Destruction* (IPA, 1978). This gives a good review of theories of how advertising works.
Wilmshurst, John. *The Fundamentals of Advertising* (Heinemann, 1985). This deals with all aspects of advertising.

Questions for Discussion

1 Evaluate the main methods of arriving at an advertising budget. Which are likely to be of most value in the case of

    (a) an established food product selling through supermarkets,
    (b) a range of machine tools marketed internationally,

  (c) the lawn mower in Question 5?

2 (IM, June 1982) How is an advertising campaign created? Illustrate your answer with examples from real life.
3 In the light of Sections 16.61, 10.1 and 10.2 write a brief explanation of how you think advertising influences people's behaviour.
4 (CAM, June 1982) As the Advertising Manager of a major toy manufacturer, you and your management have become unhappy with your advertising agency and have decided to consider moving the account.
  Write a memorandum to your Managing Director stating how you propose to go about the selection and detailing your selection criteria.
5 You are the marketing manager of a company about to launch a new lawnmower. List the categories of information you would give the advertising agency that is to prepare an advertising campaign for you.

17. *How Sales Promotion Works*

'Sales Promotion can be described as the hysterical arm of marketing operations.'
John Winkler. *Winkler on Marketing Planning*

17.1 What Sales Promotion Is

John Winkler[1] in the above quotation, and in the chapter it introduces in his book, is referring particularly to the sometimes frantic efforts to persuade customers to buy one brand rather than another. Grocery products, petrol and confectionery are areas where this kind of activity is common – premium offers, gifts, competitions, and trading stamps are typical manifestations.

Ray Willsmer[2] says that 'sales promotion' could just as easily be called 'merchandising', 'below-the-line activity', 'non-media advertising – and more'. He includes in his definition of sales promotion free circulation magazines, special discounts, exhibitions – and bribery, including special payments of all kinds to dealers! G. B. Giles[3] refers to 'consumer promotions' and under this heading includes:

(a) special price sales,
(b) free sample distribution,
(c) premium offers,
(d) contests,
(e) point-of-sale demonstrations,
(f) coupon offers,
(g) combination or banded pack product offers;

and to 'trade promotions', under which he puts the following:

(a) provision of display materials,
(b) co-operative advertising schemes, assistance with blocks or space costs,
(c) contests for sales staff,
(d) special discounts,
(e) special quantity rate terms.

Clearly there is much scope for argument as to what goes in and what is left out of a definition of sales promotion. In this chapter we include all the above but also, for convenience, sections on direct mail and P.R., although they would not necessarily be included under this heading by other writers.

Readers may find it useful initially to refer back to Chapter 8, where an attempt was made to put into perspective all the methods of communicating with customers; and to Chapter 15, which referred to the tasks for which sales promotion is generally used. A number of authorities, including the American

197

Marketing Association, refer to sales promotion as 'non-recurring and non-routine' sales activity.

17.11 *The Importance of Sales Promotion*

Sales promotion tends to be dismissed as a relatively unimportant medium, largely because, in advertising agencies, it comes under the catch-all heading of 'below the line'. In any case relatively little of the expenditure passes through agencies but tends to be spent directly by advertisers or through specialist companies. Simon Broadbent in *Spending Advertising Money*[4] gives sales promotion barely a page, under the subheading 'Peripheral Media'.

Ray Willsmer, however, speaking from long experience as a marketing executive with major companies such as Lyons, sees it as a major part of total advertising expenditure.[5]

Christian Petersen[6] was pointing out as early as 1978 the more rapid growth of below the line promotion compared with that of above the line advertising.

He quotes a Harris International Marketing Survey showing sales promotion expenditure growing from £545 million in 1974 to £1,853 million in 1977. Advertising Association figures showed a growth of advertising expenditure through agencies growing from £1,000 million to £1,630 million over the same period – a growth of only 63 per cent against the 24 per cent increase in sales promotion expenditure. Such figures have been less quoted more recently. The Institute of Sales Promotion contented itself with the claim (quoted by Alan Wolfe in *Marketing* 21 April, 1983) that 'total expenditure below the line now exceeds the money spent on media advertising'.

The fact is, it is impossible to arrive at an exact figure for the following reasons:

1 There is no easy way to collect together expenditures by individual firms on the many 'bits and pieces' that constitute sales promotion.
2 It, in any case, depends what is included under the heading. Ray Willsmer, for example, includes special discounts but not public relations. He includes exhibitions, although many would not. There is no generally agreed definition of sales promotion, at present.

17.2 What Sales Promotion is For

In Section 15.4 we listed the kind of tasks sales promotion can perform. They can be summarized by saying that sales promotion techniques are used to give a short-term 'lift' to a product, in order to achieve a tactical objective – such as getting retailers to stock, getting customers to sample, or attempting to raise sales off a plateau.

This contrasts with the long-term advertising objective of building brand recognition or creating the right associations with the product in a consumer's mind. Often a product much advertised over a long period reaches the point where there is nothing novel to be said about it. A competition or give-away reintroduces the desired novelty and excitement. Often the purpose of sales promotion is to relieve the boredom of a well established product.

Most often sales promotion is closely associated with the point of sale.

Companies have increasingly realized however that whilst sales promotion has largely tactical *uses* it has strategic *implications*. Thus there have been suggestions that a consistent policy over several years by the major U.K. petrol companies of competing largely through sales promotion had unfortunate long-term effects. The earlier 'brand image' advertising of the main petrol brands gave way to price cuts, discounting through trading stamps and a whole variety of gifts and competitions to be obtained or won by collecting vouchers. It may well be that this procedure actually reinforced a growing belief that there is no significant difference between one brand and another since customers were being urged to buy on the basis of the best sales promotional 'deal' rather than the best petrol or the best service. Clearly this is a danger and continuing price cuts in particular may convey a picture of 'cheapness' rather than of the often more desirable impression of 'good value'.

Certainly many of the big users of sales promotion techniques (Kelloggs and Heinz for example) aim at sales promotion campaigns which reinforce the value of the brand (e.g. a book on 'Fibre in your Diet' as a premium offer with Kelloggs high-fibre 'All Bran' cereal) rather than simply offering a 'bargain'.

17.3 The Importance of the Point of Sale

We looked in Chapter 1 at the sequence through which a buyer goes, from feeling a need, through a search process, to the purchasing decision. Not until that decision is made is the marketing process complete (ignoring for the moment the importance, which was stressed in Chapter 1, of the customer's post-purchase feelings).

The all-important purchasing decision takes place at the point of sale – in the shop or showroom (or less typically when the customer fills in the order form surrounded by a collection of catalogues). At this point it is unusual for 'our' product to be the only one on offer; usually there is a shop full of alternatives, and this is true whether it is the housewife buying groceries in the supermarket or the businessman buying stationery or spare parts from his supplier's showroom.

It is at the point of sale that the customer finally resolves which of the alternatives will be selected. Often he or she does not decide until this time which of the many alternatives will best meet his or her needs. Even if this decision has been made, it can be changed at point of sale by a well presented special offer, or even by a prominent and attractive display.

Most marketing organizations are well aware of the desirability of achieving special emphasis for their products. Showcards, window posters and special display material are all part of the struggle to achieve maximum point-of-sale impact.

However, the dealer often finds himself in the situation of being overwhelmed with the amount of display material offered to him by his suppliers. The more sophisticated he is, the more conscious he is that he needs to get maximum turnover and profit from each square metre of shelf space – the more selective he will be. He is not usually specially concerned with which brand sells best (his own total profit is naturally his main concern) but only with total sales. He therefore needs to be convinced that 'our' display will increase his profits. Using point-of-sale material to feature a national promotion (especially if it is to be heavily advertised) is one way of doing this but its apt design is crucial if it is to be used and not discarded.

In some cases point-of-sale promotion is used to persuade people to shop at one particular point of sale rather than another. The petrol promotions are intended to encourage people to buy their petrol or oil from one company's site rather than another's. Trading stamps are another way of achieving this. So are the 'loss leaders' which many stores feature, when one or more items are heavily marked down in price and featured in advertising, on windows etc., to tempt people into that shop in preference to a competitor's. Naturally the hope is that, once in, they will buy other items besides the featured 'loss leader'.

17.31 *Packaging*

Packaging also has a very important part to play in this area. We have already seen (Section 4.6) that its role is much wider than simply containing and protecting goods during transit. At the point of sale packaging must make the following impact:

1 Stand out clearly on the shelf.
2 Be clearly identifiable, with the brand name strongly visible.
3 Lend itself to building displays (a package that will not stack or is likely to topple or crush gives problems to the retailer's staff).

17.32 *Merchandising Staff*

So important has this whole aspect of promotion become that many large retail chains have their own teams of 'merchandisers', whose job it is to create special promotions and displays that will create fast turnover and give the store an air of excitement. Similarly, many marketing organizations have created merchandising teams as a special division of their sales staff. Salesmen secure the orders from the buying department at the retail chain's head office, and merchandising staff then ensure that goods are well displayed and stock levels maintained in the individual stores. (In 1983 this trend showed signs of going into reverse with some large chains excluding manufacturers' staff and controlling their own displays, etc.)

17.4 The Importance of 'The Trade'

In most instances marketing organizations need the assistance of third parties to complete the distribution chain carrying their products to the customers. Wholesalers and retailers for consumer products, dealers and distributors for industrial products, importers and agents in international marketing, all have to be persuaded (a) to stock the goods, and (b) to promote them to their customers. These intermediaries are collectively referred to by the all-embracing term 'the trade'.

It is customary to speak of 'trade promotions' and 'consumer promotions'. The first type are aimed at encouraging the trade to stock and display the goods, the second at encouraging customers to buy a particular type of product or particular brand rather than an alternative, or at persuading customers to shop at one establishment rather than another. These two types of promotion, therefore, correspond to (a) and (b) above. They both bring in 'the trade', since consumer promotions normally operate through the trade and are dependent on them for their success. Also, of course, consumer promotions are themselves used as an incentive to the trade to stock and display the goods (so that they can be sure of benefiting from the extra sales the promotion is intended to generate). Thus, the two distinct types of promotion are, in fact, very closely linked.

17.41 *Trade Promotions*

Special promotions, particularly those in which some kind of discount is given, are often used to encourage the trade to carry stocks of a product. The discount can be in the form of straight cash or frequently as additional merchandise (thirteen bottles or cans for the normal price of a case of twelve, six cases for the price of five, or something similar). There is a school of thought (less prevalent than it once was) which believes in 'dealer-loading' – on the basis that, if the dealer is loaded up with stock, he will have to exert himself to sell it to this customers. Clearly this can rebound on the manufacturer if the dealer in fact finds it difficult to unload the stock he has been induced to take. However, there are situations where quite genuinely the dealers need to be persuaded to carry extra stock, e.g. in preparation for a new product launch or a major consumer promotion.

Other types of promotion to the trade include incentives for dealers' staff, e.g. cash payments, holidays etc., to those responsible for achieving high sales levels. 'Mystery shoppers' may make cash payments to dealers who have the product in stock when they call or to staff who attempt to sell it to them. Window display and similar competitions encourage the display of particular products (but are now much less in evidence as national chains with their own merchandising policies take over from the independents).

17.42 *Sales Force Promotions*

Just as the trade can be encouraged to stock a particular product or range and to give it display emphasis, so a company may wish to give incentives to its sales staff. Quite apart from various types of commission structure (see Section 13.71) sales promotion techniques can be applied in this context. Thus points (or, for example, trading stamps) can be awarded for meeting targets or quotas, winning competitions etc. Prizes can be goods for the salesman and his family (often selected from a lavish catalogue) or holidays.

17.43 *Consumer Promotions*

These can take a very wide variety of forms and the following list is just a selection of the more popular ones.

1 *Premium Offers*. The consumer receives a free gift, either with the purchase or by sending in packet tops, coupons or some similar device. Self liquidating premiums are those where the consumer also sends in money, which covers the marketing organization's cost of providing the gift, though that still represents a bargain to the consumer.
2 *Money-off*. A voucher or coupon can be used to obtain a reduction in price when making the next purchase of the same product or another one in the same

manufacturer's range. Sometimes there is a money-off offer marked on the pack and relating to the immediate purchase.

3 *Banded Packs.* Two or more packs taped or wrapped together and offered at a reduced price are a variation on the theme.

4 *Sampling.* At point of sale or by door-to-door delivery, sampling is an obviously attractive way of introducing suitable new products or achieving wider recognition of existing ones.

5 *Personality Promotions.* 'Resting' actors and actresses in appropriate costume are often used as visiting personalities. They travel in decorated vehicles and visit various towns to draw attention to a particular product.

6 *Competitions.* They can be used to attract attention, provide a new advertising theme and relieve the boredom associated with a product, referred to earlier. They can be quite complicated to organize, especially as legal restrictions apply to them. Their advantage is that the cost can be known in advance (as against for example, money-off or premium offers, where the cost depends on the numbers taking up the offer). Attractive prizes can be offered (e.g. holidays), probably at relatively little cost, as the supplier of the prize (e.g. the tour operator) also gains from the publicity and may therefore be prepared to negotiate special deals.

7 *Trading Stamps* (stamps issued with a purchase and redeemable against 'gifts' when enough have been collected). These have the advantage that they are relatively cheap (and in any case represent a fixed outlay), and the whole organization is undertaken by the stamp company. They are particularly attractive to retailers, although some benefit is lost once local competitors issue stamps or cut prices substantially. (Trading stamps in the U.K. have virtually disappeared in the 80s – probably due to their very success – when most garages or supermarkets offer stamps their competitive value is lost.)

8 *Sponsorship.* This means contributing to sporting events, the arts etc., in order to gain 'spin-off'. For example, advertising displays on football stadium fences, or on racing cars often get a good showing to wide audiences if the event is televised. Supporting the arts may cause the company to be mentioned in a favourable context in important media.

17.44 *Industrial Promotions*

Sales promotion tends to be associated with consumer products marketing, but similar techniques are used in industrial marketing also. Special discounts and introductory offers are very common, as are competitions with prizes (free holidays are a favourite) for the customer's staff; 'give-aways' such as diaries, calendars, pens, calculators; annual golf or racing parties for customers; and yachts or holiday villas where a customer's staff are entertained. Sponsorship of sporting events will frequently be linked with this kind of activity. Such activities are often more *ad hoc*, less strictly evaluated and less likely to be part of a coherent plan than is the case with consumer promotions.

17.5 Evaluating Sales Promotion

As with all promotional activities, sales promotion is difficult to evaluate, but the attempt must be made. First and foremost, of course, it is, as ever, essential to be clear what is the purpose of the particular sales promotion activity being evaluated. If we cannot be sure what that is, we certainly have no chance of measuring how effective the promotion has been.

It is generally accepted that the effect of any promotional activity is likely to follow an S-curve (Figure 17.1), where increases in promotional expenditure increase the number of buyers, although, beyond a certain point, the returns from additional expenditure start to decrease.

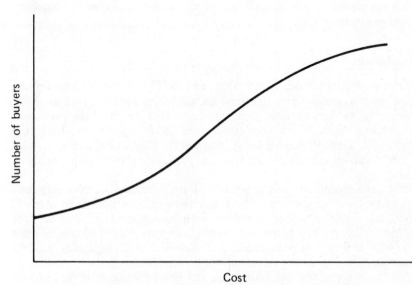

Cost

Figure 17.1 The S-curve effect of promotional expenditure

It is rarely possible, however, to relate actual purchases so directly to levels of expenditure and, normally, we need to measure some other dependent variable. Peter Sampson[7] quotes Barnes, McDonald and Tuck as giving the following list of possibles:

1 Number of 'promoted' units taken up.
2 Number of new users who repeat purchase.
3 Profit per promoted unit and profit for those unpromoted units that can be ascribed to the promotion.
4 Attitudes (short- and long-term) towards the brand (product) among actual and potential users.
5 Ascribable profit from both new and former users who take up the promotion.
6 Ascribable sales and profit against promotional cost.
7 Distribution and display increases, increases in impulse buying, sales, trade (and consumers') goodwill.

Sampson goes on to elaborate on this list, allocating the labels 'strategic' or 'tactical' to each item, and then examines ways of measuring each. He concludes that 'conducting research to determine the effectiveness of sales promotion is a viable, but difficult, field to work in'.

It is enough for our purposes to say that, clearly, while item 1 of the above list is easy enough to measure, measuring many of the others will necessitate quite sophisticated research techniques. There is a further complication. Sales promotion is rarely carried on completely in a vacuum – other forms of promotion will be happening simultaneously. There is then frequently a synergistic effect, i.e. the collective effect of the various forms of promotion is greater than their individual effects simply added together (2 + 2 = 5, as it has been graphically put). This simply reinforces the difficulty of measurement: it does not mean we should not make the attempt.

17.6 Exhibitions

Trade exhibitions, such as the Motor Show and the Ideal Home Exhibition, are a form of promotional activity that enables marketing organizations to show, and frequently to demonstrate, their products to their ultimate customers without needing retailers or other 'middlemen' to do it for them. Industrial exhibitions such as the Packaging Exhibition and the Plastics Exhibition provide a source of 'captive' potential customers for particular groups of materials or equipment.

However, exhibitions are a very expensive form of promotion. Not only does the cost of building a stand run into many thousands of pounds at a major exhibition, but they also have to be staffed, with consequent loss of normal calls by salesmen; visitors have to be entertained; large quantities of special sales literature must generally be provided; and for technical shows especially, moving and installing demonstration equipment can be very costly.

This does not mean that exhibitions are not a worthwhile activity, but that some hard-headed questions must be asked as to whether the return will be worth the cost – questions such as the following:

1 What kind of people will attend?
2 Are they in a position to buy our products?
3 What results do we expect, actual sales or merely an additional opportunity for publicity?
4 What kind of follow-up action do we need to take in order to benefit fully?

The last is a particularly important point. It is rare for sales to be concluded at an exhibition; more often it is merely a fairly superficial contact, which must be followed through hard if any business is to result. Because of these considerations, many companies explore other ways of achieving contact with customers – their own 'mini-exhibitions' in a suitable hotel; or travelling caravan, boat or even train; open days at the factory; or special seminars and symposia.

Like all forms of publicity, exhibitions must be part of a carefully worked out plan and not embarked upon simply 'because our competitors will be there'. Similarly, great care must be taken to evaluate results (difficult because of the long-term and diffused nature of the outcome) in order to be sure that the money was well spent.

17.7 Direct Mail

By direct mail we mean promotional material sent through the post to selected individuals or companies. It is often confused with mail order – the ordering by post of goods usually advertised in the press or in catalogues.

Direct mail is probably the most neglected of all the main promotional media. Many senior marketing people who should know better say 'It doesn't work, we have tried it', when the only reason it did not work was that they did it badly. Examples such as *Reader's Digest*, who for many years have sold books and records entirely by direct mail, demonstrate how effective the medium can be. But a close look at it shows also how much thought and effort must go into producing effective campaigns.

In the first place an overwhelming reason why direct mail can be so effective is that the letters are sent to carefully selected individuals by name. All too often a random list of people is used or letters are sent to companies (where their chances of reaching the right individual are very low). Secondly, the content of direct mail has to be extremely carefully worked out – a poorly worded sales letter with any old piece of literature attached will not do. It is worth looking at the *Reader's Digest* material to see how the whole sales story is stated with maximum appeal to the potential customer, how easy ordering is made (send no money, just use the 'yes' sticker), and how chances to win a prize are offered as an extra incentive.

Used in this way, with carefully selected and up-to-date names and addresses, direct mail can be very effective indeed, even though the cost of reaching each recipient is much higher than through press advertising or television. The advantage lies in much less wastage, and because much more can be said and action can be stimulated much more effectively. It is particularly valuable in situations, such as many business to business markets, where a small number of buyers can be clearly identified.

17.8 Public Relations

Much ink (and probably some blood) has been spilt trying to assign public relations its correct position in relation to marketing and promotion. As is so often the case with such arguments, semantics are a large part of the problem. The letters P.R. are used to mean 'public relations' and also 'press relations', and these two are *not* the same.

Press Relations (more accurately *media relations*) is the process and technique of providing information to the press and also to radio and television.

Public Relations is the much wider activity of communicating with the many groups of people who constitute an organization's public. (The term 'publics' is often used in recognition that each group may need such special treatment that they are best treated separately.) These groups include shareholders, employees, local communities, Government departments and many others, as well as suppliers, customers and other 'trading' contacts. A company that has established a good relationship with all its publics will find it much easier to launch new ventures and will have a firmer base from which to deal with any difficulties or disasters.

To communicate effectively with all of these may call for the use of films, house journals, advertising and many other media, as well as the use of press relations activity. The subjects on which communication takes place will also be very broad, so that public relations in this full sense is far more than just an aspect of the marketing activity.

Similarly, press relations can be used in a variety of ways, not simply to supply information about products. However, it often is a vital method of promotion, especially in the case of new products. For a car manufacturer it is just as important to get his new model into the motoring sections of the press as it is to launch an advertising campaign. Similarly, technical products rely heavily on being 'written-up' in the technical journals.

New products, especially if they involve new technologies (such as the microchip) or achieve things which could not be done before (such as a new drug) are often newsworthy and hence may be featured in the editorial columns of the press or in radio and TV programmes or news broadcasts.

As well as making products widely known (at no direct cost, by contrast with advertising which would often cost a great deal to achieve the same coverage) products featured in this way carry the authority and independent endorsement of the publication or feature writer, the broadcast channel or presenter. It is of course possible for this to backfire. The newspaper or TV programme may not like the product or may highlight its less desirable features. But good products offering genuine benefits are more likely to gain than to suffer.

Products which are no longer new may, of course, find it more difficult to be featured in this way. Then we have to look for such things as:

(a) *Application stories*. New ways in which the product is being used, new problems it is solving ('XYZ adhesive overcomes space shuttle ceramic tiles problem').
(b) *Orders and expansions*. Large overseas contracts, new factories providing employment.
(c) *Visits*. Royalty or other visiting dignitaries seen using the products ('President tries his hand with ABC Bulldozer').
(d) *Sponsorship*. (See next section)

Like all forms of promotion PR must be conducted on a planned systematic basis. The following 7-step sequence is a useful approach:

1 *State the problem or aim* (launch a new product, inform or remotivate the sales force, encourage a favourable attitude amongst potential customers).
2 *Do the research* to establish the facts about the present situation.
3 *Identify the public* (who do we need to talk to and what do we need to say to them?).
4 *Choose the appropriate media* (anything from TV to newsletters, conferences to films depending on the objective and the public concerned).
5 *Monitor the effects* to make sure the message is being received and understood in the way intended.
6 *Look to the future* – PR is never 'finished' but always part of a continuing, changing situation.
7 *Maintain financial checks* at all stages to ensure the operation is cost-effective.

The biggest danger with all promotional activity is that it will be conducted on a piecemeal basis. This is a special danger with some of the techniques referred to in this chapter. Yet to treat them as individual events is to risk losing the full return on what is often considerable outlay. We have referred earlier in this chapter to the synergistic effect. A far greater return is likely if personal selling, advertising and all other promotional activities are planned in detail as part of a totally integrated marketing campaign. Then each activity reinforces and is reinforced by all the others. The sales force is trained to seize the openings created by advertising, which is opening the way for them; exhibitions are used to generate 'leads', which are fed to the salesmen – and so on.

17.9 Sponsorship

Increasing sums of money are being invested by organizations of all types and sizes in sponsoring sporting and cultural activities. Thus something that could once have been regarded perhaps as a minor PR medium is rapidly becoming a distinct and important form of promotion in its own right. The reasons for this perhaps include a desire to contribute to the good of society (and to be recognized as doing so).

Usually, however, there are more specific objectives involved. For example, the advertising of cigarettes on television is forbidden. By sponsoring sporting activities such as cricket (e.g. 'the Benson & Hedges Cup') the manufacturers were able to retain their presence on TV, together with many mentions of their names in a wide range of other media. At the same time they stand to gain from the association of the brand name with an activity which has healthy connotations and their contribution to its success is seen by many as a laudable activity. Others, of course, may take the view that such contributions amount to a somewhat cynical flaunting of the spirit of the law. The total effect however is likely to be overwhelmingly good rather than bad for the companies and for their products.

Often the link between sponsors and the activity concerned is much more direct such as oil companies and motor racing, sportswear manufacturers and tennis, and the potential benefits of such an association are obvious.

17.10 Summary

1 Sales promotion has been defined as a 'non-recurring and non-routine sales activity'.
2 Although it is often treated as only an insignificant part of the 'below the line' advertising budget, it can be a very important activity.
3 Sales promotion is frequently used to give a short-term boost to sales of a particular product. It is usually concentrated at the point of sale.
4 It is much used to gain the support of the trade, either directly through 'trade promotions' or indirectly through 'consumer promotions'.
5 Sales promotion techniques can also be used to generate a higher level of sales force activity.
6 Evaluating the effectiveness of sales promotion is a vital activity but a difficult one, especially in view of the synergistic effect.
7 Exhibitions, direct mail and public relations are important methods of marketing communication.
8 All promotional activity must be part of an integrated marketing campaign.

References

1 *Winkler on Marketing Planning* (Cassell/Associated Business Programmes, 1972).
2 *Directing the Marketing Effort* (Pan, 1975), Chapter 17, 'Sales Promotion'. Perhaps because the subject is a diffused and 'bitty' area, books tend to be less satisfactory. Willsmer, however, clearly illustrates the marketing manager's viewpoint.
3 In *Marketing* (M. & E. Handbooks, 1976).
4 An extremely valuable, 350-page book published by Business Books Ltd (1975).
5 *Directing the Marketing Effort*, op. cit.
6 His *Sales Promotion in Action* (Associated Business Press, 1979) is a masterly review of all of the Sales Promotion area.
7 In Dakin, Tony (ed.). *Sales Promotion Handbook* (Gower Press, 1974), chapter entitled 'Evaluating Sales Promotions'. This book is useful to dip into on particular aspects, though its multiple authorship and lack of cohesive sequence make it impossible to read for anyone wanting a clear understanding of the whole business of sales promotion.

Further Reading

Jefkins, Frank. *Advertising Today* (Intertext, 1971), chapters entitled 'Sales Promotion' and 'Merchandising'. Give useful lists of the various techniques. Jefkins also has chapters on Direct Mail and Exhibitions.
Lloyd, Herbert. *Teach Yourself PR* (English Universities Press, 1973). A sound introduction to the field of public relations.

Questions for Discussion

1 Why are 'on-pack' sales promotion techniques especially prevalent in super-markets?
2 What types of sales promotion might be appropriate in selling:

   (a) office furniture,
   (b) banking services for university students,
   (c) do-it-yourself gardening products?

3 What kind of point-of-sale advertising material and displays would you recommend for the following:

   (a) children's toys such as train sets and electric racing cars,
   (b) motor car accessories,
   (c) expensive cosmetics,
   (d) moderately priced hi-fi equipment,
   (e) office calculators?

4 At any trade exhibition you have recently visited, say which in your view was the most effective stand and why, and which the least effective and why.
5 In the shopping centre you normally use, make a survey of which retail outlets do and which do not use trading stamps. Why do you think this pattern has developed as it has?

6 (CAM, Nov. 1981) 'Public Relations is an intrinsic part of the marketing mix.'
Do you support this statement?
What arguments would you use to defend *and* oppose it? Include in your
answer a clear definition of the main areas of public relations.

18. *How International Marketing Works*

'Selling abroad is not synonymous with international marketing.'

Simon Majaro. *Applying Market Segmentation on a Global Scale*

18.1 Why Not Export?

In Great Britain we constantly hear of the need to 'increase our exports', 'Close the export gap', and 'Reduce the balance of payments deficit', and during the time of the Macmillan Government British industry was told 'exporting is fun'. Probably similar things are said in other countries dependent on international trading.

Why then is this chapter not headed 'Exporting' or even 'Export Marketing'? The reason is that such terms are altogether too limiting. They make too many assumptions and rule out too many potentially profitable alternatives.

In the article quoted at the head of this chapter Simon Majaro[1] goes on: 'There is a big difference between companies that syphon off excess home production into foreign markets and companies that start ab initio, exploring world markets as part of their overall marketing strategy.' As we shall see later, if we 'explore world markets' and decide that certain of them offer profitable marketing opportunities, then bringing goods into those markets from the 'home' country is only one way in which the marketing opportunities may be exploited. Local manufacture or shipment from a third country may well be a better bet.

Therefore, in this book exporting is considered as merely one way of meeting a need in some part of the world market (see Section 18.7 below).

18.2 Is International Marketing Different?

We start, then, from the standpoint that the whole world is a potential market, or series of markets. Each country and region will offer a different range of marketing opportunities, which arise from its own particular set of needs. The analysis of these markets becomes a question of deciding which of these many opportunities offers the best chance of success, bearing in mind our company's capability and resources.

It can be argued that this is precisely what we do in analysing marketing opportunities within our country of origin – the 'home market' as opposed to the 'export market' in the old-style jargon. Perfectly true. Fundamentally, there is no difference. Analysing marketing opportunities in Wales or the Midlands (if we happen to be based in, say, Hampshire), on the Eastern Seaboard or in the Middle

210

West (if we happen to be based in California), follows the same thought process as when we analyse markets in East Africa, South America, the Middle East or Australia. If we are selling paint, we need to know that the most popular colour in Devon is not the same as that in London, just as we need to know about similar differences between countries.

Are there then no differences in approach at all? Yes, there are – of two kinds. First comes the obvious differences of language, culture pattern, distribution methods, advertising media and the like. Second, there is a difference that is not so obvious and therefore much more important to come to terms with – what James A. Lee[2] has called the 'self-reference criteria'. Unconsciously we all see things from a particular viewpoint, according to our own cultural background. Carrying out an unbiased analysis and coming to clear-headed decisions about markets necessitates stepping outside this frame of self-reference.

These two things together (really they are the same thing viewed from two different levels) mean that the collection and analysis of facts about markets becomes overwhelmingly important. Although, if we are living in a particular country, we can always make use of more knowledge, there is much we already know. Just as we acquire our native language almost unconsciously, so, and in similar ways, we learn to sense how people react to certain things, and how best to present things to them. Similarly, we develop an awareness, at least in broad principle, of how advertising media function, what the distributive system is, how people shop. Take us outside the country we are most familiar with, and many of these assumptions will no longer apply. And the danger is we may not even realize that we are making assumptions.

One interesting behavioural example is quoted by Edward R. Hall Jnr.[3] In the United States two men will typically stand 18 to 20 inches away from each other when talking; anything closer is sensed as aggressive or even sexually abnormal. Latin Americans, on the other hand, usually get much closer when they talk. 'The interesting thing is', says Hall, 'that neither party is specifically aware of what is wrong when the distance is not right. They merely have vague feelings of discomfort or anxiety. As the Latin American approaches and the North American backs away, both parties take offence without knowing why!'

The colour yellow is unpopular in Muslim Pakistan because it suggests Brahmin robes. In the Far East white means mourning and blue is associated with sorrow.

As well as such cultural differences, there are many others about which assumptions can easily be made quite unconsciously. A chemist in the U.K. deals with both prescriptions and proprietary medicines; in Holland the pharmacist deals mainly with prescriptions, the druggist with proprietaries. In the main towns in East Africa there are shops operating much as in Europe, but in the villages the typical store is an open-fronted thatched hut selling everything from local produce to Brylcreem, matches, paraffin (probably called kerosene), and Aspro in packs containing one or two tablets. In many countries the radio is the most powerful advertising medium and, where there is a high level of illiteracy, it and the cinema assume a far greater importance than in Western Europe, for example.

Ignoring such differences can lead to costly failure. Yet, becoming aware of them means making a costly effort – not only the effort of gathering information, but also that of stepping out of one's own cultural frame of reference and coming to grips with what the differences mean in terms of marketing opportunity.

18.3 Differences between Markets

There are undoubted differences between markets. This is true within national borders: for example, it took two years for the mini-skirt fashion to travel from London to Cumbria, 300 miles away, where it lingered on long after it had virtually disappeared from the streets of London.

Between countries the differences can be very much greater. Notice, however, that there will be similarities between them also. On an ever-increasing scale the large westernized cities present much the same pattern of retail trading. There is a Carousel hypermarket (originating in France) serving the big cities of South Wales and there is a Burton's and a Marks and Spencer's store in Paris.

The differences can take many forms and to detect them means an analysis of the patterns within each country, under a number of main headings.

18.31 *Economic*

1 How is the population made up and how is it growing or declining?
2 Does the country import or export raw materials and food?
3 What is the state of economic development?
4 What is G.N.P.? Is it growing, and at what rate?
5 What is the foreign trade/balance of payments situation?
6 Are there import restrictions, or incentives for foreign investment? Are foreign companies encouraged or discouraged?
8 What is the cost of energy/raw materials/labour?
9 What is the balance between public planning and free enterprise?

18.32 *Political/Social*

1 Is it basically stable? Progressive or conservative?
2 What is the political system and what other strong influences (e.g. church, army) are there?
3 What is the strength of the trade unions?
4 What is the Government's attitude to free trade?
5 What are its monetary/credit policies?
6 What is the administrative set-up (bureaucratic, efficient)?
7 Are decisions made quickly and fairly?

18.33 *Cultural*

1 What are the general cultural influences (religious, historical)?
2 Are there tribal or similar complexities or a more homogeneous society?
3 What are the present trends in spending patterns (more leisure activities, eating out, holidays)?
4 What is the balance of personal expenditure on food and drink/housing, etc?

18.34 *Distribution*

1 What is the trading pattern?
2 What are the distribution methods?
3 How sophisticated are they, what changes are taking place?

18.35 *Legal*

1 What legislation is there affecting company structure, trading methods, product formulation, performance standards, labelling?
2 Is there any restriction on advertising?

18.4 Collecting Information on Markets

As the previous section indicates, a vast amount of information may have to be compiled to carry out a proper assessment of each market. Much of this is available as secondary data (see Sections 2.5 and 12.7), but there are great variations from one country to another in what kind of data can be obtained. As a generality, most of the developed industrial nations of the West are comparable with the U.K. in the availability of information (see Section 12.7). Fairly obviously, the less developed a country, the less information is likely to be available. For 'sources of sources' a good starting point for U.K. companies is the Department of Trade. Other developed countries have their own comparable government departments, which offer guidance (and often financial support, as in the case of the U.K.) to companies seeking information about foreign markets. Commercial Attachés in the appropriate British Embassies are often a good starting point for research 'on the ground'.

18.5 A Global Marketing Strategy

The essence of successful marketing is selecting profitable opportunities of using the company's resources and capabilities to satisfy consumers' needs. It is in this light that we must view the task of international marketing.

The term 'global marketing' is used by the Department of Industry, which defines it as follows:

Global marketing is becoming the keystone of successful business operation throughout the world. It refers to an attitude of mind, reflected in organisations, which regards all markets in the same light. There is no rigid distinction in thought between home and export markets; they are all *markets* and offer scope for sales. The fact that one market is nearer to the central point of control than the others is a relevant factor in decision making and perhaps in the techniques of selling, but this should not engender any fundamental difference in approach to the marketing activity.

The potential advantages of global marketing are many, and include:

(i) a larger volume of production; this might justify investment in more mechanised production methods and might therefore increase efficiency;
(ii) increased opportunities to counter falling orders from one area by increases from other areas;
(iii) learning more sophisticated marketing from contact with a wider range of markets and competitors;

(iv) keeping abreast of world-wide technical developments;
(v) opportunities to gain experience of the design, development and production of goods and services which are not called for in the United Kingdom, thereby extending the range of knowledge;
(vi) being in a better position to compete with foreign enterprises in the home market.

It is frequently argued that the disadvantage of global marketing is that selling overseas is less profitable than selling in the United Kingdom, because sales expense is greater or more working capital is required. Profitability cannot be argued so simply; it is a function of total trade. *The real question is whether the total business of an enterprise would be more profitable if it were based on U.K. trade alone than if it were based on international trade.*[4]

Indeed, such is now the problem of international trade, especially within trading blocks such as the E.E.C., that most companies will be meeting extensive international competition even within their 'home' market. Increasingly, therefore, everyone must take part in international marketing whether they choose to or not. The very concept of a 'home market' is totally outdated.

18.6 Alternative International Marketing Strategies

If it is decided that the total business would be more profitable if conducted on an international basis, then a number of different approaches are available. W. J. Keegan[5] lists them as follows:

Strategy One: same product, same message worldwide.
Strategy Two: same product, different communications.
Strategy Three: different product, same communications.
Strategy Four: dual adaptation.
Strategy Five: product invention.

Obviously, Strategy One gives tremendous advantages in simplicity of management and in cost-savings (in the manufacturing, R. & D. and marketing areas). However, this strategy can only be pursued if the same consumer need exists in each country, it is equally well satisfied by the product, and the same form of communication is equally clearly received. Coca-Cola is an obvious example and Esso's 'tiger' campaign another, but it is hard to think of many such consumer products. In the industrial products field, especially with capital goods, this strategy is much more common, however, since the needs and thought-patterns of, say, telecommunications engineers, are likely to be universal. Also, of course, the total demand within one country for a highly specialized product may be so small as to make that country unprofitable as a separate market.

The communications may have to be changed, because of differences in the media available (so that, for example, radio or cinema may have to take the place of TV as the main medium); because of cultural differences, which affect the way a message is perceived; because of the product's position in a 'foreign' market (e.g. Gauloises cigarettes are deliberately promoted in the U.K. as strongly French to capitalize on the cachet they offer to a minority market segment); or because the product is used differently (e.g. bicycles may be used for leisure or as a main means of transport, horticultural equipment for the garden or for farming on a small scale).

Modifying the product may be necessary for a number of reasons. For example, it may have to meet different safety standards (e.g. electrical appliances), or a different climate and conditions of use (cars with left-hand drive and air-conditioning); or different cultural practices and fashion standards.

Strategy Five, starting completely afresh with a new product, is likely to be the most costly, but, of course, if it is successful, it may produce the biggest profits. In many cases 'imported' products, because they were originally designed for different market conditions, can never be successful in more than a small segment of the market.

18.7 The Global Segmentation Approach

In addition to the possible changes in product and in marketing communications between one market and another, many factors might well have to change from

Country: ABC Product: XYZ (domestic appliance)	Elements of the marketing mix				
	Product	Price	Distribution	Promotion	Selling
1 The environment					
2 Cultural factors					
3 The consumer					
4 Economic development					
5 Industrial development					
6 Competitive trends					
7 Legal constraints	Strict electrical standards	Anti-cartel law; retail price maintenance allowed	Retail price maintenance; contracts with agents difficult to terminate	Strong trade mark laws. Trade Description Act. Restriction on advert expenditure	No restrictions. Trade description regulations
8 Marketing institutions					
9 Other factors					
	General remarks				

Figure 18.1 Matrix for segmenting international markets – 1 (source: reference 1)

one country to another, price, distribution, packaging (both in size/type of pack and in surface design) and servicing arrangements among them. To attempt to make all the necessary changes for every market throughout the world could not only be very costly but lead to a situation of mind-shattering complexity. Some degree of selection will normally be necessary.

Majaro[6] suggests a way of tackling the problem by carefully choosing segments of the global market. First, he distinguishes between 'undifferentiated marketing', in which the firm places on the market one product and tries to draw as many consumers as possible with one marketing mix, and 'differentiated marketing', in which the firm modifies the product and the mix to appeal specifically to each segment. Then he discusses the 'concentrated marketing' approach, by which a firm can maximize its limited resources and avoid the risk of spreading them too thinly around the world.

To achieve this, he suggests using a matrix (Figure 18.1) to summarize and tabulate the information about each market. Against each of the main factors about the market – environment, cultural factors etc. – we list the main features that will affect the elements of the marketing mix. The 'legal constraints' line has been completed as an example; in practice, each of the other cells would also be completed.

This information can then be compared, country by country, as in Figure 18.2, and a selection made of those countries where, across the board, a high degree of standardization is possible. The 'bench-mark' country will be either the 'home' country or one selected as a sufficiently promising market to justify its own specially developed mix. A judgement is then made as to how far each country, in each element of the marketing mix, approximates to the 10-mark 'norm' of the

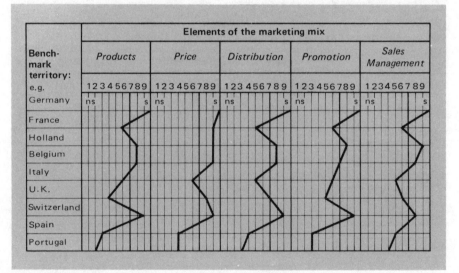

Figure 18.2 Matrix for segmenting international markets – 2 (source: reference 1)

bench-mark country. In the example shown Holland, Belgium and Switzerland all score consistently over the other countries, and therefore, with Germany, form a 'cluster' or 'segment', which could be successfully developed by means of the same mix. Other clusters of countries might be found, where a different mix could be used.

18.8 Servicing International Markets

Once it has been decided which products to sell in which markets, and how they are to be promoted, decisions have to be taken on the kind of sales organization to employ and where and how to manufacture.

18.81 *Sales Organization*

The four main ways in which the sales function can be carried out are the following:

1 *From the Home Base.* This is likely to be the situation where one or more of the following factors apply:

   (a) There is an important technical element, requiring close liaison between R. & D. and engineering staff and their opposite numbers in the customers' organizations; sales staff may themselves need to be well qualified technically.
   (b) Each customer's requirements are different, calling for a high degree of custom-building.
   (c) There are a small number of orders, each of high value.
   (d) Customers are thinly spread throughout many different countries.

2 *Using Overseas Agents*
3 *Overseas Sales Base.* These two methods represent a deeper and deeper degree of commitment to a specific country or area. They are likely to be used when there is a high level of sales in particular countries, especially when the price per unit is low and there is a large total volume through a large number of customers.
4 *Licensing Agreements.* In the long term a licensing agreement that permits a 'local' firm to produce and sell the product may well be the only way to retain a profitable interest in the market. Many developing countries, in fact, insist on the highest possible level of local manufacture – at the very least local assembly of imported components (e.g. Volkswagen cars are assembled in Nigeria from components made in Brazil).

18.82 *Manufacturing Organization*

In terms of manufacturing arrangements also there are a number of alternatives, as follows:

1 *Home-based Manufacture.* There will often be advantages in the highest possible level of home-based sales, for the following reasons

   (a) Economies of scale may apply.

(b) Fluctuations in individual markets may balance each other to give a 'steady' level of production.

(c) Management resources and skilled technical staff are less thinly spread.

Against this, stockholding and physical distribution costs may be much higher, and production planning and customer liaison much more complex. In addition, national tariffs and import quotas or pressure for local manufacture may well 'bend' the purely economic considerations.

2 *Local Manufacture.* Once the decision that local manufacture is desirable has been taken, then again a number of alternatives are possible:

(a) *Licensing Arrangement.* A local company can be given a licence to manufacture (usually where the product or its method of manufacture is patented). The 'home' company then has less commitment in terms of capital and management resources but still (through a royalty or share of profits arrangement) gets some return. Such an arrangement can often be used to overcome tariff or import restriction problems.

(b) *Manufacture under Contract.* This is an international version of the basic 'make or buy' decision. The 'home' company can concentrate on marketing and get a local company to make products to its own specification.

(c) *Partnership ('Joint Venture') Arrangement.* Together with a 'local' company a joint manufacturing subsidiary can be set up, the 'home' company supplying manufacturing expertise, the 'local' company supplying on-the-spot management knowledge of the market and some of the capital. Thus many of the burdens are shared (although so is the profit).

(d) *Wholly-owned Subsidiary.* The 'home' company can set up a complete wholly-owned subsidiary to manufacture in a particular country. Often this will take place as the last stage in a market development sequence along the lines of visiting salesman → local sales agent → local marketing subsidiary → local marketing and manufacturing subsidiary.

A company with one or more overseas manufacturing subsidiaries has a further series of options open to it. When deciding how to supply a new sales territory it can (a) ship product from the 'home base', (b) manufacture in the new territory (using the most appropriate of the methods listed above), or (c) ship product from a third country, i.e., one of its manufacturing units in a country other than the home base.

18.9 The Multinationals

The ultimate stage in the development of an international marketing policy comes when there is a substantial marketing and/or manufacturing unit in each of a number of different countries. Functions such as R. & D. product development, promotion, and market research may be developed in each 'national' unit, provided from 'home base' or from a regional headquarters. In any one territory the local unit of the multinational company may rank with, or even outrank, the big local companies.

Typical multinationals include the following:

I.C.I.   – home base U.K.
I.B.M.   – home base U.S.A.
Skefco   – home base Sweden
Philips
Electrical – home base Holland
Fiat   – home base Italy
Mitsubishi – home base Japan

Operating on this scale offers enormous advantages in terms of the flexibility referred to in Section 18.8. It opens the possibility of deciding where manufacture can most profitably be carried out. The company can also work out where tax advantages are greatest, and so where it is most advantageous to earn large profits ('transfer pricing', e.g., of components manufactured in one country for assembly in another gives a considerable measure of control over the level of profitability in any one country). Factors such as this can cause conflict between national Governments and the multinational companies, whose output can represent a high proportion of a 'host' country's Gross National Product and who may employ a significant proportion of the country's workforce. Increasingly, therefore, decisions cannot be taken solely in the company's own best interests, but must have regard for the possible social and political implications (see Section 10.6).

18.10 Summary

1 International (or 'global') marketing is much wider than simply exporting, which is merely one way of servicing a market.
2 While the fundamental concepts are the same, marketing internationally does call for a special approach in order to step outside one's normal cultural frame of reference.
3 Each market has its own special characteristics, determined by social, economic, political and cultural factors.
4 The global marketing approach regards all markets in the same light. There is no distinction between home and export markets; they are all markets and offer opportunities for profitable sales.
5 To service each potential market profitably, a choice has to be made between a number of alternative manufacturing and marketing organizations.
6 One approach to serving many markets profitably is the global segmentation technique, which 'clusters' countries into groups, each offering profitable opportunities for a given product or range of products.
7 The ultimate stage of development for a company successful in international marketing is likely to be the development of multinational status.

References

1 In 'Applying Market Segmentation on a Global Scale', *Marketing* (October, 1970).
2 In *Harvard Business Review* (March–April 1966).
3 In 'The Anthropology of Manners', *Scientific American* (April 1955).
4 In Annexe, 'Organisation for Overseas Marketing', in *Case Studies in Export*

Organisation (Department of Industry, 1971), p. 147. This booklet gives excellent summaries of the alternative sales/marketing organizations that are possible. The case studies themselves are unfortunately rather heavy reading, and should be approached with care.
5 In 'Five Strategies for Multinational Marketing', *European Business* (January 1970), pp. 35–40.
6 In 'Applying Market Segmentation etc.', op. cit.

Further Reading

Keegan, W. *International Marketing: Text and Cases* (McGraw-Hill, 1966). The classic general text.
Majaro, Simon. *International Marketing* (George Allen & Unwin, 1977) gives a far clearer conceptual approach than any of the earlier books.
Thorelli, H. B. (ed). *International Marketing Strategy* (Penguin Management Readings series, 1973). This book gives a clear view of many important aspects, and contains some excellent articles, most of them short and readable.
Tugendhat, Christopher. *The Multinationals* (Pelican, 1971). A very readable account of the development and significance of the multinational corporations.
Walsh, L.S. *International Marketing* (M & E Handbooks, 1978). A very comprehensive 'students notes' type book with useful chapters on marketing in six widely different countries.
Wilmshurst, John. *The Fundamentals of Advertising* (Heinemann, 1985). This has three chapters on advertising internationally with some useful comparisons.

Questions for Discussion

1 What is the difference between 'exporting' and 'international marketing'?
2 (IM, June 1981) Marketing principles suggest that the fact that a marketing programme is successful in one country gives little reason to suppose that it will be equally successful in another. Give a few of the major reasons why this should be so and show what practical steps can be taken to overcome these.
3 (CAM, Nov 1982) An American manufacturing company has asked for your guidance as to the most probable areas of concern for them should they decide to start trading in the United Kingdom. State the product they have selected and give the main headings in segmented order, indicating how these problems may be overcome.
4 What situations are you aware of where the interests of a multinational company are in conflict with those of a national Government?

19. *How Marketing Planning Works*

'To make the future happen one has to be willing to do something new. One has to be willing to ask: What do we really want to see happen that is quite different from today? One has to be willing to say: This is the right thing to happen as the future of the business. We will work on making it happen.'

Peter F. Drucker. *Managing for Results*

19.1 Making the Future Happen

This title of a film about marketing encapsulates a very important aspect of what marketing, indeed of what business as a whole, is all about. Unfortunately far too much of the average executive's time is spent reviewing the past or dealing with today's problems. Yet only action that affects tomorrow's situations can secure tomorrow's vital profits. As Section 10.3 stressed, marketing deals with a dynamic situation.

Drucker also says in the book quoted above: 'To try to make the future happen is risky; but it is rational activity. And it is less risky than coasting along on the comfortable assumption that nothing is going to change, less risky than following a prediction as to what "must" happen or what is "most probable". '[1]

Drucker has touched here on two very important points:

1 We cannot safely assume that things will continue exactly as they are, nor that present trends will continue.
2 Taking steps to control the future can be a rational activity.

The word normally used in management terms to describe this rational approach to controlling future events is 'planning' (the dictionary definition of 'plan' is 'arrange beforehand'.) Planning is an essential aspect of marketing and a prime function of marketing management.

Drucker particularly stresses the importance of identifying discontinuities in the way that economic and social trends are developing and then exploiting the time lag between the appearance of the discontinuity and its full impact. This he calls '*anticipation of the future that has already happened*'. Obvious examples of this in the mid-80s are the changes which must follow the 'microchip revolution' and the impact of population and employment change, in countries such as the U.K. where the proportion of older people who are 'retired', i.e. no longer holding jobs in the formal economy, is increasing rapidly.

The main areas in which we find these discontinuities which give rise to marketing opportunities are:

221

1 *Population and employment*, as in the above example. These changes suggest developing markets in such things as specialized leisure facilities; building and/or managing homes with warden/nursing care available.
2 *Changing social customs* (often associated with growing affluence) such as the trend in the U.K. to much greater frequency of eating out of the home.
3 *Technology* and the resulting changes in the way things can be done (automatic banking has developed rapidly and computer-operated shopping from home is beginning). However, we must not only look at 'high tech' developments but also at less spectacular improvements in ways of doing things. For example, growing garden plants in pots rather than in the ground has sparked off a whole 'instant gardening' trend where things can easily be planted at any time of year with a much increased success rate. Vastly increased sales – largely through garden centres rather than from traditional nurseries – has resulted.
4 *Structural change* such as 'convergence' where new technologies blur the edges between existing ones until eventually they disappear (e.g. adding machines and typewriters were quite separate developments, but there is now no clear division between a 'smart' typewriter – with a memory and possibly a small display screen – a word processor and a computer with visually displayed or printout information).
5 *Changes already happening elsewhere* – what is already happening in other countries, especially those more affluent and more 'advanced' might be capable of being 'made to happen' here, wherever 'here' is. The U.K. fast food revolution had already taken place much earlier in the U.S.A.

All such changes pose threats to existing businesses which do not react to the changes. However, they represent great opportunities to people able and willing to foresee the way the changes are likely to develop and to reallocate their own resources to take advantage of the opportunities.

Drucker comments:

' . . . tomorrow always arrives. It is always different. And then even the mightiest company is in trouble if it has not worked on the future. It will have lost distinction and leadership – all that will remain is big-company overheads . . . Not having dared to take the risk of making the new happen, it perforce took the much greater risk of being surpassed by what did happen. And this is the risk that even the largest and richest company cannot afford and that even the smallest business need not run'.

A much more recent study confirms Drucker's view. *In Search of Excellence*[2] reports on research carried out in the United States in 1977 through to 1980, to establish what are the factors that make some companies clearly more successful than others. The research, carried out by two senior McKinsey consultants, indicated that 'the excellent companies were, above all, brilliant on the basics'. They 'insisted on top quality. They fawned on their customers . . . They allowed their innovative and product "champions" long tethers. They allowed some chaos in return for quick action and regular experimentation.' In other words they did not allow themselves to get stuck in a complacent rut or become sleeping giants out of touch with the changing market-place.

19.2 Corporate Planning

It has become fashionable for the term 'corporate plan' or 'corporate strategy' to be used to describe a plan for the whole future activity of a business. Generally the plan is for 5 years (although it depends on the industry and the particular needs of the company concerned). More detailed 1- and 2-year plans are then developed.

The planning process comprises a sequence of steps along such lines as the following:

1 Assessing political, economic, social and technological trends on a national and international basis.
2 Evaluating the company's own particular strengths and weaknesses.
3 Relating these to the likely situation developing from (1). In particular, trying to pinpoint opportunities the company's strengths are well suited to exploit.
4 Setting quantified objectives.
5 Working out strategies to achieve these objectives.
6 Preparing detailed plans and assigning tasks in order to carry out the strategies.

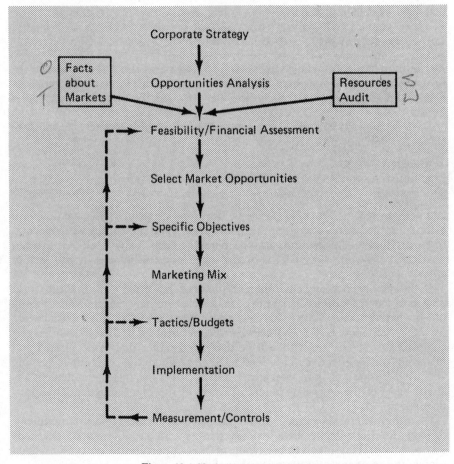

Figure 19.1 Marketing planning process

Clearly, as time goes on, the assessments of likely trends will need to be modified. The company's relative position – its strengths and weaknesses in relation to competition and to the developing situation – will change. So the corporate plan must be regularly up-dated.

Only the most sophisticated companies use this approach in its most developed form, although more and more are moving towards it. If, however, we are to control the development of the company to any extent at all and not simply be carried along by events, then some degree of planning is surely essential. Quite apart from anything else, we must assume that if we do not plan for change we shall eventually run out of business. The life-cycle of our existing products (Section 4.4) will have run its full course.

19.3 The Marketing Planning Process

The planning process outlined in Section 19.2 can be usefully explored in more detail with the help of Figure 19.1.

19.31 *Corporate Planning*

Marketing plans are a detailed expression of 'how to get there' (how to make the future happen). But first there has to be a corporate vision of where 'there' is. Thus top management must take a clear view of where the company as a whole is heading.

Ansoff[3] suggests that the successful management of a business depends on successful decisions at three levels:

1 strategic
2 administrative
3 operational

and goes on to point out that 'Strategic decisions are primarily concerned with external, rather than internal, problems of the firm and specifically with selection of the product-mix of the firms and the markets to which it will sell'. Or in other words 'What business the firm is in and what kinds of business it will seek to enter'.

In the rapidly changing environment, pictured in Section 19.1, that the world now represents, decisions do have to be made. No company can simply drift along doing whatever comes next. There needs to be a clear idea of 'what business are we in?' (See Section 1.2.) Otherwise the necessarily limited resources any company has to operate with will be dissipated rather than concentrated and hence not totally effective. This need to be clear where the company is heading and what business it is in (sometimes referred to as a 'mission statement') is at the heart of the corporate planning aspect of top management's long-range decisions.

Once this general direction has been clarified (our business is in entertainment, or food and drink, or business systems) then specific product/market decisions can be taken. This involves balancing market opportunities on the one hand against the company's resources on the other.

19.32 *Resources Audit*

A key aspect of successful management is to ensure that on the one hand a company's resources are fully employed in profitable ventures. On the other hand disaster can come if it takes on ventures which overstretch its resources.

A careful review or audit of resources needs therefore to be carried out on a regular basis so that management is very clear what resources it does and does not have to operate with. It is convenient to carry out this audit under a number of headings:

1 *Production capability*. What experience/equipment/know-how do we have in providing particular products or services and in what other areas could these be relevant?
2 *Marketing capability*. Similarly what is our experience in distributing and promoting to particular markets, what distribution channels and systems do we have available?
3 *Manpower resources*. What kind of people do we have, with what skills, experience and abilities?
4 *Financial resources*. Any new project is almost certain to need both capital investment to launch it and continuing finance to see it through the early stages of the life-cycle and into a profitable state; 'over-trading' – taking on more trade than a company can finance is still one of the commonest causes of bankruptcy – stock manufactured but not sold and goods delivered but not yet paid for can be voracious eaters of capital.
5 *Image*. Most companies have an 'image' of some sort – that is their market sees them in a particular light and this can be a valuable asset. New ventures therefore should when possible reinforce this clear and favourable image not conflict with it and thus confuse the customers (see Section 19.4).

The above concentrates on knowing positively which resources we have but it is of course also important to be clear what resources we do *not* have. A common experience of the author and other consultants is to be asked to advise on marketing a new product and to find that the company can easily manufacture it but is in no way geared to market it (and is usually also short of finance for the long haul required to establish itself in a market which is totally new to it).

19.33 *Selecting Marketing Opportunities*

Alongside the resources audit an analysis of market opportunities will be taking place. This is based on a constant review of 'facts about markets' (see Figure 19.1) provided by the company's marketing information system (see Section 2.5).

Out of these many opportunities a selection has to be made of those which are:

(a) feasible, given the company's resources (see Section 19.32) (for example the fast food boom provides many market opportunities, but they may not be feasible for a company whose experience is in some totally different direction such as heavy engineering).
(b) potentially profitable.

The latter needs to be established as early as possible. Often no-one does any figuring until enthusiasm for the project has caused many hours of precious manpower and much expenditure has been committed. If the project is then aborted because it is not financially attractive all of this time, effort and money has been wasted. It should therefore be established at the outset whether the venture looks likely to be profitable (the calculations will need refining at least once as the project goes along).

One common failing in this area is that many people only look at those opportunities that are obvious extensions of what they are already doing. There are often other more profitable opportunities which would be preferable if only some-one had established that they existed. This is why 'facts about the market' must be gathered on a continuing basis and market opportunities compared as against another.

19.34 *Where the Marketing Department Comes in*

In the sequence shown in Figure 19.1, the first steps are mainly the responsibility of top management (often assisted in large organizations by a 'corporate planning team'). They will call on the marketing department for facts, figures and forecasts and will draw on past marketing experience. But the direct responsibility is theirs. When we get into deciding on which marketing opportunities to go for, the marketing department becomes more deeply involved, although top management would normally take the main decisions. Once, as a result of the feasibility and financial studies, specific opportunities are selected, then it becomes primarily a marketing task to elaborate those decisions into specific objectives and to work out and implement the details of how they are to be achieved.

19.4 The Central Importance of the Marketing Mix

Chapter 3 discussed the necessity of using the marketing mix – the 4 P's and the S – as a kind of check-list to ensure that we can deliver customer satisfaction in all the key aspects of the total marketing activity. Section 1.9 showed how a company's 'competitive differential advantage' can derive from any one of the key elements in the marketing mix. The time has come to examine another dimension of the marketing mix. This is that in practice it is not possible to examine one element such as price without considering possible effects on other elements. For example, if we decide that the price must be substantially reduced we may have to reduce the quality of the product to help make it possible. If a product needs heavy promotion to help establish it in the market-place with a strong image to which customers can relate, the price may have to be increased to help finance it.

Figure 19.2 indicates the different approaches or strategies that can emerge from varying combinations of high/medium or low price with high medium or low product quality. At one extreme we can offer a low-priced, low quality product. In some situations many people will happily opt for this combination. But others will prefer the opposite extreme of top quality at a premium price. 'Fly-by-night' street traders may operate with high prices and low quality but that will not be a suitable strategy for companies wanting repeat business from an established and loyal clientele.

An interesting pattern has emerged when a wide range of marketing executives (male and female, old and young from all sectors of British industry) attending the

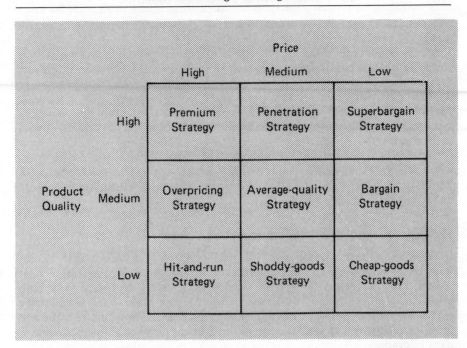

Figure 19.2 Nine marketing mix strategies (from: P. Kotler, *Marketing Management*, Prentice Hall, 1976)

author's 'Fundamentals of Marketing' seminars over the period 1981–3 were asked to say how they as customers perceived the trading policies of three major U.K. retail chains.

Marks and Spencer were always placed towards the top left-hand corner but with much discussion over which part of which square.

British Home Stores were placed, virtually without exception, firmly in the middle of the middle square.

Woolworths posed great problems and it was seldom possible for the groups (with numbers ranging from 12–30 in each group) to reach agreement. Some people still saw Woolworth as pursuing a 'cheap goods' strategy (firmly and clearly their policy at one stage but far from the facts of the 1980s). Some had been impressed by the 'Wonder of Woolies' advertising which showed a wide range of merchandise in an exciting 'show business' atmosphere but had then been disappointed by the merchandise, store layout and staff behaviour when they actually visited a store.

Further discussion elicited the feeling that both Marks and Spencer and British Home Stores had 'got it all together' with merchandise, pricing, store layout, staff and promotion all of a piece and each presenting a coherent believable consistent story which appealed to many people. Woolworths on the other hand were still struggling (under a recently appointed new management) to 'get their act together' in a changing environment already very different from the one they had once dominated with their clearcut '3d and 6d' (cheap goods strategy) approach of many years earlier.

A very important aspect of the whole marketing planning process is thus arriving at that emphasis right across the marketing mix which enables customers to relate strongly and firmly to the company and its products and thus be happy to do business with them. A low price alone, a good product or a fantastic advertising campaign by itself will not do unless *all* the elements of the marketing mix are individually correct but also reinforce each other and are consistent with each other.

The tactics to be used and the budgets to be allocated (what needs to be done, when, and by whom, using what resources) depend on this clear establishment of what is to be communicated. (The 'competitive differential advantage' referred to in Section 1.7.)

19.5 The Importance of Measurement and Control

In drawing up the marketing plan, it is vitally important to include at the outset ways of knowing how the implementation of it is proceeding against pre-set targets. For this reason the Specific Objectives in Figure 19.1 need to be both quantified and measurable. Otherwise it will be impossible to tell whether the plan is working or not. The quantified objectives can be based on revenue and profit targets, market shares, return on investment or whatever combination is most relevant.

Measurement may involve rapid feed-back of sales figures, retail audits (to give both turnover at point of sale and also market share information) and sometimes opinion survey type research – especially when the selling process is a lengthy one.

Figure 19.1 shows this information being 'fed back' up the line. Thus in the light of actual achievement, tactics may have to be changed or objectives revised. It may even be necessary in the light of experience 'in the field' for the whole feasibility and financial viability of the project to be reviewed. It is better for this to be done early on and the project terminated so that losses can be cut rather than for the juggernaut to roll forward consuming resources to no ultimate purpose.

19.51 *Contingency Plans*

Sometimes, it can be foreseen that the original plan may have to be changed if certain situations are encountered in the market (e.g. a known possible competitor does in fact enter). In this case plans can be made in advance against such a contingency and swung in to replace the original plan when the situation changes. The availability of such contingency plans prepared in advance can avoid the necessity for hasty re-planning in a 'panic' situation.

19.52 *Sub-divisions of the Marketing Plan*

The marketing plan, itself ideally developed within the total corporate plan, will contain a series of sub-plans. Generally the corporate plan is designed for a lengthy term (say 5 years), and the marketing plan for a shorter term (say 2 years).

The sub-plans will often be short-term (1 year or less). The following sub-plans are usual, with others perhaps being added in particular situations:

1 The Sales Plan will detail how the selling effort is to be deployed – balancing servicing existing accounts against gaining new ones, detailing the relative effort to be put into each part of the product range. It will indicate call rates, journey cycles etc. Items such as conversion rates of orders to calls and new accounts opened will be quantified.
2 The Advertising Plan will indicate matters such as target audiences and the relative importance to be attached to them, expenditure in the various alternative media etc. Quantification will be in terms of number of new users of the product, increase in brand awareness, coupon response rate, or other criteria, depending on the situation.
3 A Sales Promotion Plan.
4 A Market Research Plan.

19.6 The Importance of Budgets

We have referred to the importance of quantifying targets. Another aspect of this is that all phases of the marketing plan must be budgeted as accurately as possible, in terms both of costs and of anticipated income. Since there eventually must be a profit (even though in the short-or-medium-run a loss might be acceptable) it is essential at all stages to know what are the expectations in this respect. Incidentally, an important aspect of the 'controls' will be devoted to methods of monitoring income and expenditure against budgets. Break-even analysis (Section 6.31) may play an important part in the development of plans and arriving at acceptable budgets.

Another aspect of budgeting, which has assumed increasing importance in recent times, is 'cash flow'. Not only is it vital than an adequate profit should ensue from any marketing activity, but also the necessary funds to finance each stage of the operation must be available without undue cost and without crippling the firm in other directions.

With new ventures particularly it is almost a certainty that in the early stages there will be a net outflow of funds (i.e. outgoings will exceed income). The timing and level of the flow of money in each direction – the cash flow – must therefore be carefully predicted and monitored if serious hold-ups and/or expensive borrowings are to be avoided. In all marketing planning, a key factor will almost certainly be the level of profit a project is likely to generate, either in the short-or in the long-term. (See Section 4.52.)

19.7 Marketing Forecasting

Forecasting demand is an important aspect both of arriving at a total long-range corporate plan and of preparing detailed shorter-term marketing plans. In the first case management must have an idea of the size of any predicted market developments, in order to estimate the resources needed to seize the opportunity presented. In the second case distribution, price, and promotional resources (including size of sales force, level of advertising budget) all depend on an accurate assessment of the likely level of sales.

How then can accurate forecasts be made?

William J. Stanton[4] suggests that there are basically two approaches – the 'top-down' and the 'build-up'.

The 'top-down' approach works as follows:

1 Start from a forecast of general conditions (stage 1 of the corporate planning approach outlined in Section 19.2).
2 Use this to estimate the total market potential for the product in question.
3 Apply to this figure the proportion of market share the company can expect to achieve.

The 'build-up' approach, instead of starting from broad economic estimates, begins with separate estimates for each of a number of market sectors or organizational units within the company. These are then added together to form the total market estimate. For example, a company might be selling electronic components to a number of different industries – home entertainment, tele-communications, aerospace etc. A projected new range of components could have a number of different applications within each industry. Estimating each and collating the estimates gives the total forecast.

It is of course likely that the 'build-up' approach will be more applicable where the new ventures are developments of existing business and that the 'top-down' method may have to be used for a completely new departure. Note too that, inevitably, there is a fair amount of intuition and 'guesstimating' in these approaches. There is no way that we can achieve certainty about the future. All we can do is to be systematic instead of haphazard, and to subject all our guesses to careful scrutiny, to compare the unknown with the known to see if it appears reasonable. There are a number of well established forecasting methods we can use.

19.8 Forecasting Methods

19.81 *Survey of Buyer Intentions*

Since forecasting is an attempt to gauge the quantities of future purchases, the most obvious method is to ask buyers what they intend to buy. In some cases this is a perfectly reasonable approach. For example, component and sub-assembly suppliers to major industries often work on a forward contract basis or at any rate work in close liaison with their major customers.

More often, however, buyers may be unwilling to disclose their intentions. In a volatile industry they themselves may not know what their future buying pattern is likely to be; even when they are clear on their future intentions, they may in the event not carry them out. In many cases, too, where there are many buyers with diverse interests, the cost of collecting the information may be too high relative to its value. It is thus likely to be of the greatest value in a fairly stable industry with few buyers.

19.82 *Composite of Sales Force Opinion*

Since salesmen or middlemen (agents or distributors, for example) are closest to the market, they can be said to be in a good position to make reliable estimates. Clearly there are potential problems, in that salesmen are not generally trained to make unbiased estimates, and indeed may have (or believe they have) reason to introduce bias (e.g. they may want to minimize likely demand so that their performance will show up well against the targets set). But, especially where there is a high technical element, the salesman, from his close personal knowledge of and relations with his customers, may well have a contribution to make, even if his views have to be weighed rather carefully for possible bias in one direction or another.

19.83 *Expert Opinion*

Particularly where a new venture is concerned, or where long-range forecasting is employed, past and present experience may be largely irrelevant. How do you estimate what the consumption will be in 10 years' time for a product that does not exist yet? How do you calculate the off-take of as yet undesigned components for engineering projects themselves still in the preliminary consideration stage?

One approach is to consult a number of experts in the field and ask them to guess what the future situation is likely to be. One refinement of this is the 'Delphi Technique' (the name derives from the Delphic oracle of ancient Greece). A number of expert 'guesses' are built into a combined 'scenario', which is fed back to the individual experts for comment and revision. Stage by stage the scenario is modified until a 'consensus' is reached. Sometimes a number of alternative scenarios are developed, so that alternative plans can be built upon them.

19.84 *Time Series Analysis*

This method goes right to the other extreme and attempts to use past patterns to project future trends. The simplest example is the sales graph over a number of years, showing a consistent trend, which is then extrapolated to indicate the likely future development of the trend. This method has considerable attraction because at least in its basic form it is simple and also because it is based on facts. However, it has considerable inherent dangers, unless the underlying factors producing the trend are clearly understood. Otherwise an unanticipated change in one of the factors will completely wreck the forecast.

Philip Kotler[5] points out that a series of sales figures plotted over time (time series analysis) contains the three following components:

1 *Trend*. The result of basic developments in population, capital formation, technology.
2 *Cycle*. House-building, for example, shows swings (undulations in the curve) related to the general level of economic activity, which itself tends to have a cyclical pattern.
3 *Season*. Many products show distinct seasonal peaks and troughs – some, like toys for obvious reasons, others less obvious.

Time series analysis uses mathematical techniques to separate out these components, and also to isolate any extraneous or 'random' factors (such as strikes, price wars, fads, abnormal weather conditions) which obscure the underlying patterns. Detailed analysis of this kind, which can be a formidable undertaking, is often only possible by the use of specially developed computer programs.

19.85 *Market Factor Analysis*

A market factor is an element in the market which can be quantitatively measured and which has a direct relation to the demand for a particular product. For example, the number of housing starts is a market factor contributing to the demand for plumbing components, the number of two-year-old cars is a market factor in the demand for replacement tyres. When the relation is as obvious as this, market factor analysis can be a very cheap and reliable method of forecasting.

19.86 *Statistical Demand Analysis*

Unfortunately in many cases the factors contributing to demand are not so obvious as those just cited. However, by means of statistical techniques, one can develop equations that may demonstrate a correlation between past sales figures and a single variable (simple regression analysis) or a number of variables (multiple regression). The variables may be population figures, income levels etc.

Depending on the precision of the 'fit' between sales and those predicted by the equation, the equation may then possibly be used to predict future sales on the basis of the variables in question. However, a high volume of computer analysis is needed for these calculations, and figures over many years are necessary before a 'fit' good enough to ensure accurate prediction can be obtained.

19.87 *Executive Judgement*

Stanton[6] makes the point that 'all the previously discussed forecasting methods should be tempered with sound executive judgement. Forecasting should not be done solely by slide rule, computer or mathematical model'. He goes on: 'On the other hand, forecasting by executive opinion alone is a risky technique. In some instances, it is simply intuition or guesswork.' Perhaps in the end, the purpose of the more sophisticated techniques is to reduce the possibility of some of the wilder guesses being acted upon.

19.88 *The Role of Marketing Research*

It will be realized that many of the above forecasting techniques depend on the availability of suitable information. Often marketing research techniques will have to be used to gather and analyse this data. In Section 19.6 we see the importance of controls as part of the marketing plan. Here, too, marketing research normally plays a vital role in providing a flow of data, which enable performance to be continuously monitored.

19.9 Estimating Market Potential for a Civil Engineering Contractor

A U.K.-based company was involved in large design and construction projects.

Analysis showed that most of its work had been in three main areas – off-shore oil rigs, nuclear power stations and petro-chemical plants. Its particular experience, know-how and equipment therefore gave it a competitive edge in these markets. However, all three had gone into the doldrums by the end of 1980, owing to the recession and to the fact that the off-shore oil rigs building boom had peaked in the U.K.

So, virtually for the first time, business had to be sought elsewhere. Teams had been sent to various other countries on a rather ad hoc basis and and an office established in Saudi Arabia. These however, were panic measures and a planned campaign to seek overseas business was necessary.

Fortunately, such major projects are announced well ahead; for example *Nuclear News* publishes twice a year a 'World List of Nuclear Power Plants and *Ocean Industry* a yearly list of 'Offshore Platforms under Construction and Planned' (based on a survey of 128 oil companies and 89 designers and fabricators).

Based on these and other sources a table was developed showing the approximate value of all projects, listed by stages, for 1981 through to 1985, country by country. This immediately made clear which were the countries with the most potential (the U.K. market showed a continuing dramatic decline).

Two other factors needed to be considered. The first was competition. All main competitors were known and their strengths in the various countries could be estimated (although to a large extent this is a truly international market).

The other factor was to assess how much of the value of each project was the kind of work that the company's resouces were geared to. So a number of calculations were done (based largely on past projects) to work out the main elements involved in each type of project and then the projections re-worked in terms of the total potential value *to the company* country by country.

Thus a clear picture was developed showing, over a 5-year period, fairly precisely how much business was likely to be available country by country. This enabled a very detailed marketing campaign to be developed for a carefully planned approach to the market.

At another level of planning, individual large customers were identified and a dossier prepared on each. This included details of the company's past dealings with that customer (where they had occurred), who were the relevant executives, what were their links with customers and so on.

So not only could rational decisions be made on which countries to tackle, but the sales team could be given very specific targets to attack, with precise turnover figures to aim for.

19.10 Conclusion

In this chapter and throughout this book we have seen that marketing is a vital aspect of the managementof any business. Because it is concerned with the future and with the behaviour or many individual people, it can never be an exact science. However, that does not mean that it should ever be irrational. The use of careful study, logical thought-patterns, detailed monitoring of results and quick reaction in the light of experience can avoid many costly mistakes and add greatly to profitability.

19.11 Summary

1 A prime function of all management, and of marketing in particular, is to take rational steps to 'make the future happen'.
2 The ideal starting point is a corporate plan setting out quantitative objectives and strategies for achieving them.
3 From this a marketing plan can be developed, with sub-plans for sales, advertising, market research etc.
4 Forecasting likely demand is a vital activity of marketing, both in providing a basis for the long-range corporate plan and in working out the shorter-term detailed marketing plan.
5 There is a range of methods of forecasting demand, with varying degrees of accuracy and levels of cost.
6 All plans must include budgets, and these form a vital element in the control procedures, without which no plan can function properly.
7 We conclude with the thought that marketing can never be an exact science but nevertheless is a rational, as well as a vital, activity.

References

1 In *Managing for Results* (Pan, 1967) Peter F. Drucker has been described as the 'guru' of modern management. This book is a very readable statement of his main ideas. His starting point is that 'Results depend not on anybody within the business. They depend on somebody outside – the customer in a market economy'. The book is really therefore all about marketing, but viewed from the standpoint of general management rather than as a specialist activity. Any marketing man should have his own copy and read it regularly.
2 *In Search of Excellence* by Thomas J. Peters and Robert H. Waterman Jnr. (Harper & Row, 1982).
3 *In Corporate Strategy* (Pelican, 1975).
4 In *The Fundamentals of Marketing* 3rd ed. (McGraw-Hill, 1971).
5 In *Marketing Management* (Prentice Hall, 1977). There are many books on methods of forecasting, but Chapter 7 of Kotler's book goes into sufficient detail for all but the specialist.
6 In *The Fundamentals of Marketing* op.cit.

Further Reading

Coventry, William F. *Management Made Simple* (W H Allen, 1970). Chapter 7 is a brief introduction to setting objectives in planning.
Winkler, John. *Winkler on Marketing Planning* (Cassell/Associated Business Programmes, 1972). Up-to-date, practical in its approach and carrying many interesting examples. Chapters 2–4 are particularly relevant to planning. Chapter 8 deals briefly with marketing models.
Wilson, R.M.S. *Management Controls and Marketing Planning* (Heinemann, 1979) is particularly useful on the financial control aspects of marketing planning.

Questions for Discussion

1 What are some market factors you might be able to use in estimating the market

potential for the following?

(a) Indoor television aerials.
(b) Marketing textbooks.
(c) Domestic electric cookers.
(d) Oscilloscopes.

2 (IM, June 1983) How is an annual marketing plan created and what is it used for?
3 What do you see as the importance of executive judgement in the marketing planning process?
4 (CAM, June 1982) You are a shoe manufacturer whose sales are restricted to your own region. You wish to become a national brand. You are the Marketing/Sales Director. Explain your strategy and what you hope to achieve in a given time.
It is important that you state clearly any assumptions you consider necessary to develop your arguments to the other members of your board. The company is privately owned, largely by members of one family.
5 How far do you agree with the statement that marketing can never be an exact science?

Index

Acquisition of new products, 51
Ad hoc research, 125
Added value, 7
Advertising, 18,92,173–96
Advertising agencies, 19, 188–91
Advertising budgets, 186–8
Advertising planning, 185–6, 193–5
Advertising research, 129–31
Attitudes, 114
Audits, 126–8

BARB, 131
Behaviour, customer, 8, 112–14
Bias, 143
Brand image, 177
Brand personalities, 115
Brand manager, 109
Branding, 94
Break-even analysis, 66–8
Budgets, advertising, 186–8
Budgets, marketing, 229
Business ethics, 119
Business to business marketing, 13
Buyer behaviour, *see* Customer behaviour

Campaigns, advertising, 193
Campaigns, integrated, 98
Case histories, 57, 137, 182, 232
Changing needs, 36–8
Channels of distribution, 79–88
Cluster sampling, 143
Codes of practice, 119–22
Cognitive dissonance, 152
Commission for salesmen, 160
Communication, methods of, 97, 214
Communication, two-way, 98, 151
Communication process, 97
Communications with sales force, 170
Competitive differential advantage, 10, 65
Competitors, 18, 70
Consumer attitudes, 180
Consumer needs, *see* Customer's needs
Consumerism, 116–19
Controllable variables, 11
   see also marketing mix
Cost, 10, 63, 66–70
Cost-plus method of pricing, 66
C.T.N., 84
Customer behaviour, 8, 114
Customer-oriented, 3

Customer's needs, 5, 26, 36–8, 112, 114, 118

Data, primary and secondary, 20
Decision-making unit, 154, 155
Demand, 63
Demographic segmentation, 45
Differential pricing, 73
Direct mail, 205
Direct marketing, 80, 177
Discount, 72–3
Distribution, 29–30, 78–89
Down-market, 94

Economic model of customer behaviour, 63–6, 112
Ethics, 119–22, 181
Exclusive distribution, 86
Exhibitions, 204
Export, 210

Forecasting, 229–33
Four P's, *see* Marketing mix
Franchising, 82

Gap analysis, 55, 135
Global marketing strategy, 215
Group discussions, 22, 129

Hall tests, 133
Hierarchy of needs (Maslow), 8
Hypermarkets, 82

Industrial marketing, 13
Innovation, 3, 49
Innovative products, 50
Innovators, 57
Integrated campaigns, 98
Intensive distribution, 86
International marketing, 210–19
Interviewing methods, 21

Key accounts, *see* National accounts

Laggards, 57
Life cycle, customers', 113
Life cycle, product, *see* Product life-cycle
Loss leader, 200

Marginal cost pricing, 69
Market research, *see* Marketing research

Market segmentation, 45, 54
Marketing concept, 2–7
Marketing communications, 96
Marketing, definition of, 1
Marketing department, 101–10
Marketing mix, 11, 26–33
Marketing process, 11
Marketing research, 16–24, 124–48
Marketing research (organization of), 18
Marketing services, 2, 104
Mark-up, 72–3
Maslow's hierarchy of needs, 8
Media planning, 191
Merchandisers, 96
Merchandising, 200
Middlemen, 80–3
Mix, marketing, *see* Marketing mix
Mix, product, 42
Mix, promotional, 91, 175
Models of customer behaviour, 112–14
Motivating salesmen, 159–61
Motivational research, 20, 117
Multinationals, 199
Multi-stage sampling, 143

National accounts, 73
Needs, 5–8
Needs, hierarchy of, 8
Negotiation, 73
New products, 49–60
Nielson retail audits, 126
Non-controllable variables, 11

Omnibus surveys, 129
Organization of marketing departments, 106–10

P's, four, *see* Marketing mix
Package testing, 131
Packaging, 43, 200
Panels, 21, 126
Penetration pricing, 71
Personal selling, 91, 98, 150–63
Physical distribution, 86
Place (in the marketing mix), 29–30, 78–89
Placement tests, 133
Plateau effect (on price), 63
Point of sale, 199
Positioning, 94
Postal questionnaires, 21
Post-purchase feelings, 8, 199
Price, 27, 62–76
Price brackets, 63
Price changes, 73–5
Price-setting, 75
Price sructures, 72
Pricing policies, 29
Pricing strategies, 70–2

Primary data, 20
Product, 10, 27, 35–45
Product, definition of, 35
Product development, 49–60
Product differentiation, 44
Product elimination, 42
Product life-cycle, 38–42
Product manager, 109
Product-market strategies, 35
Product mix, 42
Products, new, 49–57
product-oriented, 3
Product range, 29, 42
Product testing, 131
Production-oriented, 103
Profit, 2, 6, 32, 39, 41, 49, 52, 56, 69, 166, 229
Promotion, 10, 28, 90–9
Promotion, definition of, 90
Promotional aims, 92
Promotional methods, selection of, 97
Promotional mix, 91
Psychographic segmentation, 45
Public relations, 175, 182, 205–7

Qualitative research, 117
Quantitative research, 117
Questionnaires, 143–5
Quota sampling, 141

Random sampling, 141
Recruiting salesmen, 155–7
Resources, 11, 225
Retail audits, 126
Retailers, 80–3
Risk and uncertainty, 11
Risks, 16

Sales force management, 164–71
Sales force organization, 162–7, 217
Sales force performance evaluation, 170
Sales promotion, 98, 174, 178–9, 197–207
Sales territories, 169–70
Salesman, role of, 95, 150–3
Sampling, 141–3
Secondary data, 20, 146, 213
Segmentation, 45, 54
Selective distribution, 86
Selling, 91, 98, 150–63
Selling process, 152
Service, 10, 31
Services marketing, 13
Skim-the-cream pricing, 71
Social marketing, 7
Social-psychological model of customer behaviour, 113
Social responsibility, 119
Socio-economic classification, 145
Sponsorship, 207

Stratified sampling, 143
Supermarkets, 82
Survey methods, 21
Syndicated research, 128

Telephone interviewing, 21
Telephone selling, 168
Test marketing, 56, 133
Timing, importance of, 31
Trade promotions, 201

Training salesmen, 157–9

Up-market, 94

Value, added, 7
Value, concept of, 6
Voluntary chains, 82

Warehousing, 86
Wholesalers, 79
Word-of-mouth, 97

GLOSSARY OF MARKETING TERMS
Norman A. Hart and John Stapleton

This book contains a comprehensive selection — over 2,000 entries in the second edition — spanning the complete range of present-day marketing and associated terminology including research, management, export, packaging, advertising, raw materials, selling, public relations, law etc. It may be used equally as a source of reference and instruction and will prove invaluable to marketing professionals throughout the world not to mention students learning the profession.

'I consider that the authors, are to be warmly congratulated on their efforts to satisfy a real need of the students of marketing with this pioneering work. A start has to be made somewhere and they have given us the lead.' Professor Michael Baker
Quarterly Review of Marketing
Second edition 1981/208 pages/183 × 123/434 91861 X

ECONOMICS: AN INTRODUCTION FOR STUDENTS OF BUSINESS AND MARKETING
Frank Livesey

Frank Livesey believes that producers are at the heart of the economic system, and he discusses both the way their activities — including the marketing process — affect the community and the way they respond to the community's needs. In doing so he demonstrates the close relationships between producers and consumers on the one hand and producers and government on the other.

The book comprises four main Parts. The first examines the elements making up the economic system, the second and third cover micro-economics and macro-economics respectively, and the last takes a critical look at the current economic policies and institutions.
'Students will find this an easy textbook to use: the style is clear and leisurely, the index comprehensive, the subheadings are liberal, the diagrams large and accurate . . .'
Marketing Forum
1986/272 pages/254 × 159/434 91156 9

MANAGEMENT CONTROLS AND MARKETING PLANNING
R. M. S. Wilson

Effective management implies skilled planning and control. This book which supersedes *Management Controls in Marketing* describes the techniques available to the marketing executive. It emphasises the importance of strategic planning and deals with the application of models, the use of information systems, and the likely problems to be encountered in marketing practice.

It will be invaluable reading for students taking the Diploma examination of the Institute of Marketing. It will also appeal to those on related courses including HND/HNC Business Studies, Diploma in Management Studies, and the professional stage syllabuses of the Institute of Cost and Management Accountants and Association of Certified Accountants; Marketing practitioners will find in it much of value.

Reviews of *Management Controls in Marketing:*
'Mr Wilson's book is a thorough, comprehensive compendium of useful check-lists, relevant questions and helpful techniques, all carefully set out and applied to the various facets of marketing.'
The Economist
'This book is happily not just another recital of available techniques; nor is it uncritical of system for system's sake.'
Management Review and Digest
1979/240 pages/254 × 159/434 92266 8

MARKETING PLANS: HOW TO PREPARE THEM, HOW TO USE THEM
Malcolm H. B. McDonald

Crucial to a company's success is the definition of objectives that are achievable and realistic and the development of a business plan that sets out in detail what elements of the marketing mix are necessary to bring them about. This book, based on much practical research in industry, describes the marketing planning process, how a thorough marketing audit is carried out, how strategies are evolved and costed, and how aspects such as price, distribution, information systems, and forecasting, often overlooked, are an integral part of the marketing plan.

The book is written in clear straightforward style with many examples and case studies. It is above all practical and systematic and will provide essential guidance on a complex subject.

For students following IM Diploma, MBA, BA BSc Business, Management and Marketing Courses and practising marketers in private and public sectors.
1984/224 pages/234 × 156/434 91230 1

BEHAVIOURAL ASPECTS OF MARKETING
Keith C. Williams

Explains clearly the application of the main behavioural concepts in the marketing arena in relation to both consumer behaviour and employee interaction.

For students following IM and CAM Certificate and Diploma, HNC/HND, BTEC National and Higher National Awards, DMS and BA/BSc Business Studies (with marketing options) courses.
1981/240 pages/234 × 156/434 92300 1

THE PRACTICE OF PUBLIC RELATIONS
Edited by Wilfred Howard

The second edition of this established text incorporates essential up-dating but has not changed the basic approach of the original. Revisions include up-dated newspaper circulation figures in the section on the media; a description of the reorganized Central Office of Information in the chapter on central government public relations; and recent trends in the public relations practice of various voluntary organizations. The section on ethics includes amendments to codes of conduct for public relations practitioners, and recent legislation is incorporated in the chapter on the law and public relations.

For students following IM Certificate and Diploma and other related courses.
'An authoritative across-the-board survey of the current "state of the art" in public relations.'
The Media Reporter
1985/250 pages/234 × 156/434 90785 5

THE MARKETING OF SERVICES
Donald W. Cowell

This is the first text to apply and adapt current ideas in marketing, developed for a product-orientated market, to the service-orientated market. The service economy covers diversity of interests and businesses, which need the ideas and techniques given in this book applied for their needs.

For students of marketing and business studies at BTEC, undergraduate, postgraduate and diploma level as well as marketing practitioners engaged in marketing services.
'I have awaited Donald Cowell's book eagerly and I am not disappointed. The whole is based upon an extensive literature study with full bibliographics, is clearly presented and offers questions for discussion'.
QRM
1984/378 pages/234 × 156/434 90263 2

MARKETING RESEARCH FOR MANAGERS
Sunny Crouch

The purpose of the book is to enable managers to become more informed research users and buyers. The more managers know about how marketing research works, the more effective they can be in using it as a management tool.

Marketing Research for Managers is an easy-to-read introduction, covering the range of marketing research techniques and describing how each stage in the research process is carried out, with an appreciation of their strengths and weaknesses.

It is a practical handbook for managers and students of BA Business Studies, BSc Management Science, BTEC, HNC/HND Business Studies. Other readers of this book are likely to be students taking the Diploma of Marketing, Diploma of the Market Research Society, and officers with managerial responsibility in local and national government.
1984/336 pages/216 × 138/434 90282 9

CASE STUDIES IN MARKETING, ADVERTISING AND PUBLIC RELATIONS
Edited by Colin McIver

This is a collection of 20 case studies based on actual events taking place in the British and European marketing world. Each case study is presented in a lively readable manner suitable for class tuition or private study. They cover the full range of marketing activity as it relates to consumer and industrial products and services, as well as a number of causes and ideas affecting public interest and voluntary organizations.

For students following IM and CAM Certificate and Diploma, BTEC National and Higher National Awards and other professional courses.
1984/240 pages/234 × 156/434 91235 2

THE FUNDAMENTALS OF ADVERTISING
John Wilmshurst

This book provides a comprehensive coverage of the whole business of advertising and its associated promotional areas (including public relations, sales promotion and sponsorship). Advertising is viewed from the points of view of advertisers, advertising agencies and the media, with the main emphasis on practical application in the current marketing scene.

The author uses a wide range of examples to illustrate his themes and an informative series of guidelines and check lists of value not only to students but to those trying to apply the various techniques.

For students following the IM Diploma (Marketing Communications), BTEC Higher National and BA/BSc Business Studies courses.
'More than adequately covers the subject in the certificate areas . . . references are very thoughtful . . . I particularly like the way in which the author positions research in the book . . . a most effective addition to any student bookcase.'
QRM
1985/272 pages/234 × 156/434 92330 3

PROFITABLE PRODUCT MANAGEMENT
John Ward

Profitable Product Management has been written as a basis for product managers to manage, efficiently and profitably, the products or services for which they are responsible or may become responsible. The accent is on the management of the many marketing factors with which they must continuously juggle. The role of a product manager, the creation of a marketing strategy, the annual Marketing Plan of Action, the management of the product range, are some of the topics discussed.

The book is directed at students taking the diploma examination of the Institute of Marketing, and those following Business Studies courses at degree or diploma level. It will also help to refocus and give added expertise to product managers, brand managers, sales managers and those executives or supervisors responsible for large manufacturing companies.
1984/304 pages/234 × 156/0 434 92215 3

CASE STUDIES IN INTERNATIONAL MARKETING
Peter Doyle and Norman Hart

Investigates British firms in a wide variety of international marketing situations and presents the multifaceted challenges of overseas marketing in a way that gives the reader an opportunity to participate in the decision making process.

Areas covered include: Environment of International Marketing; Identifying International Marketing Opportunities; Developing the International Marketing Programme; Organization and Control of the International Effort.

All the case studies have been extensively tested in class.

A Teachers' Manual is available to accompany the case study material which highlights the key issues in each case study.

For students following IM, IAA Certificate and Diploma, BA/BSc Business Studies, Institute of Export and BTEC courses.
1982/272 pages/234 × 156/434 90370 1

INTERNATIONAL MARKETING
S. J. Paliwoda

Changing world conditions affect the ways companies, large and small, are able to operate internationally. This book, one of the first texts to reflect the European perspective, takes account of these changes and introduces strategies that marketers can adopt to take advantage of evolving market trends.

The recommended text for the I.M. Diploma International Aspects of Marketing syllabus, *International Marketing* will also be essential reading for Business Studies and Marketing Degree students, those following DMS and MBA courses as well as Institute of Export and other related courses as well as international marketing executives in every type of organization.
1986/352 pages/234 × 156/434 91509 2

THE PRINCIPLES AND PRACTICE OF EXPORT MARKETING
E. P. Hibbert

The complexity of any marketing operation is dramatically increased when the market concerned is overseas. This practical and comprehensive volume covers all aspects of international trade and export administration and has been welcomed by the Institutes of Marketing and of Export alike.

For students following IM Diploma + Part II professional examination of the Institute of Export.
'good value for money'
Export
1985/352 pages/234 × 156/434 90746 4

HOW TO SELL A SERVICE: GUIDELINES FOR EFFECTIVE SELLING IN A SERVICE BUSINESS
Malcolm H. B. McDonald

There are numerous books on how to market products effectively but in the fast-growing service industry a new approach is needed. Malcolm McDonald, author of the highly acclaimed Marketing Plans, now demonstrates how to sell services successfully.

The book will prove invaluable to students of business, management and marketing who are interested in organizations that market services rather than goods and practitioners in all service industries who are responsible for marketing.
1986/140 pages/234 × 156/434 91231 X

LEGAL ASPECTS OF MARKETING
John Livermore

Marketing law in general and the new commercial law syllabus for the Institute of Marketing are covered for the first time in this book.

A useful reference for marketing and purchasing executives, the third edition takes into account changes which have occurred in the areas of the Consumer Credit Act, Employment Protection Act 1975, Unfair Contract Terms Bill 1977, restrictive trade practices, EEC, Trade Descriptions, Competition Act 1980, Sale of Goods Act 1979, and Companies Act 1980.
'Marketing law in general and the new Institute of Marketing Part II commercial law syllabus in particular are covered for the first time in *Legal Aspects of Marketing . . .*' *Co-operative News*
3rd Edition 1981/300 pages/254 × 159/434 91144 5

BARGAINING FOR RESULTS
John Winkler

The author outlines, in his informative and lively style, how the bargaining process works under different management situations. He shows individuals what they can do to obtain better results and how they can handle opposition tactics. With this book you can check how good a negotiator you can become and how your skills can be developed to their best advantage.
1981/288 pages/216 × 138/434 92350 8

BUSINESS ORGANIZATION
R. J. Williamson

Modern business techniques are presented in sufficient detail for them to be applied as well as understood; theory and practice are linked in such a way that the reader has a working handbook which will give him a clear picture of any organization that employs him, and will also enable him to improve his job-performance. The revision exercises for each chapter, given at the end of the book, will be an additional help to students preparing for examinations.
1981/352 pages/254 × 159/434 92262 5

The complete range of Heinemann books is available, on request, from:
The Marketing Department
Heinemann Professional Publishing Ltd
Halley Court, Jordan Hill, Oxford OX2 8EJ